612-810-6586

Trial
and Error

Trial and Error

The EDUCATION *of a* COURTROOM LAWYER

John C. Tucker

CARROLL & GRAF PUBLISHERS
NEW YORK

TRIAL AND ERROR
THE EDUCATION OF A COURTROOM LAWYER

Carroll & Graf Publishers
An Imprint of Avalon Publishing Group Inc.
161 William St., 16th Floor
New York, NY 10038

First Carroll & Graf edition 2003

Library of Congress Cataloging-in-Publication Data is available.

ISBN: 0-7867-1113-2

Interior design by Simon M. Sullivan

Printed in the United States of America
Distributed by Publishers Group West

For Katie Tucker Trippi, Cynthia Tucker Nau, Laura Tucker, Michael Tucker, Nancy Moran, Robin Tucker, and Jayne Barnard, who each lived through some or all of the moments described in these pages and whose support and forbearance were essential to everything I accomplished as a lawyer.

CONTENTS

Trial
and Error

⚔ CHAPTER 1 ⚔
LEARNING THE ROPES

As I stood behind the solid oak lectern facing the judge's bench in a courtroom of Chicago's Criminal Court building, a keening wail rose from the spectator benches, striking the back of my neck with jarring force. Its volume and pitch increased to an anguished scream, pressing me forward until I was leaning against the lectern.

Fifteen minutes earlier, a jury had found my client guilty of armed robbery. After brief arguments, the judge had just pronounced sentence on Roosevelt Andrews[1], a slim nineteen-year-old black man-child. He had several arrests as a juvenile, but this was his first adult conviction. The judge had sentenced Roosevelt to "not less than six nor more than nine years in the penitentiary." The scream that now filled the courtroom came from his mother.

As a bailiff slapped handcuffs on her son and escorted him toward a door leading back to the lockup, the mother's scream gave way to loud sobs, and when the boy neared the door, he stopped, turned back toward his mother, and called out, "I'll be awright, Mama." The bailiff shoved him forward, and they disappeared through the swinging door.

The judge announced a fifteen-minute recess, banged his gavel, and was gone before the clerk could finish shouting, "All rise! This

---

[1] For a variety of reasons, I have sometimes changed the names of real people. Whenever a substitute name is used in this book for the first time, as in this case, it will be marked by an asterisk.

court is now in recess." Then he followed the judge through a door behind the judge's bench.

A few people who had been waiting for the next case filed out, leaving only the mother, a friend or relative who was trying to comfort her, and me. I walked from the lectern to the counsel table where my papers and briefcase rested. To the still-sobbing mother, I said something like "I'm sorry. I don't know what to say."

"It's not your fault," she responded between sobs. "You did the best you could."

She was right, but even as I stood there, I knew that the "best I could" had been woefully inadequate. My cross-examination of the gas-station attendant who identified Roosevelt as the robber was full of open-ended questions that allowed the attendant to assure the jury he was certain of his identification. My effort to demonstrate that conditions were too dark and the encounter too brief to permit a reliable identification had been clumsy and unconvincing. My client's testimony on his own behalf was inescapably weak—he claimed he was at home and his only alibi witness was his mother—but I had failed to prepare him for some routine cross-examination traps which made his testimony even weaker. Worst of all, I had not appreciated how nearly certain it was he would be convicted, and how much additional time this judge would give him if he insisted on a trial rather than pleading guilty. As a result, when my client quickly rejected the prosecutor's pretrial offer of a sentence of "one to three" for a plea, I simply accepted his decision without presenting him with the stark realities of his situation.

The first rule in the American Bar Association Model Rules of Professional Conduct—the ethical bible of the American legal profession—is titled "Competence." It announces: "A lawyer shall provide competent representation to a client. Competent representation requires the legal knowledge, skill, thoroughness and preparation reasonably necessary for the representation." Unfortunately, the ABA does not tell a new lawyer how or where to obtain the tools to satisfy the rule I had just violated, but with a mother's scream still piercing my spine, I was determined to find out. I vowed I would never again feel so monstrously responsible for a client's tragedy, and I never did. What I did not know then, however, was that I would never try a case without knowing afterward there were some things I could have done better.

Every good trial lawyer says the same thing: The only way to learn how to try cases is by trying cases. You can learn a little bit from reading books, and a little more from watching trials (if the lawyers are good), and a little more still from law-school and post-law-school trial-practice courses—but in the end, you learn trial strategy, the way to prepare and examine witnesses, and how to handle the surprises and pressures of a real trial for a real client, only by "doing it" and learning from your mistakes. It is a process of trial and error.

The two most common fields for a newly minted lawyer to begin learning how to try cases are criminal law and personal-injury law. Many new lawyers who think they want to try cases begin in a prosecutor's office, a public defender's office, or a firm that specializes in criminal defense, insurance defense, or plaintiffs' personal-injury cases. Soon they find themselves in court, handling minor misdemeanors or fender benders. From there, some discover quickly that trying cases is not for them, and move on to another calling. (The sooner the better—there are few occupations as miserable as trying cases when you have no talent for it and are likely to be scared to death every time you go to court.) Others move up to trying midrange cases, and a few reach the top of their field, trying the most important and complex cases.

But for the law graduate who begins his career in a general-practice law firm in a large city, the road to competence as a courtroom lawyer is likely to be slower and harder. Many such firms do not handle the kind of small cases which could provide training for a novice trial lawyer—their high hourly rates would often result in the fee exceeding the amount in controversy.

The firm I joined when I graduated from Michigan law school in 1958 was a medium-large general-practice firm with an emphasis on trial work. Senior partner Floyd Thompson had read law in a small town in central Illinois. He became a county prosecutor, the youngest ever Chief Justice of the Illinois Supreme Court, and in 1928 the (unsuccessful) Democratic candidate for Illinois governor. After that loss, Thompson returned to private practice. Rough and plainspoken in manner and personality, he became one of the toughest and most respected trial lawyers in America, especially in complicated high-profile cases for clients in real trouble. Thompson had successfully defended Samuel Insull against the fraud charges that followed the collapse of his utility empire, and Preston Tucker when his car company failed. Thompson was nearing the end of his career when I joined the firm, but Albert E. Jenner Jr., college boxing champion and son of a Chicago cop, was well on his way to becoming his recognized successor in the Chicago legal community. Smoother than Thompson and an obsessive workaholic, by 1958 Jenner had already served as president of the Illinois Bar Association and was beginning a term as president of the American College of Trial Lawyers, the most prestigious organization of trial lawyers in the country. Although a generation younger than the other named partners of the firm, Jenner was already its biggest revenue producer. His practice consisted primarily of commercial litigation, much of it referred by lawyers in other cities whose corporate clients found themselves in court in Chicago. Between the cases referred to Thompson and Jenner by other lawyers and the cases generated by the firm's regular business clients, litigation accounted for well over half the firm's revenue.

Despite this emphasis on litigation, the firm's practice provided few cases for its young trial lawyers to learn on. The firm had decided not to take on routine insurance-defense work lest it create a group of "insurance-defense" lawyers who would be viewed as second-class citizens. Neither did it represent any of the major utilities or other companies whose business generates a body of small cases to provide a learning experience for young lawyers.

As a result, several of the younger lawyers had seized upon

another way to obtain firsthand trial experience: the acceptance of court appointments to defend indigent persons charged with serious crimes. Somewhat surprisingly, most of the senior partners supported this work even though it provided no fees at all and often required unreimbursed out-of-pocket expenses.

Bert Jenner approved of this work, as did Jim Sprowl, the senior trial lawyer I was assigned to assist when I joined the firm. Sprowl's other assistant, Jerry Solovy, was already involved in indigent-criminal-defense work, as were Prentice Marshall and Tom Sullivan, Jenner's principal assistants among the younger lawyers. In addition to helping Jenner, Marshall and Sullivan had already begun to establish their own reputations as promising trial lawyers.

With those examples before me, and the independent belief that lawyers have an ethical duty to serve the indigent, I quickly volunteered to join them. Which is how I came to be standing in a courtroom of the Criminal Court building when young Roosevelt Andrews was sentenced to the penitentiary and his mother filled the room with a scream which still echoes in my mind forty years later.

It wasn't supposed to happen that way. Inexperienced lawyers who volunteered for appointed criminal cases were not supposed to try cases alone. Rather, an experienced lawyer would be appointed to the same case to serve as lead counsel and provide guidance to the neophyte as he began learning his way around a courtroom. A more experienced lawyer was appointed with me in the *Andrews* case, but when the trial date arrived he was unavailable—and the judge flatly refused my request for a continuance. When I told him I had never tried a case of any kind, or even examined a witness before a jury, he said I had a law license and had to start somewhere. The fact that a young man was on trial for his freedom with a lawyer who had never handled so much as a $500 fender bender was of no concern to the judge. The law said anyone charged with a felony was entitled to an appointed lawyer if he could not afford to pay one. I was a lawyer. End of story.

The *Andrews* case did not deter me from accepting pro bono

criminal cases, but it did cause me to resolve I would never again try a case I was not competent to handle. The next time I appeared in the Criminal Court of Cook County it was to assist a more experienced lawyer who had recently joined the firm after several years as a prosecutor in the State's Attorney's office.

John Crown was the son of Colonel Henry Crown, Bert Jenner's most important client. Colonel Crown was one of the richest men in America. The Crown family owned, or had owned, a vast empire of businesses and properties ranging from the Empire State Building in New York and thousands of acres of prime real estate on Florida's southeast coast to Material Service Corporation, a huge sand, gravel, and cement company that originated the ubiquitous trucks with rotating drums which enable cement to be transported long distances without "setting up." A tall, heavyset man with thick glasses and a perpetual air of impatience, John sometimes seemed disorganized and even indifferent to the world around him; but when he agreed to represent an indigent defendant he would focus on the case immediately, and with great intensity. His years with the states Attorney's office had not made him a great courtroom lawyer—from the prosecution side, street-crime cases generally pose few problems requiring sophisticated arguments or witness examination—but he brought other important resources to our work as appointed defense lawyers.

For one thing, as a former assistant states attorney John enjoyed the deference generally afforded graduates of that office by its current members on such matters as continuances, favorable plea bargains, and access to information about the state's case.

For another, John's experience had taught him, and he taught me, a crucial fact that law schools seldom mention: the importance of the secretaries, clerks, bailiffs, and other courthouse personnel whose knowledge and cooperation are vital to any lawyer hoping to practice effectively and efficiently in "their" courthouse. It is these men and women who can quickly find—or not find—a file you need to examine; tell you or not tell you about some development in the judge's schedule that will affect your case; inform you or not inform you of a particular judge's idiosyncrasies and preferences regarding the many practices and procedures on which judges have individual discretion; and help or hurt your client in a dozen other ways. As a member of a rich and powerful family, John could easily have alienated everyone in the courthouse with an arrogant and dismissive attitude. Instead he treated everyone from the lowliest file clerk to the chief judge with courtesy and respect. You didn't need to be terribly perceptive to see how important that was, yet some lawyers acted as though the court personnel were peons whose only function was to respond smartly to the lawyer's every command. Theoretically, that may have been true, but lawyers who adopted that attitude paid dearly for the privilege—as did their clients.

The most significant lesson I learned from John Crown was the importance of prompt and thorough investigation of the facts of each new case. John was a dogged, determined, even compulsive investigator, and between the resources of a major law firm and the special resources which came with John's family connections, we had advantages many lawyers representing indigent defendants did not have. Unlike the states attorneys, who had both the police department and their own staff of investigators, we had to do our own investigations; but unlike full-time criminal defense lawyers, who had to meet a monthly payroll, our firm (if not all of its partners) supported our spending as much time on a case as needed to do a thorough job.

The first thing to be done in every case was to find out as much as possible about the state's evidence and its theory of the case. The indictment and arrest report provided basic information, but not nearly enough. At that time, the only other information the law required the state to provide the defense was any statement or confession made by the defendant and access to any physical evidence and scientific reports the state had obtained. Not until the Supreme Court decision in *Brady v. Maryland* in 1963 was the state required to disclose exculpatory evidence, and even the *Brady* line of cases are of limited value since they leave it to the prosecutor to determine what is exculpatory or helpful to the defense, and his views on the subject are likely to be considerably narrower than those of a defense lawyer. It is one of the inexplicable ironies of American justice that if someone brings a civil action over a few thousand dollars, both sides are entitled to learn every detail of the facts surrounding the dispute, including not only information relevant to the case but any information that might lead to relevant information, while a man on trial for his liberty, or even his life, has no right to that kind of full disclosure from the police and prosecutor.

When I began trying indigent-criminal cases in 1959 a few judges in the criminal court occasionally ordered a prosecutor to provide more information to the defense than the law required, usually in the form of statements made to the police by the most important witnesses, and sometimes a prosecutor would allow a defense lawyer to look at some or all of the police reports as a way of persuading him that the state's case was so strong the defendant should accept a plea bargain.

But our most valuable tool—to be used only when other efforts failed and circumstances suggested there likely was material in the police file that could be important to our defense—arose from John's family ties. The top criminal-defense lawyers in Chicago—the ones who handled the highest-profile cases for the wealthiest clients—all had a "contact"—someone at police headquarters who could and would, for whatever reason, provide the lawyer with a copy of the police investigative file—a service seldom available to lawyers representing indigent clients in run-of-the-mill street-crime cases.

Fortunately, however, the man in charge of investigations and security for Material Service Corporation had a frequent, ongoing need for access to police records in his work, and saw no reason to turn down an occasional request from the owner's son to use his contacts on our behalf. In the time John Crown and I tried criminal cases together, our access to police files never turned up a dramatic piece of information which by itself enabled us to win a case, but sometimes it provided facts and names of potential witnesses we otherwise would not have known about, and that information allowed us to give better advice and service to our client. Not infrequently, it revealed a weakness in the state's case which we could use to obtain a more favorable plea bargain, or better defend the case at trial.

Another resource John brought to the table was his secretary, an intelligent and energetic woman. In interviewing witnesses, it is essential to have someone take accurate notes, and equally important to have someone present who can testify to what the witnesses said if their stories change at trial. Because lawyers are not supposed to testify in cases they are trying (or to try cases when they know their testimony is needed), when a client can afford it, lawyers employ paid investigators to take witness statements or accompany the lawyer who wants to do his own questioning of a witness. The investigator can then testify if necessary. For John and me, his secretary served as both expert note taker and potential witness.

Every crime has a "scene," a physical location or locations where events important to the alleged crime took place. Once we knew the basic facts alleged by the state, one of the first things we did was to visit and thoroughly investigate those scenes. John was a skilled photographer with equipment capable of capturing understandable images of almost any scene in any condition of light, and we never visited a crime scene without cameras, tape measures, and paper on which to draw a rough diagram we could later convert to scale if necessary.

Almost all our clients were African-Americans and almost all the witnesses and crime scenes were located in the black ghetto that occupied much of Chicago's south and west sides. Many of the crime scenes had to be visited at night, when the crime occurred, in order to understand the light conditions, and many of the places we visited were not hospitable to white folks in business clothes, even during daylight. Apart from safety concerns, it was a guaranteed waste of time for a stranger to knock on the door of a ghetto apartment and ask for Witness X. The universal presumption was that you were a cop or a bill collector, and the answer was, "He doesn't live here and I never heard of him." Not infrequently, the purveyor of this noninformation was X himself. The solution to these problems was to obtain the assistance of the client's friends or family to escort us on our investigative forays, and there was almost always someone willing to do so. Occasionally, however, our escort would not show up at the appointed time and place, and the only alternative was to go home or go alone. If we were looking for witnesses to interview, we usually just went home—it was a waste of time unless the witness was friendly and already expecting you—but if it was a crime-scene visit we went ahead, and never had a problem.

In the eight years I tried indigent-criminal cases, first with John Crown and later by myself or with a younger assistant, I visited basement apartments where the only heat in January was from the open flames of a gas stove; single rooms which served as the living quarters for a mother and three children who took turns sleeping on one or two urine-stained mattresses laid on the floor; single-room-occupancy hotels where everyone you saw, including the witness you were looking for, had the jaundiced yellow eyes and spaced-out demeanor of heroin addicts; and high-rise housing projects in which all the elevators were broken, the stairwells were full of garbage, the smell of human feces and urine was overpowering, and law and order—to the extent it could be said to exist—was administered by the street gangs. Everywhere in and around these places were children, little children four, five, and six years old, playing in the streets and gutters and junk-strewn parkways and lots. Children as bright eyed and intelligent and inquisitive as my own children and those of my friends and neighbors in the suburbs, and playing the same children's games.

Over the years, I was appointed to represent indigent defendants charged with felonies in the Criminal Court of Cook County in fifteen or twenty cases. I volunteered for those cases in part because I thought it was my duty as a lawyer, and in part because I thought they would help me learn to be a trial lawyer. I visited those filthy streets and grim apartments because that's where my clients and witnesses lived and the crimes occurred. But those experiences did much more than help me learn how to try cases. They caused me to understand that if I had been born and raised where my clients were, I would probably have become a criminal or a drug addict myself. And worst of all, they made me realize that in the absence of enormous luck, tremendous willpower, or an extraordinary parent, by the time they reached their teens, most of those curious, bright-eyed children would turn out that way too. Those experiences, more than anything else, shaped the social and political views I have retained ever since. It would be a wonderful thing if every businessperson, professional, and politician in America had similar experiences when they began their careers.

In the meantime, I also learned quite a bit about trying cases. I soon learned to tell a story—not give a lecture. I learned to discard the stilted language of law school and police reports and use plain words. A gun is a gun, not a weapon. And when you pull the trigger, it does not discharge, it shoots.

I learned to stand up to a judge and protect my clients rights' without being offensive, but to be offensive if necessary. I learned the basic rules of cross-examination: Don't ask open-ended questions. Don't ask questions unless you know and can prove the answer or don't care what it is. Don't ask a question unless you can articulate a reason for doing so. And, once you have established the facts you need to make a point, don't try to make it with another, argumentative question—save that for your closing argument. And I learned enough to sense that some day, if I became experienced enough and good enough, I would know when it was all right to break those rules.

I learned that juries are not stupid and the vast majority of cases that go to trial turn out the way you would expect them to turn out from a rational weighing of the facts. But I also learned that when cases turn out differently than you would expect, they are lost more often by bad lawyering than won by a lawyer's brilliance, and that even good lawyers can make a bad mistake.

In a case where a young black man was on trial for auto theft, there seemed little doubt the jury would return a guilty verdict until the experienced white prosecutor mocked the defendant's alibi testimony by repeating it in a thick accent reminiscent of "The Kingfish" on the *Amos 'n Andy* radio show. The four black jurors were furious, and three of them held out and hung the jury. When an angry judge asked the prosecutor what the hell he thought he was doing, the prosecutor was mortified and swore he did not realize what he had done. Unspoken was the fact that the white prosecutors and judges who occupied the vast majority of those positions in the criminal courts told each other racist jokes every day, using exaggerated imitations of the accents of the defendants who appeared before them. The prosecutor had momentarily forgotten where he was and who he was talking to.

The hung jury enabled John Crown and me to negotiate a plea agreement for probation, which the prosecutor had previously refused to consider.

Several years later, a murder case I was defending ended with a similar result, not because of a lawyer's mistake, but from pure luck. Luck is as much a fact of life in court as in all endeavors, and lawyers are as anxious for her favors as poker players and presidents.

The trial was expected to last about five days, and the judge had seated an alternate along with the twelve regular jurors. After the first day of trial, several of the jurors reported that one of their fellow jurors was complaining in the jury room that it was obvious the defendant was guilty and sitting through the trial was a waste of his time. After a brief hearing, the juror was removed and the alternate moved into his place. On the morning of the third day, a distraught juror reported her home had been burglarized the night before while she and her children slept upstairs. The incident had so traumatized her that she no longer believed she could be fair to the defendant in the case we were trying. The judge tried mightily to change her mind and get her to say she could put the experience aside and be fair, but she resisted bravely and the judge finally had to excuse her. When I refused to proceed with eleven jurors, a mistrial was required. The case involved a black-on-black murder arising from a bar fight, not considered a major crime by most prosecutors in the overtly racist world of the Chicago criminal courts in the early 1960s. Rather than start over, the prosecutor agreed to reduce the charge to manslaughter, with a sentence that would have my client out of prison in less than a year. My client still insisted he had acted in self-defense, but it was an offer he could not refuse.

A lawyer's mistake in one case and a piece of luck in another resulted in mistrials for two clients—but why would the prosecutors accept such dramatically more favorable plea bargains instead of simply retrying the cases? For one thing, the cases were now old and newer cases had crowded onto the schedule behind them, making it seem even more important than usual to dispose of them quickly to prevent the system from collapsing under the weight of a huge backlog. Moreover, the defendants and their lawyer had proved that they were willing to try the case rather than accept a harsh sentence. (Many private lawyers, having long since used up the fee they collected, would have moved heaven and earth to avoid another trial by persuading their clients to plead guilty; but to the intense displeasure of prosecutors and judges, pro bono lawyers were often perfectly willing to try the case again. After all, we were in it for the experience, not the fee.)

But there was another factor at work. In both cases, the state had already put on all or most of its case. Their theory of the case was fully exposed and their witnesses had testified, every word put down by a court reporter and available to defense counsel before a second trial. No prosecutor likes to try a case a second time, when his or her witnesses' stories have already been told. The advantage gained by defense counsel in his or her ability to challenge details of the story on cross-examination and through other witnesses can dramatically improve the argument for reasonable doubt.

For the same reason, no competent criminal-defense lawyer ever allows a client (suspect) to give a quick statement to the police, no matter how innocent the client claims to be. Even if the lawyer believes, after careful investigation, that the client's story is good enough to satisfy the police, it should be presented by the lawyer—not the client—so no record is made of the client's words that can be used to impeach him later if the effort to avoid prosecution fails. For month after month, police, prosecutors and editorialists across the country excoriated the parents of Jon-Benet Ramsay for following their lawyers' advice against giving a statement to the police, but innocent or guilty, if they had given statements before the police had completed and documented their initial investigation, there is a strong possibility one or both of them would have been indicted, and perhaps even convicted, of participating in their daughter's murder. For the same reason Monica Lewinsky's lawyers refused to let her talk directly to Kenneth Starr's prosecutors until they had an enforceable promise of complete immunity so long as her statement did not vary materially from the version of events her lawyer proffered.

Another pro bono criminal case provided my first exposure to expert witnesses. Several years after we tried our first case together, John Crown and I were appointed to represent two young men charged with murder. They were our first and only white clients, nasty and snarling with the arrogance a twenty-year-old affects to conceal his fear and uncertainty. In fact, our clients were scared silly, and for good reason. Following the classic rumor that a reclusive, elderly woman in their neighborhood had a significant hoard of cash, the two punks invaded her apartment one afternoon, bound and gagged the woman, tied her to a chair, and ransacked her apartment looking for the nonexistent stash. Departing, hurriedly and empty-handed except for a few dollars from her purse, they left the door to the apartment ajar. When a neighbor returned home from work several hours later, she noticed the open door, and after the old woman failed to answer her calls, the neighbor looked inside. The chair was tipped over with the woman still bound to it. She had bled from a cut on her forehead, and she was now dead. When the crime hit the newspapers and television, one of the boys couldn't resist bragging to friends. One of the friends told a cop with whom he had been cooperating to work off a marijuana charge. Under questioning, the first boy denied killing the woman but admitted trying to rob her and named his companion. Matching fingerprints were found in the apartment, and the two were charged with first-degree murder. To make matters worse, the prosecutor announced he would ask for the death penalty, which scared me almost as badly as it scared my two clients.

The prosecutor's theory was that the boys, frustrated by their inability to find the money and the woman's failure to tell them where it was, had beaten her to death. That scenario was supported by the coroner's autopsy report, which claimed the woman's death was caused by a blow to the head with a blunt instrument.

After our client's arraignment, the court proceeding at which a defendant is formally told of the charges against him and asked to enter a plea, the prosecutor suggested we talk. After decrying the brutality of the crime and pronouncing his certainty of obtaining a death sentence, he said it was barely possible he would be able to persuade his boss to accept a negotiated sentence of life in prison in return for a prompt plea of guilty.

There was nothing new or unusual about a prosecutor's using the threat of death as a club to extract a plea and a long sentence, and if the facts were as the prosecutor claimed, it was a somewhat tempting offer. That the defendants would be found guilty seemed a foregone conclusion, and the prosecutor was right that juries would not look kindly on two young men who had brutally beaten a seventy-eight-year-old woman to death in her own home. Our clients, however, vehemently disputed the state's theory of the case. They did not deny they had tried to rob the woman and had bound and gagged her; but interviewed separately, they both insisted that neither of them had ever hit her. She was sitting upright in the chair, alive and not bleeding, when they left.

We needed an expert to examine the autopsy report and tell us if there was any way to attack the coroner's conclusion about the cause of death. Over the years I had come to know Jim Dougherty, a large, red-faced Irishman who was the chief deputy public defender. Jim had endless enthusiasm for his job, and more than anything else enjoyed battling with prosecutors tooth and nail, no quarter asked or given. He also knew just about everyone who had any contact with the criminal-justice system in Cook County. When I told him my problem, he immediately suggested contacting Dr. Victor Levine, a former chief pathologist in the Cook County coroner's office who had lost his job for political reasons. Dr. Levine had a national reputation among pathologists and, according to Dougherty, was completely honest, very competent, and very willing to testify against the current coroner's office, which he thought was filled with incompetent political appointees. Jim said he would probably be willing to look at the report, and even testify without compensation if he believed the report was inaccurate.

Several days later, I met with Dr. Levine at his office at a major area hospital where he was serving as a staff pathologist. I had previously sent him a copy of the report and a letter describing what we knew about the case. When I arrived at his office and introduced myself, Levine, a small man in his early sixties wearing a white coat and a gleeful smile, pulled a copy of the coroner's report from a manila file on his desk. "I don't know if the guy who wrote this report is dishonest or just incompetent," he said, his smile growing even brighter, "but I can tell you one thing: This woman did not die from a blow of any kind, blunt instrument or otherwise. She died from congestive heart failure, and she'd been dying of it for a long time."

The first part of his statement, Dr. Levine explained, was apparent more from what the autopsy report *omitted* than from what it said. The pathologist had recorded the presence of a contusion and laceration of the right forehead, and gone on to report that there was no fracture of the skull. Most important was the fact the report made no reference to bleeding or swelling of the brain—and it's pressure on the brain caused by bleeding and swelling that is lethal. According to Levine, it is routine—and essential—for the pathologist to determine the presence and extent of these factors in any autopsy where a blow to the head is the suspected cause of death. Either the pathologist made the examination and didn't mention it because it showed no evidence of pressure on the brain and thus contradicted the prosecutor's theory of the case, or he didn't do it because he realized from examining the victim's forehead that the injury was so superficial it could not have caused such pressure. Either way, the prosecution theory was contradicted by the autopsy report.

On the other hand, Dr. Levine declared, it was clear from the facts recited in the report that the true cause of death was heart failure. The pathologist had removed the heart and reported its weight and dimensions. In relation to the victim's body size, it was enormous—a sure sign that for many years her heart had been failing, causing it to become larger as it worked harder to perform its vital function. Based on autopsy photographs of the victim's forehead and crime-scene photos of the victim lying on the floor, still bound to her overturned chair, Dr. Levine thought the slight injury to her forehead might have occurred when her chair tipped over as she had tried to free herself.

Could Dr. Levine say there was no connection between the burglary and the victim's death? No. In fact, the doctor explained, the reason the victim's heart finally failed when it did was probably because of the physical and emotional stress caused by the burglary and being bound to the chair.

We thanked Dr. Levine profusely and asked if he would be willing to testify to what he had told us if the case went to trial. He said he would.

Returning to the office, my first task was to determine if Dr. Levine's analysis of the autopsy report was as clear and indisputable as he had asserted. A quick reading of the authoritative medical literature indicated it was. Under the felony-murder rule in effect in Illinois and most states, our clients were still guilty of murder if the jury believed the victim died of heart failure caused by the burglary instead of a beating, but the sentence was likely to be far less severe.

Two months later, after an unsuccessful effort to persuade the prosecutor to agree to a reasonable sentence in return for a guilty plea, the case went to trial with the state still insisting the cause of death was a blow to the head, and still seeking the death penalty. As a result, any juror who admitted opposing capital punishment on religious or moral grounds was summarily dismissed from the jury pool.

On direct examination, the state's pathologist repeated his assertion that the cause of the victim's death was a blow to the head. Forewarned of our opposing theory by the plea negotiations, the prosecutor also asked the pathologist about the report's failure to mention any swelling of the brain. The witness said he had indeed examined the brain and found no bleeding or swelling (which, he claimed, is why he didn't mention it)—but insisted that a blow to the forehead could cause death even without increased pressure on the brain. On cross-examination, I confronted him with several medical texts confirming Dr. Levine's claim that the only way a blow to the head can be the direct cause of death is if it causes pressure on the brain. The witness did not deny the texts were considered authoritative, or that they said what I suggested they said, but continued to insist that in his opinion even a blow that caused no pressure could kill a frail elderly woman like the victim. He was sure, he said, that his theory was supported in the medical literature, but he could not cite any source.

To my eye, several of the better-educated members of the jury gave the witness a dubious look when he failed to provide any support for his opinion, and I sat down feeling considerable confidence we had won this point. Nevertheless, after the state rested its case, we called Dr. Levine as our only witness. After detailing his impressive credentials, he asserted emphatically that the blow to the victim's head could not have been the cause of her death, and went on to explain his own theory that she had died of heart failure. The prosecutor had apparently found no medical literature to contradict him, and was wholly unprepared for the heart-failure theory (which we had not mentioned in the plea negotiations when it became apparent the prosecutor was determined not to accept anything less than a very long sentence, regardless of the facts). As a result, his cross-examination was limited to establishing that Dr. Levine had not himself examined the victim's body.

In his closing argument, the prosecutor abandoned his request for a death sentence, asking instead for a sentence of life in prison. I devoted most of my time to the cause of death and to asking the jury, if they found the defendants guilty, to give them a sentence that would allow them to emerge from prison with time to make a life for themselves. Less than two hours later, the jury returned to find both defendants guilty of murder and sentenced them to four-teen years in the penitentiary—the minimum for first-degree murder in Illinois at the time.

Confronted with an expert's report on an unfamiliar subject, it is tempting to assume that the issue is settled. Dr. Levine taught me always to get a second opinion. In a way, however, my experi-ence with the excellent Dr. Levine was misleading. It would take many more years to learn the problems (and opportunities) associ-ated with the arrogance of so many experts, especially their inability to say "I don't know" in answer to any question.

While my adventures in the Criminal Court building were pro-viding an early opportunity to examine witnesses, argue to juries, and deal with the staggering pressures of responsibility for the freedom and even the life of a client, the majority of my time was spent in my office learning the skills of a big-firm, big-city civil liti-gator, primarily under the tutelage of James A. Sprowl, the partner I was assigned to assist when I joined the firm. Like me, Jim Sprowl had attended the University of Michigan Law School on scholar-ship; but unlike me, he had reputedly graduated first in his class, with the highest grade-point average in the law school's history. We had both made high enough grades in our first year to be selected for the law review, but from that point my grades had slipped as I devoted more time to poker and parties than studying law.

Sprowl was a big man, somewhat overweight, with a relaxed, garrulous personality strikingly at odds with the fierce intensity of most of his partners, especially the trial lawyers. His clothes looked as though they had been tailored by someone who didn't see very well, and his habit of wiping his mouth with his tie after finishing a meal gave new meaning to the term "paisley." Even in the middle of an important trial, when everyone involved was working eighteen-hour days, Sprowl could usually be found in his office after dinner, leaning back in his chair, solving a crossword puzzle. When he finished the puzzle, he would pack his briefcase with whatever papers he had that were relevant to the next day's court session and announce to his assistants that he was going home—and they should too. Of course, we never did—working into the night to find some case or document that might help with the next day's cross-examination or legal argument. The next morning, he would gratefully accept whatever material we had developed and then perform a near-perfect cross or argument from a few frag-mentary notes he had made himself, sometimes incorporating one of the suggestions you had made that morning but were not even certain he had heard.

Sprowl's cases—mostly for his own clients—were a mixture of almost every type of dispute that brings people and businesses together in American courtrooms. Early on, I was assigned to assist in preparing the defense of an antitrust case brought against Young's Rubber Corporation, then the country's largest manufac-turer of condoms, claiming our client was attempting to monopo-lize the business by persuading state legislatures to ban condom sales in vending machines. The case was already pending when I joined the firm, and Jerry Solovy had been assisting Sprowl on the matter for some time. Ultimately we won the case without a trial, but in the meantime Jerry and I traveled around the country interviewing and taking depositions from legislators and drugstore owners. It was a great lesson in how to prepare friendly witnesses to say the right things and avoid saying the wrong things without lying. It was also a great lesson in the virtues of law-firm seniority. In January and February Jerry conducted a series of depositions in Florida and Puerto Rico while I held the fort in Minnesota and North Dakota.

In another antitrust case, Sprowl represented a small food jobber who had been cut off by Kraft Foods, the supplier of our client's most important product. Our legal theory was difficult in the extreme, and the facts necessary to prove it were largely under the control of our opponents. Responsibility for developing the facts was left entirely to me, and the many long and difficult depositions I took from Kraft executives and the lawyers who advised them taught me the virtue of exploring every conceivable fact and theory when examining hostile witnesses in pretrial proceedings. My lengthy depositions often infuriated opponents (and sometimes judges), but not infrequently uncovered important evidence that a less persistent examination would not have discovered.

Sprowl had a number of friends from law school who practiced alone or in small firms and would hire him to handle cases too complicated to handle themselves. Early on, I assisted him in litigation arising from a dispute between family members over the operation of a family owned chain of small department stores and shoe stores in central Illinois. From that and several similar cases, I learned over the years that few cases are so predictably bitter as business disputes among family members.

I also learned the value of "smoking gun" evidence, however obtained. The company had been started by two brothers. Our client, the son of one of the founders, now deceased, was president. His uncle—the company's co-founder—was chairman of the board and our bitter opponent. During a trial over the issue of whether our client had the authority to take certain actions on behalf of the corporation without board approval, Mr. Sprowl, cross-examining the chairman, showed him a copy of a document our client had taken from his uncle's files in the corporate office just as the dispute was beginning. The document was devastating to the chairman's position in the case, and when he saw it he began shouting that it had been stolen from his office by our client. Red-faced and indignant, he demanded that the document be returned to him at once and our client charged with theft. Sitting at counsel table I was momentarily stunned and worried. Had we done something awful and put our client in danger of criminal prosecution?

Mr. Sprowl, on the other hand, stood calmly in front of the shouting witness, smiling. When the chairman's outburst finally subsided, Sprowl turned to the judge (it was a bench trial) and said, "Your Honor, we dispute the characterization of our means of obtaining the exhibit as theft, but that is not an issue for this court. The question is whether it is authentic, and while I suppose the witness's outburst effectively provides the answer, I would ask the court to instruct him to answer the question—did he prepare it, and does it bear his signature?" The judge did as Mr. Sprowl asked, the chairman yelled some more and refused to answer, his lawyer asked for a recess to confer with his client, and before the trial resumed, the dispute was settled on terms we had suggested weeks earlier.

In 1960 Floyd Thompson, our senior partner, died suddenly, and Jim Sprowl took over a case Thompson had been handling for a Bermuda-based entrepreneur who had purchased the remains of a bankrupt retail hardware chain. The Marshall-Wells Company had been in business since the late 1800s selling hard goods through stores in the rural Midwest. Much of its merchandise was sold under its own trademarked brand names, including "Zenith." Once our client acquired the company, he closed down what remained of its failing hardware business and concentrated on selling private-label refrigerators, freezers, and washing machines through independent appliance and hardware stores. The appliances were sold under the Zenith name.

It was not long before Zenith Radio Corporation, then the country's largest and most successful manufacturer of radios and televisions, sued Marshall-Wells for trademark infringement and unfair competition in federal court in Chicago. The complaint asked that our client be prohibited from using the name Zenith in its business and pay Zenith Radio several million dollars in damages. Zenith Radio was represented by its regular Chicago trial counsel, Tom McConnell, one of the most unpleasant lawyers in the city. Marshall-Wells hired Judge Thompson, a man who was not quite as unpleasant as McConnell, but just as tough.

The first thing Thompson did was file a counterclaim for Marshall-Wells, alleging that Zenith's use of the name on its radios and televisions violated Marshall-Wells's Zenith trademark, which it had used on wringer washing machines and similar products before the Zenith Radio Corporation was even founded. Thompson and McConnell sincerely despised each other, and some who knew them believed the case was a factor in Thompson's death. Whether that was true or not, when Sprowl took over the case McConnell's continued nastiness made little apparent dent in Sprowl's relaxed demeanor. Inwardly, Sprowl came to dislike McConnell as much as Judge Thompson had, but he seldom showed it.

Another associate in the firm had been helping Thompson on the case and stayed on to help Sprowl, but as the trial approached and the pace of discovery increased, I was enlisted to take some of the remaining depositions. A major issue was whether people who bought our client's appliances were confused by the name Zenith into thinking they were made by the same company that made the popular radios and TVs. Many of the stores that sold our client's appliances were located in Appalachia, and for several weeks one fall I traveled around Tennessee, Kentucky, and West Virginia interviewing and then taking depositions from people who had bought the appliances and said that they had not been confused or misled by the name. After an investigator located enough such witnesses to occupy a few days of short depositions, we would serve notice of the depositions on our opponents. McConnell had a young partner named Philip Curtis who attended the depositions for Zenith. Curtis was almost as unpleasant as his boss, and one day, as we were riding through the countryside between depositions we got into an argument. I was in the front seat of the car, which was being driven by our local investigator. Curtis was in the backseat, along with the court reporter who traveled with us to record the testimony. I was turned facing Curtis in the back when he suddenly grabbed my tie and twisted it, choking me. I returned the favor, and we were face to face, red-faced, choking and sputtering threats of greater violence. The court reporter screamed and the investigator stopped the car and separated us. The two of them surely wondered if this was the way Chicago lawyers acted all the time. Mobsters they knew about, but lawyers?

Actually, it was the only physical confrontation I had with another lawyer in thirty years. The closest I came thereafter was with a truly obnoxious assistant state's attorney in the Criminal Court building. Leaving the courtroom, furious, after an especially outrageous encounter, I ran into another assistant state's attorney I knew, waiting for an elevator. "What will you charge me with if I throw that little son of a bitch down this elevator shaft?" I fumed.

"Littering," he replied.

In due course, *Zenith v. Marshall-Wells* went to trial before U.S. District Court Judge Hubert Will. On the third day of trial, Will, who was known for asking his own questions during trials, addressed one to a Zenith executive who had just finished his testimony on direct examination. The witness had described the history of the company's use of the name Zenith on its products, the tens of millions of dollars it had spent promoting the name, and the tremendous value it had in the marketplace as a symbol of the highest quality in radios and televisions. "What about the defendant's claim they have been using the name Zenith on washing machines and other products for some forty years longer than you've been in business? Do you challenge that claim?"

"Well, Judge," the witness responded, "I don't have any personal knowledge of that, but I understand it may be true."

"Well, what about that, Mr. McConnell—do you dispute that claim?"

When McConnell said no, and began to explain why it didn't make any difference, the judge interrupted him, saying he understood that our prior use of the name didn't necessarily mean we had an exclusive right to use it now, but that it could be awfully important. "Did the president of Zenith know that it's at least possible this case could result in the company losing the right to use that extremely valuable name your witness just described?"

McConnell hemmed and hawed, insisting such a result was inconceivable. Judge Will said he understood McConnell didn't think it would happen, and that he wasn't saying he thought so either, but before going any further he wanted to be sure the company's top executives understood it was at least a possibility. Will ordered McConnell to have the company president in court the next morning, so he could explain the possibilities.

That night Jim Sprowl called Murray Gurfein, our client's chief counsel in New York, and described the day's events. Gurfein understood at once what was happening, and wanted to participate personally in the settlement discussions he and Sprowl believed would begin the next day. He would fly out on a late plane that night.

Three days later, the case was settled, with Zenith Radio dismissing its case and paying our client a large sum for whatever rights it had in the name Zenith. Judge Hubert Will, whatever else you thought of him (and many lawyers disapproved of his intervention in the questioning of witnesses) was a master at stimulating settlements, and Murray Gurfein was hands down the best negotiator I ever watched in action. In truth, as Tom McConnell insisted loudly until his face grew purple with anger, our overall position in the case was weak, and the chance that Zenith would end up losing its trademark extremely slim, but Gurfein was fearless in pressing his position. However small the risk, Gurfein knew that Zenith management could not afford to take it, no matter how insistently their lawyer promised to win the case. Three times the Zenith side walked out of the negotiations and said they would resume the trial, but Gurfein stood his ground, even though the Zenith offer he had refused seemed to me a miraculously favorable disposition of the case. Each time, Zenith came back to the table, until finally Gurfein sensed he had all he could get.

Despite this early exposure to the work of a master negotiator, it was a skill I never developed. I did, however, learn one thing from the experience that would prove extremely valuable over the years: It's a lot easier to remain tough in settlement negotiations if you're not the person who has to try the case the next day if it doesn't settle. If settlement talks began during or on the eve of trial I always tried to get someone else to negotiate while I continued my trial preparations.

Although most of my work in my first five years of practice was for Jim Sprowl, I was occasionally called on to assist other partners. One such assignment was to represent a world-famous Chicago architect who was a client of Sam Block, a senior partner in the firm. The architect had been sued by a structural engineer he had hired to work with him on a major architectural commission. The engineer claimed he had not been paid in accordance with an oral agreement. Our client disputed the terms of the alleged agreement, but in going through his files, I came upon a letter addressed to the engineer which described the agreement just as the engineer alleged. Apparently, the letter was never sent, as the original, signed by our client, remained in the file along with several copies. I showed it to the client and told him it would make defense of the case more difficult. Our client pointed out that the letter had apparently never been sent, and claimed it was therefore irrelevant and should not be produced to the other side. I had given him the original to read, and he told me to give him the copies and he would "handle it." When I told him it was indeed relevant, whether or not it was sent, and had to be produced, he angrily demanded the copies. When I refused, he told me I was fired from the case and he was going to call Sam Block. I said fine,

I would take the copies to Mr. Block so he could decide what should be done.

As soon as I got back to the firm I went to Block's office and explained what had happened. He already had a message from the client, but had not yet returned the call. When I told him the story, half-fearful I would be fired from the firm as well as the case for offending one of his good clients, Sam laughed. "Don't worry about it," he said. "You did the right thing, and I'll take care of it right now." He told his secretary to get the architect on the telephone, and when he picked up the phone, he went right to the point. "Bert" he said, "I have John Tucker here and he's shown me the letter and told me what happened. You have to produce it, and I'm sending John back to pick up the original and all the other documents he gathered today. We're supposed to produce them next week and that's what we're going to do, unless you want me to settle the case on whatever terms I can get before then." The architect protested loudly. "I don't care about all that," Sam replied. "You have to produce it, and I'll tell you why. If you don't produce it, you'll get caught, and then it will cost you a hell of a lot more money, and you might just go to jail. You have no idea how many copies of that letter are lying around somewhere, and believe me, one of them will surface. So that's that." And it was.

"With guys like that, 'you'll get caught' is a lot better argument than 'the law requires it,' " Sam said. "In the end, if they don't buy it, you have to make them do what's right or resign from the case, but it's always worth making the other argument first—it usually works, and they like you better."

Over the next twenty-seven years similar situations arose on several occasions with my own clients. Each time I followed Sam Block's advice, and it always worked.

In early 1960 I accepted an appointment by the Illinois Supreme Court to represent a man in his appeal from a conviction for selling narcotics. Unlike trials, the moot-court program in law school taught me something about appeals, and the legal research and brief writing I had done for firm clients was also helpful experience. Nevertheless, when the time arrived to travel to the state capital in Springfield to present my oral argument, I was both excited and apprehensive.

The Illinois Supreme Court, like the United States Supreme Court, hears oral arguments with all of its members present, sitting behind a long, elevated bench in a huge, ornate, high-ceilinged room designed to impress lawyers and spectators with the majesty of the law and the power represented by the black-robed justices who administer it. My case was to be the first argued one morning, so I took the train to Springfield the previous day, having booked a room at the Statehouse Inn, a hotel that was close to the Supreme Court building and locally famous as the place for legislators and lobbyists to meet, eat, drink, argue, and take prostitutes when the legislature was in session. Fortunately, they were not in session, or I could not have gotten a room.

After checking into the hotel I went to the courthouse to reconnoiter the room where I would present my argument the next morning. I had been there once before, to be sworn in as a member of the Illinois bar, but on that occasion I had paid no attention to such crucial matters as where the lawyers sit, and by what route they can move from there to the podium where they present their arguments. The courtroom was empty when I arrived, the arguments for the day having ended, and it seemed even more cavernous and imposing than I remembered. I now noticed there was a rail between the spectator benches and two tables which sat in front of the judges' bench. Each table was flanked by a half dozen leather-upholstered chairs which, I later learned, were made by prisoners in the state penitentiary. I could see how to get to the tables, and how to get from there to the rostrum, but the experience left my concern intact when I realized that I had no idea which of the two tables I was supposed to sit at, or even whether it mattered.

That night I stayed up past midnight going over the outline of my argument: Thirty minutes, with some space left to answer the questions appellate judges often ask during oral argument.

The next morning, as instructed, I arrived a half hour before the court convened and checked in with the clerk, who answered my inquiry about where I should sit and explained a few other procedural matters as well.

I was momentarily relieved, but as I sat at my assigned table, looking through my outline one last time while waiting for the justices to appear, my nervousness returned full force. Suddenly the bailiff banged his gavel, everyone rose, as he demanded, and the seven justices filed in and took their places in seven massive high-backed chairs behind the bench. As soon as they were settled, the clerk called out the name of the first case to be argued that day: "*People of the State of Illinois, defendant in error, vs. James Strong, plaintiff in error*"—meaning that Strong, my client, was the appellant, the party who was claiming there had been a mistake during the trial which the Supreme Court should reverse. Chief Justice Schaefer, a man highly regarded for his honesty and intellect, invited me, by name, to begin my argument. As I approached the podium, I somehow allowed my outline to get underneath my other papers. It took a few seconds to fumble through the papers and find the outline—I knew what I intended to say first, but in my mind the outline was an essential crutch—and then I began, speaking the words which lawyers use throughout the country when beginning an oral argument before an appellate court: "Chief Justice [Schaefer], may it please the court . . ."

As I spoke those words, my anxiety miraculously dissolved, as it would at the beginning of every argument I would present for the rest of my career.

For the next ten minutes or so, my argument progressed essentially as I had prepared it, without interruption from the justices. My primary contention was that the heroin Mr. Strong had been convicted of selling to a state narcotics agent had been supplied to Strong shortly before the sale by a state informant, and that for an agent of the state to supply my client with the drugs used to arrest

him was entrapment. It was essential the court believe the evidence
was undisputed that the informant supplied the narcotics, as any
dispute would be resolved in favor of the state—appellate courts
do not reevaluate disputed issues of fact. (Prosecutors, commenting on claims of innocence based on evidence discovered after
a trial and conviction, often say that the finding of guilt has been
reviewed and approved by numerous other courts during the
process of appeals and postconviction proceedings. Such claims are
simply false, as the prosecutor well knows. Except in the most
extraordinary circumstances, appellate courts do not reconsider
questions of guilt or innocence.)

I had just finished that part of my argument when one of the justices rose and disappeared behind a black curtain. I was stunned. I
had no idea what was happening, but kept on with my argument.
A minute or two later, another justice left. Now throughly confused, I wondered if I had somehow offended the judges. Finally,
addressing the chief justice, I asked if I should go on or wait until—
what, I didn't really know—but the chief justice interrupted: "No,
no, go on. They can hear you back there." So I did, learning later
that such conduct was common on the Court, as judges left to use
the bathroom, or look at a case that had been cited, or just make a
phone call or dictate a letter. The argument was piped back into the
chambers behind the curtain. It was a rude and unsettling practice
I have never seen in any other court—and one that the Illinois
Supreme Court finally ended some time later.

In those days, the Illinois Supreme Court was also unusual in
the paucity of its questioning of lawyers presenting oral arguments.
I finished my presentation in the *Strong* case without a single question, even though the legal issue I was raising was one that had not
previously been decided. There were very few Illinois cases on
entrapment under any circumstances, and none dealing with the
claim that it was entrapment for a government informant to supply
a suspect with narcotics.

The idea of the state supplying someone with drugs in order to
set up his arrest impressed me as grossly unfair, and in January

1961, the Illinois Supreme Court agreed and unanimously reversed Strong's conviction. Needless to say, I was delighted with the result, and still believe the decision was right. Today, however, in the wake of the "war on drugs" and the politicalization of criminal law, it is unlikely the result would be duplicated. An examination of references to the *Strong* decision in subsequent cases reveals it has often been cited, but almost never followed.

Winning the *Strong* case provided a needed boost to my confidence that I would someday become competent to handle cases on my own—a confidence shaken by the disaster of my first criminal trial and little improved by my work with Jim Sprowl and the other partners, all of whom appeared to enjoy a level of skill and easy self-confidence beyond anything I could ever hope to achieve. It also improved my reputation with the partners in a firm still small enough that a young associate's victory in the Illinois Supreme Court would be favorably noticed by most of the lawyers who worked in litigation.

Most important, although I did not know it until later, the *Strong* case helped me with Bert Jenner, the firm's most important partner. Sprowl had not told me about it at the time, but some months earlier Jenner had asked him how I was doing, and when Sprowl reported I was doing fine, Jenner sounded dubious, saying that whenever he saw me I seemed to be wandering aimlessly down the hall with my head down. He told Sprowl I might be smart, but he doubted I would make a trial lawyer. After the *Strong* decision was announced, however, Jenner had a conversation with Chief Justice Schaefer, who volunteered, "The young man in your firm who argued that entrapment case did a fine job—his argument changed the minds of several of the judges"—or so Jenner reported to Sprowl, who shared it with me as part of my next evaluation.

Sprowl did not wait for the mandatory annual associate evaluations to let you know what he thought of your work. Generally, he commented to his assistants about their work on a case as it progressed. Some of the other partners, however, hardly ever said a word until the required report, which left the younger associates who worked for them in the same state of anxiety they had experienced in their first year of law school, when no one had the faintest idea how he was doing until the first exams were given in January. Despite my own self-doubts, Sprowl's frequent and generally favorable comments kept me reasonably free of worry.

In early December 1963, John Crown and I tried our last criminal case together. The charges were kidnapping and aggravated rape. Our client had been identified by the victim in a lineup, over a month after the crime. He was put in the lineup after he was picked up for another rape in the same neighborhood. John and I were appointed in both cases, but the state elected to try the second charge first when evidence emerged that tended to support our client's claim that the first complainant was his ex-girlfriend who claimed rape only after he dumped her for another woman. Our client vehemently denied any contact at all with the second complainant, but having been charged so long after the Friday night when the crime allegedly occurred, he had no clear recollection of where he had been that night. He did say he had probably been at one or another of two local taverns he frequented.

After investigation failed to find any witness who could credibly say he or she had been with our client on the night in question, we settled on the defense that the complainant was simply, but understandably, wrong in her identification. Our client and the complainant lived in the same neighborhood, within two blocks of each other, and frequented the same neighborhood stores, restaurants, and bars. Our theory was that the victim had seen the defendant in the neighborhood, and when she was called down to police headquarters to view a lineup she knew would contain someone the police thought was her attacker, she picked out the one familiar face in the lineup.

Our client was employed, presentable, and had no prior record, so he was able to testify, deny the crime, and say that although he didn't know her, when he saw the complainant in the courtroom, he recalled seeing her around the neighborhood. When the evidence and arguments were completed, the case was submitted to the jurors on a Thursday morning. They were still deliberating at 3:00 P.M. when the sound of a loud, angry argument could be heard through the closed door of the jury room. After fifteen minutes or so, the argument subsided, and not long thereafter the jury informed the bailiff that they had reached a verdict. The jury filed back into the courtroom, and at the judge's request identified their elected foreman, a white, middle-aged salesman named Klein.*

"Has the jury reached a verdict?" the judge asked.

"We have, Your Honor," Mr Klein replied.

"What is your verdict?"

Reading from a verdict form the jury had filled out by placing an X in the appropriate boxes, Mr. Klein announced: "On count one of the indictment, aggravated kidnapping, we the jury find the defendant not guilty. On count two of the indictment, aggravated rape, we the jury find the defendant not guilty."

The prosecutor looked stunned, the judge annoyed. Instead of the effusive thanks usually showered on juries that return guilty verdicts, the judge thanked them gruffly for their service and announced they were discharged and could return to the jury room for their belongings and then leave. As the jury filed out, the judge called on our client to rise, and after announcing that a judgement of not guilty would be entered on both counts of indictment, directed the bailiff to take him back to the lockup for return to the county jail, where he would remain pending disposition of the first rape charge. "You're a lucky man," the judge intoned. "If it had been up to me, I'd have found you guilty. Court is adjourned." He banged his gavel and was gone.

As soon as the judge disappeared into his chambers, the prosecutor made a beeline for the jury room where, I knew, he would tell the jury about the other rape charge and berate them for their verdict. (Many judges would not allow such contact today, but at the time it was standard procedure for some prosecutors, aimed at making sure the next time the jurors were called for duty, they would start out determined to make up for the "error" they made in this case.)

John and I followed the prosecutor into the jury room and when he was done we tried to reassure the jurors their verdict was correct, and asked them to tell us how they had reached it—what arguments and evidence had been most persuasive. Most of the jurors said the differences between the description the complainant gave the police on the night of the crime and our client's appearance, together with the logic of our argument that she selected him because he looked familiar, had caused them to have reasonable doubts about the correctness of the identification. But the most surprising story emerged from two jurors who held out for a guilty verdict until the very end. It was their holdout that caused the hot argument we could hear—but not understand—through the jury-room door. They had finally been persuaded to vote not guilty when one of the other jurors came up with an argument which had not been mentioned during the trial. It was now December 5, 1963, only thirteen days after the murder of President John F. Kennedy in Dallas. Among the widely reported evidence that Lee Harvey Oswald was the killer was the fact that Oswald's trigger hand had been tested and telltale traces of the chemicals in gunpowder had been found. One of the jurors pointed out that the prosecutor had produced no evidence that gunpowder was found on our client's hand, despite testimony that the person who kidnapped Mrs. Y had a gun, and had fired warning shots at her husband when he tried to rescue his wife. Surely such a test would have been conducted on our client, and the results put in evidence by the prosecution if they were positive. That the defendant had no gunpowder on his hands was strong evidence he was not the kidnapper.

It was enough to persuade the two holdouts. The problem was no such test had been done for the simple reason that our client was not arrested until over a month after the crime. Had there been gunpowder residue on his hands on the night of the crime, it would have been gone long before he was arrested.

Studies of juries conducted by Professors Harry Kalven and Hans Zeisel of the University of Chicago Law School have shown that once the number of holdouts to a verdict supported by the majority is reduced to one or two members of a twelve-person jury, the jury seldom hangs. Alone or with only one supporter, holdout(s) soon give in, and probably would have in this case. Nonetheless, it was a strange (and unusual) way to win a case. At the same time, self-evaluation of my performance during the trial persuaded me that at long last there was reason to hope that one day I would become a competent trial lawyer.

While I was trying the rape case in Chicago, Jim Sprowl had begun the trial of another case in central Illinois. Late one afternoon, less than a week after my trial was over, Jerry Solovy came into my office, white-faced, to tell me he had just learned that Mr. Sprowl had collapsed in the courtroom that afternoon and been rushed to a hospital. He had a ruptured aorta, and although by some miracle he did not bleed to death before reaching the hospital, he was in critical condition. Two days later, he died.

CHAPTER 2
PROGRESS

Jim Sprowl was my friend, a fine lawyer, my first professional mentor, and one of the nicest men I have ever known. His death was an enormous personal loss with professional consequences as well. Some things were obvious and immediate. Sprowl was the only senior partner in the firm with sufficient knowledge and appreciation of my work to act as my advocate when yearend evaluations and bonuses were passed out and, most important, when the discussion turned to the subject of whether an associate was "making progress toward partnership."

Then, as now, "making partner" was the holy grail for young lawyers joining large firms in big cities, and while in those days firms in Chicago (unlike New York) claimed that as a matter of policy they expected every associate they hired to become a partner, everyone understood it was not quite true. If the people you worked for liked you and thought you were a good lawyer, and if the firm's business held up well enough that making you a partner did not adversely effect the income of the existing partners, and if you had or seemed likely to develop some significant clients of your own (or had developed an expertise so essential to servicing existing business that the firm could not afford to let you go), then yes, you would likely become a partner between eight and ten years after you graduated from law school—but those were quite a few ifs. Jerry Solovy had been approved for partnership before Jim Sprowl died, effective January 1, 1964. Jerry and I had become personal friends and I knew he thought well of my work, but as a new partner he would have little influence. Four and a half years after joining the firm and without a senior supporter, I would have some making up to do.

Today, of course, the chances of making partner would be much worse. Large firms in Chicago and every other major city now hire many more associates than they expect to admit to the partnership. Efforts are made to weed out those who will not make it before the year of final decision, but it is not unusual for a large firm to have a dozen or more associates still hoping to make partner after eight or nine years with the firm—and then admit only a handful of them. Some of the rest may be offered salaried positions as permanent associates (or some euphemism for that job), and some firms will attempt, with varying success, to place their partnership rejects in the law departments of their major corporate clients; but inevitably others will simply be told to "take the time you need" to find another job—law-firm-speak for "you're fired." That message comes as quite a shock to young men and women who since grammar school have been at the top of their class, always gotten into the best schools, always gotten the best jobs, and always seen themselves as superior in work and intellect. Anyone who accepts a high-paid job with a large urban law firm should understand the odds and be prepared to accept the results. For young lawyers with the credentials to be hired in the first place, there will be many attractive alternatives available if they fail to make partner, but every year there are some who never recover from the rejection.

Another problem arising from Mr. Sprowl's death took longer to appreciate. While I received assignments from other partners while he was alive, Sprowl always knew what I was doing, and was in a position to protect me from the impossible demands of other partners who, inevitably, thought their assignment was all I should concentrate on, and should have been finished yesterday. Now the bulk of my assignments would have to come from a broad range of partners, and only I could keep track of what I was supposed to do and establish priorities for doing it. The problem was complicated by the need to gain the confidence of partners who had little previous contact with me. I knew they would not be impressed by my declining their assignments, and even less so if I accepted an assignment and failed to complete it on time, or did it poorly. The inevitable result was a lot more nights and weekends at the office until I finally learned to risk saying no.

In retrospect, the problems I encountered in the years following the death of Jim Sprowl are nothing compared to the demands on today's large-firm associates. While Sprowl was alive, my "chargeable hours" probably averaged between 1,600 and 1,800 per year. After his death they rose to about 2,000 for a few years until I gained the self-confidence to take more control of the assignments I would accept. Today, associates in many of the large firms in major cities are expected to charge a minimum of 2,200 hours to paying clients every year. Given the time required for administration and other nonchargeable matters, you can't do it in less than 60 to 80 hours a week.

For all the problems, as time passed, some positives emerged. As I began to receive assignments from a broader range of partners, my exposure to different practices and personalities provided ideas I could try to incorporate (or not incorporate) in my own approach to handling legal disputes.

My experience in trying pro bono criminal cases had given me enough confidence to handle some of the firm's civil cases on my own, and lawyers who handled the firm's business and real estate clients began sending me some of the smaller cases their clients were involved in. I also "inherited" several cases I had been working on with Jim Sprowl where the client had come to trust me enough to let me take charge of the matter rather than insisting that it be reassigned to an older lawyer. As a result, I had to exercise my own judgment about how to prepare the case for trial, whether or not to settle it, and how the case should be tried.

In addition, I was increasingly enlisted by Prentice Marshall and

Tom Sullivan to help them in their own cases and in cases Jenner had turned over to them, or where Jenner was still involved but a third lawyer with trial experience was needed. Marshall and Sullivan were great trial lawyers, and I learned an enormous amount from each of them. They also became two of my closest friends.

Thus it was that over the five years following Jim Sprowl's death, my education as a courtroom lawyer progressed in ways that were sometimes painful, often stressful, but always fascinating.

I learned the importance of knowing as much as possible about your judge, and conducting yourself accordingly. In a case for a major airline company, I watched Bert Jenner treat Judge Julius Hoffman with elaborate courtesy (some would say blatant flattery), and saw Hoffman respond like a four-month old puppy, grinning and wagging his tail while peeing copiously on opposing counsel. At the time Jenner was chairman of the American Bar Association Committee on the Federal Judiciary, and I later realized that Hoffman may have been responding more to the hope that Bert would help him advance to the Court of Appeals than to the flattery.

Nevertheless, it was a useful tactic with Hoffman, a despicable man who was widely rumored to have purchased his federal judgeship with a $50,000 contribution to Everett Dirksen's senatorial campaign and who regularly turned the concept of justice on its head, bullying lawyers and litigants alike while consistently catering to the powerful and treating the weak with disdain.

The great master at handling Hoffman was Maury Walsh, one of Chicago's best criminal-defense lawyers, who regularly won acquittals for his clients despite Hoffman's efforts to signal the jury that they should convict. Hoffman despised him, but Walsh responded with elaborate deference to every sneering insult and insinuation Hoffman could deliver, until finally the jury would begin to feel sorry for Walsh and his client and treat Hoffman's transparent bias as reason enough to acquit.

Hoffman himself took pains to ingratiate himself with the jury, treating them with feigned but convincing courtesy and respect, so his efforts to sway the jury's verdict could be dangerous to your case, especially in a short trial. If the case lasted long enough, however, his bias would eventually show through. A classic example was the criminal trial of the "inventors" and promoters of the phony cancer cure Krebiozen. A major reason Krebiozen achieved widespread fame was its support by Dr. Andrew Ivy, a highly regarded medical researcher and head of the Department of Clinical Sciences at the University of Illinois. The government concluded that Ivy's support of the drug was corrupt, influenced by payments from the inventors, the Durovic brothers, and an overweening ambition to win the Nobel Prize in medicine. Thus Ivy was included in a mail fraud indictment along with the Durovics and another doctor who had tested the drug and allegedly falsified the results. The cast of defense lawyers was as odd and varied as the cast of defendants. John Sembower, a lawyer who had little previous criminal-defense experience represented the distinguished, scholarly-looking Dr. Ivy, Maury Walsh represented the other doctor, and the Durovics were represented by a lawyer named Julius Sherwin, whose demeanor toward Hoffman was the opposite of Walsh's, nasty and confrontational.

Some time earlier, the chancellor of the University of Illinois had written a book about the Krebiozen controversy in which he strongly criticized Ivy, and Ivy had sued for libel. Pren Marshall and I were defending the libel case, and we both spent some time attending the criminal trial to gather information that might be useful to us. From the start, Judge Hoffman did everything he could to belittle the defense and sway the jury in favor of the prosecution. Sherwin loudly protested every adverse ruling and met every insult and snide comment in kind, leaving no doubt of his opinion that Hoffman was biased and unfair. Walsh met every flare-up between Hoffman and Sherwin with a courteous, soft-spoken renewal of his request that his client's case be severed from that of the other defendants. At first I thought Sherwin's insulting treatment of the judge was bound to backfire, especially since the judge was even more elaborately concerned with the jury's every comfort than usual. As the trial wore on, however, Hoffman, infuriated by Sherwin's insults, and apparently even more infuriated by Walsh's polite but repetitious requests for a severance, became more and more blatantly biased in his rulings and treatment of all the defendants.

In the end, the jury returned a verdict of not guilty for everyone. Hoffman was furious, and when one of the marshals reported that after the jury was discharged he had found a newspaper in the jury room containing an article favorable to Krebiozen, he ordered the U.S. attorney to investigate how it got there. When one of the jurors admitted that he had brought in the paper, Hoffman held him in contempt of court. Thereafter, when he sentenced the juror to a substantial term of imprisonment and the juror's wife cried out in protest, he sent her to prison as well. It was a classic Julius Hoffman result. It also demonstrated that sometimes there is more than one way to skin a cat. Nonetheless, the Sherwin approach is not recommended for everyday use—and unfortunately, some lawyers tend to use it every day.

Jenner treated every judge he appeared before in the same obsequious way he treated Julius Hoffman, and while some of them undoubtedly recognized his flattery for what it was, no one seemed especially offended by it, and a surprising number appeared to be influenced by it.

Not long after Jim Sprowl died I discovered that Jenner was not the only lawyer who believed there is nothing to be lost by playing to the human ego in dealing with judges. For some time I had been working with Sprowl in defending the primary-school district in the Chicago suburb where I lived against a personal-injury claim arising from an onstage explosion during a children's theater production. When Sprowl died, I took over the case, and as a result of a recent Illinois Supreme Court decision I had filed a motion to dismiss the claim on the basis of the doctrine of sovereign immunity. My opponent was an older lawyer named Louis Davidson who was one of the city's leading plaintiff's-personal-injury lawyers. Davidson, a soft spoken man with thinning hair, glasses, and a pleasant smile, was nevertheless a feared advocate, known to the personal-injury bar as "Whispering Lou" for his habit of situating himself close to the jury so he could mutter derogatory comments about the testimony of his opponent's witnesses loud enough for the jury to hear, but too soft to be heard by the judge or opposing lawyer.

The Circuit Court of Cook County, Law Division, had recently inaugurated a policy of having a group of judges assigned full time to hear and decide "dispositive motions"—that is, motions which, if granted, would end the case. Since these matters did not require a full courtroom with jury box, witness chair, and other furniture, the judges assigned to hear them were instead assigned to smaller rooms, informally laid out with a desk for the judge and a single table where the lawyers could sit and lay out their papers.

The judge to whom my motion was assigned for hearing and decision had been on the court for many years and was highly regarded for his fairness and knowledge of the law. Before this assignment, he had been one of the judges who handled the trials of important personal-injury cases, and Davidson had tried jury cases before him many times. I had never seen him before, and perhaps for that reason he went out of his way to make me feel comfortable as we sat before him—expressing sympathy about Mr. Sprowl's death and engaging in a few minutes of small talk on various subjects before asking me to proceed with my argument in support of my motion to dismiss. Sitting on one side of the table, with Davidson sitting across from me, I spoke for perhaps fifteen minutes. When I finished, the judge asked if Davidson wanted to respond.

"Yes, I do, Your Honor," Davidson replied, rising from his chair as he spoke, "but I wonder if Your Honor would permit me an indulgence. You know, I have appeared before Your Honor so many times, over so many years, and I have so much respect for Your Honor that it just doesn't seem right to me to address you without standing. I wonder if it would be all right if I stand while I make my argument."

The judge, who was no fool, grinned at Davidson, and then at me, but I could see that beneath his amusement he was pleased. "Certainly, Lou, if that makes you more comfortable." The judge's grin seemed reassuring, but I knew I'd been trumped, and I couldn't help wondering if it would affect the outcome.

When the arguments were over, the judge said he would take the case under advisement and inform us of his ruling in a few weeks. Afterward, in the hall, I kidded Davidson about his ploy, but he could see I was concerned, and angry I had permitted myself to be made to look less respectful of the court. He told me not to worry, this was a judge who would call the case the way he saw it—he'd just wanted to have a little fun with me, and with the judge. "But you know," he went on, "the truth is it was more than that. I really did feel uncomfortable not standing up."

The importance of knowing as much as possible about the judges you appear before extends far beyond issues like their susceptibility to flattery. In the state courts in Chicago, and to a lesser extent the federal court, almost all of the judges owed their seats to the boss of the local Democratic organization, who, from 1955 until his death in 1976, was "Da Mare"—Richard J. Daley. The question was not what would happen in a case with obvious and important political consequences—that was a given. The hard part was to figure out whether your case involved some kind of political issue that wasn't obvious. With some judges, almost any case might have some aspect that was likely to influence the judge—was your opponent "connected" and your judge the kind who always ruled in favor of such a lawyer? If so, and the case warranted it, you needed to hire an equally or more connected co-counsel. (Some lawyers made large fees for doing little more than putting their names on pleadings.) If the case would not support a co-counsel, and you couldn't get rid of the judge, you needed to explain the facts of life to your client, and either settle or prepare to appeal.

In personal-injury cases, some judges were reliably pro-plaintiff, others the opposite, but since I rarely handled such cases (the school-board case was an anomaly) that didn't matter. In state court, almost all the judges assigned to the Criminal Court of Cook County were former prosecutors and generally favored the prosecution, but some were worse than others, and you had only one chance for a change of venue from an especially bad draw.

No judges liked lawyers to be late for a scheduled appearance, but some were fanatics, and would accept no excuse, even if you called chambers in advance to explain your problem. One federal judge with whom I tried a case imposed a fine on any lawyer who showed up in court so much as a few seconds late. If it happened more than once during the same case, the amount of the fine increased each time. There were multiple defendants in the case, and when one of the lawyers was a tiny bit late for the third time, the fine was more than he could pay out of his pocket. We waited anxiously to see what the judge would do next, but fortunately one of the other lawyers always carried a large sum of cash and bailed out his colleague before the judge announced what he would do. It was the last time anyone was late.

Another federal judge made a practice of convening court precisely on time. If one of the lawyers was late, he would nevertheless bring the jurors into the courtroom. Informed by the judge of the reason for the delay, the jurors would be kept sitting in their seats with nothing to do until the tardy lawyer finally arrived. I knew about the practice and always tried to arrive at least fifteen minutes early to avoid any unexpected problem. Despite that precaution, I arrived late one day during the trial of an important civil case when I was stranded on the wrong side of the Chicago River from a drawbridge that was stuck open. "How nice of you to join us, Mr. Tucker. We've been waiting for you," the judge declared with heavy sarcasm. Prompted by the judge, several of the jurors looked mightily impatient, although they could not have been waiting more than five or six minutes. I apologized profusely and for the rest of the trial arrived a half hour early in the morning and ate lunch in the courthouse cafeteria.

Before Jim Sprowl died, the firm had planned to add his name and Sam Block's to the firm name after the first of the year.

Instead, only Block's name was added, and a few years later, the name was shortened permanently to Jenner & Block. Sam Block was a brilliant lawyer whose practice was primarily the handling of complicated business transactions, but he had been trained as a trial lawyer and still handled business litigation as well. Not long after Sprowl's death he asked me to take primary responsibility, albeit under his supervision, for a case involving patent royalties owed to our client. Before the case came to trial I arrived at a settlement which involved drafting a new agreement between the parties to clarify their rights and avoid any future dispute about the amount of payments due.

Some years later, the company again stopped paying, claiming, among other things, that the contract I had drawn was ambiguous and contrary to public policy. This time the case fell entirely into my lap. The truth was the claims the company raised to justify stopping its payments to our client were entirely spurious—the company was in financial difficulty and simply stopped making payments in the hope that delay and the possibility of obtaining a reduction in another settlement would solve its problems.

In the end, my client refused to modify the agreement or settle for anything less than all he was owed. After a week's bench trial before a federal judge, we won a complete victory. Even so, as the trial unfolded, I came to realize I probably should not have handled the case myself. For the same reason it is a mistake to try a case for a beloved family member, it was a bad idea for me to defend an agreement I had prepared myself—one of my firstborn legal children. The level of anxiety is high enough in any trial without adding that additional element.

I didn't fully recognize the problem until the opposing lawyer, who had a weak legal position, decided to have some fun at my expense during the trial, and in the process see if he could unnerve me into agreeing to a settlement. The defendant had hired Max Wildman, one of the city's best and most experienced courtroom lawyers to defend the case. Max had been the most active trial lawyer in the largest law firm in Chicago, then known as Kirkland,

Fleming, Green, Martin and Ellis. Several years earlier, he left Kirkland and formed his own firm, taking with him several other experienced litigators.

A delightful man with a wicked sense of humor, Max showed up unexpectedly (to me, at least) on the day the trial began, after all the pretrial work had been done by an associate closer to my age and experience. He immediately set out in a variety of ways to try to shatter my confidence, which was already a little fragile as a result of the sudden appearance of an opponent who was twenty years older and fifty times more experienced. His main tactic was to accost me in the corridor before court opened each morning and describe in lurid language the havoc he intended to wreck on my case with his cross-examination of my client. Without, of course, disclosing the facts he was relying on, he supported these threats by displaying a copy of my client's deposition with dozens of pages folded over, and, I could see, heavy underlining of some of the text on those pages. It was with the ammunition of the testimony on those pages, he let me know, that he expected to destroy my client's credibility and win the case.

While I did my best to appear unconcerned, I was terrified. Every day after court I would pore over the deposition, and insist that my client once again rehearse with me the testimony I intended to adduce from him the next day, watching for anything that might be contradicted by what he had said in his deposition, which by now I knew almost by heart.

When, after two days of direct examination I turned my client over to Max Wildman for cross-examination, my heart was in my throat. Max rose, gathered up the several volumes of the deposition, laid them out on the podium in what appeared to be a carefully chosen order, and began his cross-examination. For the next fifteen minutes or so, he made three or four fairly innocuous points, and then, for the first time, reached for the depositions. He picked them up, walked back to his table, and announced he had no further questions.

There had been no realistic way for Max Wildman to win the

case—unless he frightened me into finding a way to lose it. He frightened me plenty, but fortunately it was a nearly impossible case to lose.

Over the years that followed I tried several other cases with or against Max Wildman or one of his partners, and ultimately began to receive client referrals from his firm and to represent the firm itself when it had legal problems, but Max never let me forget what he described—accurately, I suspect—as the look of panic that crossed my face every time he showed me the turned-down pages of my client's deposition.

While the vast majority of my work continued to be assisting older lawyers in a variety of major civil cases and trying some smaller ones myself, I continued taking on one or two pro bono criminal cases each year. In March 1964, I was appointed by the United States Court of Appeals for the Seventh Circuit to represent an indigent prisoner who was serving a life sentence for murder in the Illinois State Penitentiary.

Theodore Robinson had been convicted of killing his girlfriend in 1959 and his conviction was affirmed by the Illinois Supreme Court in 1961. Thereafter he filed a *pro se* (acting as his own lawyer) petition for a writ of habeas corpus in the federal district court in Chicago, alleging that his federal constitutional rights had been violated in his state trial. After reviewing the record of the state court proceedings, Julius Hoffman had dismissed the petition without an evidentiary hearing, without appointing counsel, and without even requiring the state to respond to it.

An examination of the trial record revealed a wealth of evidence in support of the proposition that Robinson was insane at the time of the murder, and was probably still insane at the time of his trial. What a federal court could do about it, given that both issues had been considered and rejected in the state court, was less apparent. In two landmark cases decided in 1962 and 1963, the Supreme Court had emphatically stated the duty of federal courts to use the historic writ of habeas corpus to protect the constitutional rights of state-court criminal defendants, even if doing so requires an evidentiary hearing on issues already considered by the state court, and even if the issue has been waived under state procedural rules by the failure of defense counsel to raise it during the state court trial and appeal. Only a defendant—not his counsel—can waive a constitutional right, the Supreme Court declared, and he must be shown to have done so knowingly. Commencing with the ascension of William Rehnquist to Chief Justice of the United States, the writ of habeas corpus has been steadily emasculated, and today neither of those principles has survived, but in 1964 recognition of the powerful role of the "Great Writ" in protecting constitutional rights was at its apex.

Still, there had to be a constitutional right to protect. Two theories suggested themselves: that the trial court had deprived the defendant of due process of law by refusing him the opportunity to call an expert witness on the question of his sanity at the time of the crime, and also by failing to conduct a hearing into his sanity at the time of his trial. Both claims were problematical—the foundation for the claim that the defendant could have presented an expert if given a short midtrial continuance was weak, and neither the defendant or his trial lawyer had asked for a hearing on his sanity at the time of trial. Moreover, the trial judge had observed the defendant during the trial, and his conduct arguably suggested the defendant understood the proceedings.

The answer, it seemed to me, was to emphasize the many facts that showed that regardless of whether he could have produced an expert witness or could understand the charges and cooperate with his lawyer, Theodore Robinson was surely insane when he killed his girlfriend, and probably during his trial as well.

When Robinson was seven or eight years old, he was struck on the head by a brick dropped from a third-floor window. Thereafter, his mother testified, he acted peculiar and suffered from headaches. Later, home on leave from the army, he flew into a rage for no reason and kicked a hole in his mother's breakfront. When his mother came into the room to see what had happened, he stared at her without speaking and paced the floor. From then on, he seemed lost in himself, glaring and refusing to speak. In 1951, at his aunt's house, he began pacing the floor and saying someone was after him. His aunt called Robinson's mother, but when she arrived, he would not let his aunt open the door, saying someone would come in and shoot him. When his mother finally got in and went to hug him, he pushed her away, saying someone was about to shoot him. He was agitated and foaming at the mouth. The police were called, and he was taken to the psychiatric ward at Cook County Hospital. He was diagnosed as schizophrenic, and after a week he was transferred to the Kankakee State Mental Hospital. At the request of his wife he was released after six or seven weeks, but he continued to act strangely, and his mother believed he was still insane. A year and a half later, he shot and killed his eighteen-month-old baby and then attempted suicide by shooting himself in the head.

Robinson spent four years in the penitentiary for the killing of his baby. When he was released, he still did abnormal things and appeared to have a disturbed mind. In late 1957 or early 1958, his mother went to the police and asked them to pick him up and have him sent back to a mental hospital, but the warrant that was issued was never served. In 1959, shortly before the murder of his girlfriend, his mother again obtained a warrant to have him picked up and committed, but the murder occurred before he was picked up. In addition to his mother, three other relatives testified to incidents of Robinson's behavior up to three or four days before the murder which led them to believe he was insane. The stipulated testimony of a police officer revealed that after shooting his baby, Robinson had not only shot himself, but when that failed to kill him, jumped into a lagoon to try to drown himself.

The evidence of Robinson's conduct at the time of his girlfriend's murder also suggested insanity. He had walked into the restaurant where she worked and pointed a gun at her from a few feet away. He stared at her for a minute or more without saying a word, and then walked some twenty feet away, to the far end of the restaurant counter, and leaped over it. By going to the end of the counter, Robinson had placed two other restaurant employees between himself and his girlfriend, but he rushed past them in the narrow space behind the counter and fired his gun. His girlfriend jumped over the counter and ran out the door, where she was found dead on the sidewalk. Robinson had also leaped the counter, rushed out behind her, and continued down the street.

In addition to the evidence of insanity, the record showed that the trial judge had consistently devoted more energy to demanding that the lawyers hurry the case to conclusion then to a full and deliberate consideration of the relevant facts. On several occasions he berated counsel for causing a few minutes' delay, reminding them that there were thousands of other cases that had to be tried. Despite the evidence of Robinson's extensive history of mental illness and his inexplicable behavior at the time of the murder, at the close of his case, the trial judge summarily refused a request that he adjourn the trial until the next morning so a psychiatrist could be called to testify on Robinson's sanity at the time of the crime. And the instant defense counsel spoke his last words in closing argument, the trial judge passed judgment:

> THE COURT: Very well. All right, bring up the defendant, please. The defendant is found guilty of the crime of murder. He is sentenced to the State Penitentiary for a term of his natural life. Take him away.

If I could persuade the appellate judges that Robinson had been the victim of the trial court's rush to an erroneous judgment that he was sane, I thought, they would be far more willing to accept the harder argument that this miscarriage of justice amounted to a violation of his right to due process of law under the United States Constitution. Thus, in preparing my brief to the Court of Appeals, I discussed the facts in great detail.

Oral argument in the case was set for November 19, 1964, and after filing my reply brief on November 12, I began preparing my argument. There are almost as many ways to prepare for a courtroom argument (trial or appellate) as there are courtroom lawyers, and no one of them is the "right" way. There is, however, a "right" result: a planned speech that fits comfortably into the time allowed and that the lawyer knows well enough to deliver without reading, to return to after being interrupted by questions or objections, and to shorten as necessary without leaving out something crucial. In addition, for an appellate argument, one must have a sense of what questions are likely to be asked by the court and how to answer them, and a sufficiently comprehensive knowledge of the facts and relevant cases to answer questions you did not anticipate. And, in my opinion, you should also have planned and memorized a concluding sentence or two that persuasively summarize the most important reason the court or jury should decide the case in your client's favor.

I began preparing to argue *Robinson v. Pate* in the Court of Appeals the same way I had prepared for arguments in the state courts: by writing out my complete argument in longhand, and then reading it to myself, editing it, and then reading it again against the clock. It would inevitably be too long, so I would edit it again to bring it within the allowable time, and then have it typed. Next I read the typed copy several more times, underlining the points I wanted to emphasize, and then dictated an outline, based on the points I had underlined. Using the outline, I would deliver the argument to myself often enough to be comfortable that I could hit all the important points with only the outline, and then I would outline the outline, reducing it to its essence as reflected by a short sentence or two for each major issue. Finally, I would again deliver the argument to myself with only that final outline to look at, until I felt comfortable that I could say everything I wanted to say, in the time available, without any crutch but the one- or two-page final outline to glance at once in a while to be sure I hadn't left out an important point.

I was now prepared to make the kind of uninterrupted argument I would make in a closing argument to a jury, but this was to be an argument to a panel of judges, who might interrupt and ask questions. Indeed, while very few questions had been asked in the arguments I had previously made in the Illinois Appellate and Supreme courts, lawyers who had argued in the United States Court of Appeals warned me that depending on which three of the Court's judges were assigned to hear the *Robinson* case, I was likely to be asked lots of questions, especially questions about what authority the federal courts had to effectively second-guess a decision of the Illinois courts in an Illinois murder case. With this in mind, I tried to think of all the questions I might ask if I were a judge—and then, how I should answer them. When I had thought of everything I could, I enlisted Jerry Solovy and Pren Marshall to read the briefs and propose additional questions they thought might be asked. It was a sobering experience. There were, I realized, a lot of problems with the case which had not been fully developed in the state's brief and which I had not considered. The judges, however, might well raise them on their own. With the help of Jerry and Pren, I prepared to give the best answers I could to the anticipated questions.

One thing I did not do was to argue the case aloud, to my wife, a friend, or a mirror, or to a panel of lawyers primed to ask the likely questions and force me to answer them on my feet. Over the years I tried these ideas and found I could not summon the necessary adrenaline rush to make a competent performance, and that failing to do so simply made me more nervous about the real thing. However, many lawyers employ these techniques and find them useful.

In consulting with Pren and Jerry, I revisited the question of whether, in my argument, I should emphasize the facts of the case, as I had in my brief. In my own mind I had concluded that I should, but I knew that doing so was contrary to the advice of some judges and texts on appellate advocacy. In many appellate courts, counsel are specifically informed that the judges will have read the briefs before argument and will be familiar with the facts of the case. Sometimes a note sent to counsel before argument or posted on the lectern states expressly that counsel need not discuss the facts. In the same vein, many law-school courses, especially those taught by the increasingly numerous professors who have had little or no experience in the actual practice of law, pay scant attention to the facts of the cases their students are asked to read, as though the legal principles set forth in the opinions sprung fresh from the minds of the judges, uncluttered by the real-world problems that brought the parties to court in the first place. As a result, surprising numbers of top graduates from top law schools begin their careers writing research memos and briefs which display an utter lack of understanding of the fact that in arguing a real case, an abstract statement of the law is of no value unless there is a logical connection between the facts of the case cited and the facts of the case at hand. Even some experienced lawyers seem to believe an appeal to the equities of a case has no place in an argument directed to judges, as though a judge is some kind of different creature than an ordinary flesh-and-blood human with flesh-and-blood biases, sympathies, and emotions.

It seemed to me the opposite must be true—hence the axiom that bad cases make bad law—or, on a more positive note, that good cases, cases with facts that appeal to the human instinct for fairness and logic, make good law for the party whose cause is so blessed. Pren and Jerry assured me that at least in this case I was right, and I resolved to begin my oral argument the same way I had begun my brief, with a detailed recitation of the evidence of Theodore Robinson's insanity.

On November 19, 1964, the United States Court of Appeals for the Seventh Circuit still sat in a converted mansion tucked in the midst of luxury residences and apartment buildings on Chicago's North Side "Gold Coast." The courtroom itself was a beautiful chamber, well up to the task of impressing those who entered it with the power and majesty of the law (an essential element of courtroom design) while at the same time possessing a kind of warmth missing from the oppressively vast courtroom at the Illinois Supreme Court. Three weeks later, the court moved to new quarters in a Mies van der Rohe high-rise. By comparison, the courtrooms in the new building were cold and sterile, with full-ceiling fluorescent lighting that would prompt Abbie Hoffman, on trial five years later in the "*Chicago Eight*"[2] conspiracy case, to call Judge Julius Hoffman's courtroom "a neon oven." I have always been grateful for the chance to argue my first federal appeal in the gracious setting of the older courthouse.

There were seven active judges of the Seventh Circuit at the time, and although I knew my case would be heard by three of them, I did not know which three until I arrived at the courthouse, so I had learned as much as I could about each of the seven from older lawyers who had argued before the court. As it turned out, the panel for the day consisted of Judge Roger Kiley, who was reputed to be a good "draw" in a criminal case, Judge Win Knoch, a law-and-order conservative, and Judge Elmer Schnackenberg. "Schnack," as he was not very fondly called by the lawyers I talked to, was said to be a wild card whose most reliable characteristic was a nasty temper and a tendency to try to embarrass the lawyers who argued before him.

Given the complexity of the issues and Schnack's reputation, I was even more nervous waiting for my argument to begin than I had been before previous arguments. The wait seemed to last forever. Then, at last, the clerk called *Theodore Robinson v. Frank J. Pate, Warden* for argument. (In habeas cases, the warden of the prison where the petitioner is held is the nominal defendant.) I gathered my outline and other papers, stepped to the lectern, and discovered to my great relief that once again, as soon as I spoke the magic words "May it please the Court," adrenaline took over and my nervousness vanished.

Those who had warned me that the questioning was likely to be more lively than I had encountered in the Illinois courts were cor-

---

[2] The Chicago conspiracy case is more widely referred to as the "Chicago Seven" case, due to the midtrial severance of the eighth defendant, Bobby Seale, after he was notoriously bound and gagged in the courtroom on Judge Hoffman's orders. However, throughout this book I refer to it as the "Chicago Eight" case.

rect, although Judge Knoch did not participate. As predicted, Schnack was the most persistent questioner, but his legendary nastiness did not show itself until the assistant attorney general, arguing for the state, took his turn. At that point the judge made it quite clear with a series of acid questions that he thought the state's claim that there was insufficient evidence to overcome the presumption of Robinson's sanity was nonsense. Under Illinois law at the time, if there was sufficient evidence to overcome the presumption, the state was required to prove beyond a reasonable doubt that the defendant was sane at the time of the crime. In fact they had put on no evidence at all on the subject.

The state's argument was presented by Richard Michael, a lawyer who had recently succeeded William Wines as the state's primary appellate advocate. Wines was legendary for his brilliant arguments and sharp wit, which were all the more impressive because he suffered terribly from cerebral palsy. Watching him drag his twisted and apparently uncontrollable body to the lectern, it seemed unlikely he could speak at all, much less make a coherent argument; but once he began, few could match him. Interestingly, Michael, too, had a problem which made it hard to believe he would be an effective oral advocate: a serious stutter that sometimes made it difficult to talk to him in a normal setting, even without the pressure of an appellate argument. In fact, however, just as Bill Wines's palsy disappeared, so did Dick Michael's stutter when he began an argument. Michael made no headway with Judge Schnackenberg on the question of whether the evidence of Robinson's history of mental illness and strange conduct at the time of the crime were sufficient to overcome a presumption of sanity, but he was forceful in presenting the better argument that the Illinois rule shifting the burden of proof to the state was not required by the Constitution, and thus there was no basis for federal court intervention under the habeas corpus act.

All in all, when the arguments were over, I felt reasonably good about the case based on the questioning. "You can't tell how the case is going to be decided from the questioning" is a maxim of the legal profession; but when an argument is over, most appellate lawyers will nevertheless examine each question that was asked by each judge, turning it over and over like some ancient rune, trying to decipher its message about the judge's likely vote to affirm or reverse.

Right or wrong, I concluded that Judge Kiley was going to vote for some kind of relief, that I should count Judge Knoch as a loss even though he had not asked a single question, and that I had a better-than-even chance with Schnack, since he seemed to believe the case had been badly handled in the state courts. My confidence was bolstered a few days later when Bert Jenner stopped by my office and told me that a friend who had been in the courtroom had praised my argument. I was delighted that someone had given a favorable review of my argument to Jenner, who seemed impressed. By then I had come to understand the importance of his opinion to my future with the firm.

The *Robinson* case remained under advisement in the Court of Appeals for nearly six months, a period only a little longer than usual for the Court in those days, but so long that by the time the decision was finally announced on May 3, 1965, I had almost forgotten it was pending. By a vote of two-to-one, Judge Knoch dissenting, Judge Hoffman's denial of the writ was reversed. The case was remanded to the district court for evidentiary hearings on the question of whether Robinson was sane at the time of the crime, and whether he was denied due process of law by the failure to have a jury determine whether he was sane at the time of trial. If found insane at the time of the crime, Robinson was to be released. If found sane at the time of the crime, but denied due process by the failure to determine his sanity at the time of trial, he was also to be released, subject to the state's right to conduct a new trial within a reasonable time.

It was a terrific result, I thought, and I immediately wrote Robinson, predicting that although the state had a right to petition the U.S. Supreme Court for a writ of certiorari (the process by which the Supreme Court is asked to exercise its discretion to consider a case), I doubted certiorari would be granted, even if the state asked. My prediction was not unreasonable. Certiorari (always shortened to "cert" by lawyers) is granted in only a tiny percentage of cases—those which at least four of the nine justices believe are so important that review in the U.S. Supreme Court is justified. A fact-specific case like *Robinson* didn't seem to me to fit that profile, but to my great surprise my prediction was wrong. The state's cert petition was filed in July, after the Court adjourned for the summer, and therefore would not be acted on before the first Monday in October, when the Court always reconvenes.

There was no word on the first Monday, but three weeks later, a newspaper reporter called and asked my reaction to the Court's announcement that it would hear the case. I was flabbergasted, and said so. What I didn't say was that I was also enormously excited. Even including the lawyers in the solicitor general's office who argue the government's cases before the Court, far less than one percent of American lawyers ever have the opportunity to argue a case in the Supreme Court. So far as I knew, the only lawyers in my firm who had argued in the Court were Edward R. Johnson, a former senior partner who had argued a famous early antitrust case, and Tom Sullivan, who had argued another appointed criminal case a year or two earlier. Not even Bert Jenner, whose name was frequently mentioned as a possible appointee to the Court, had ever argued before it. Now, only seven years out of law school, I would have that opportunity. In my excitement, I nearly forgot that the Court's decision was a defeat. For my client, it meant the possibility of losing the victory we had won in the Court of Appeals, and at best, a delay of many months before he would be released from prison.

The reporter had told me the order granting cert included a request that the parties submit briefs on another issue in addition to those presented in the state's petition, but he could not quote the order. After calming down some I called the Supreme Court and got one of the clerks to read me the order, which instructed the parties to brief the additional question of whether "any of the further proceedings contemplated in the opinion of the Court of Appeals should be conducted in the appropriate Illinois courts rather than the District Court."

Now I understood. The Warren Supreme Court's recent decisions expanding federal court oversight of state criminal convictions had come under increasingly virulent attack by law-and-order conservatives and Southern states' righters. The Court of Appeals decision ordering a federal district court judge to reconsider the state-court decisions that Robinson was sane at the time of the crime and competent to stand trial was certain to engender a howl of protest, and the Supreme Court wanted to consider whether the ruling violated the principles of federalism, a doctrine that requires the federal courts to defer to state-court rulings in the absence of a clear violation of the U.S. Constitution.

John Stifler, who had worked on the Court of Appeals brief as a summer associate, had now graduated from law school and joined the firm, and I called him at once to enlist his assistance, especially regarding the additional issue the Court had inquired about. John was a brilliant lawyer who, in years to come, would work with me on a variety of other cases until he developed cancer and died tragically in his midthirties. In a short time, he produced a memo covering the relevant cases on federalism and providing an argument we were able to use with little change when the time came to respond to the state's brief.

The state filed its brief in early December, just as I was starting a short trial in another case. I obtained an extension of time to file a response until January 19, and was surprised to receive word from the Court that the case had been set for oral argument a week later. Several days before it was due we sent galley proofs of our brief to the state so they would have time to file a reply before the hearing. Then I began preparing my argument. For a week I did nothing else, first preparing my outline and then trying to anticipate and answer potential questions. Then, as now, the Supreme Court is notorious for its intensive questioning, sometimes filling so much time that the advocates are unable to give more than a sentence or two of their prepared remarks. Being questioned by Earl Warren, William O. Douglas, Hugo Black, and John Marshall Harlan about federalism, a subject that I had never seriously considered before this case, was daunting, and I devoted myself to the subject with great intensity while trying to maintain the outward appearance of calm. Fortunately, the number of relevant Supreme Court decisions was quite small, and with patient coaching from Stifler and another firm associate, Tom Eovaldi, both of whom had researched the issue and understood it better than I did, I finally began to feel moderately confident.

The argument in *Frank J. Pate, Warden v. Theodore Robinson* (the names were now reversed as a result of my victory in the Court of Appeals) was originally scheduled for Wednesday, January 25. In early January I was informed that the case would not be reached until January 26. I was not yet admitted to the bar of the Supreme Court and would have to be sworn in on or before the morning of the argument. I had already decided I wanted to watch another argument to familiarize myself with the Court's procedures and the courtroom itself, so I decided to go to Washington on Tuesday, January 24, and be sworn in the next morning.

My friend Donald Page Moore had temporarily left his law practice in Chicago to join the Justice Department in Washington and he was still there, completing his work on the prosecution of Teamsters' president Jimmy Hoffa. I knew he was acquainted with Thurgood Marshall, who was then Solicitor General of the United States and one of the great heroes of American law. To be admitted to the Supreme Court bar, a lawyer must be sponsored by someone who is already admitted. At my request, Don arranged for Marshall to be my sponsor, which meant I would be able to meet him and introduce myself, a thrill for me almost as great as the opportunity to argue before the Court.

Most Americans have seen TV or news photographs of the white marble building that houses the United States Supreme Court, but no photograph can convey the grandeur of the massive flight of marble stairs that lead into that building, nor can I imagine anything an American lawyer can do that compares with walking up those steps for the first time to argue a case inside. When I climbed the stairs on the morning of January 25, I was not going to argue my case until the next day, but that did not change my feelings. I was about to enter the highest temple of American justice. I had been invited, and would soon be part of it.

Once I walked between the sixteen huge white Corinthian columns that dominate the entrance to the building and through the open brass entrance doors, I was directed to the clerk's office to sign in. From there I was told to enter the courtroom itself, where I would sit on the spectator bench closest to the front of the room in the section reserved for members of the Supreme Court bar, and wait for my sponsor. Several other lawyers who were to be sworn in that day also waited on the front bench, but they already had their sponsors with them, and as the time when the Court would convene approached with no sign of the Solicitor General, I became convinced he was not coming, that I would not be admitted and would not be able to argue my case. Then he arrived, a tall, distinguished-looking man who, I knew, was raised in modest circumstances in Baltimore, but appeared born to the striped pants and morning coat worn by the Solicitor General of the United States when appearing in the Supreme Court. I rose to introduce myself, and before we could say more than a few words, the marshal bid everyone rise, thus announcing the imminent arrival of the Justices, who appeared almost by magic from behind a black curtain and took their seats on the high bench that filled the front of the room.

One by one, we applicants were called to the lectern with their sponsors, who vouched for our character and learning. Quickly, but with great warmth, we were each welcomed to the Court's bar by Chief Justice Warren. When it was over, I went to the clerk's office to be formally enrolled, and then returned to the courtroom where arguments were to begin in a landmark case brought by voters challenging the constitutionality of the Virginia poll tax. A three-judge district court had upheld the Virginia statute and the

Supreme Court had granted a full hearing on the plaintiffs' appeal. The United States had filed an amicus brief supporting the voters. "Amicus" briefs are filed by "friends of the court" who have an interest in a case, but are not actual parties in the lawsuit. In an unusual order the Court had granted the Government's request that additional time be allotted for oral argument on behalf of the amicus—to be presented by the Solicitor General himself.

As I had hoped, I learned some useful things about the Court's procedures, but watching that argument was probably not the best thing I could have done that day. Listening to the Court's piercing and persistent questioning of the Solicitor General and Marshall's prompt, learned, and precise answers was humbling enough, but he was one of the most famous oral advocates in American legal history, and I could hardly be surprised that his performance made me feel as though I had never been to law school, much less argued a real case before. If Marshall's performance made me feel inadequate, it made me feel almost sorry for the man who would have to stand up next and argue against him, even though I had no sympathy for Virginia's position. That man was George Gibson, a much smaller man than Thurgood Marshall, thin, gray-haired, and elegant, with that soft First-Family-of-Virginia accent that exists only in Richmond and its immediate vicinity. There were still a few private counsel who wore morning suits to argue in the Supreme Court in those days, and while I no longer recall if Mr. Gibson was wearing one, it would have been entirely consistent with his manner and appearance. But the amazing thing was that not long after George Gibson began his argument, it became apparent that he was every bit the equal of Thurgood Marshall as an advocate. His effort to defend a law whose result (and transparent purpose) was to discourage poor blacks from voting enjoyed little sympathy with the majority of the Justices, and Gibson was peppered with hostile questions from the moment he rose to argue. Somehow he answered all of them calmly and directly, while weaving a seamless defense of the statute out of his answers and the few moments of "free" argument time allowed him by the Court. He was not going to win the case, and everyone in the courtroom knew it, but his performance was stunning. When the Chief Justice abruptly adjourned court for the day and continued the case until the next morning with Gibson still on his feet, the only thing I could think was "What the hell am I doing here with men like this? I'll make an utter fool of myself."

My wife, my mother, and my sister were all arriving in Washington that afternoon to attend the momentous occasion of my argument the next day. I canceled our planned dinner together and dragged Stifler and Eovaldi off to my room to ask me more questions and help me with the answers. We ate room-service sandwiches and worked until nearly midnight, when I finally concluded that sleep was more important than any more cramming.

Near the front of the Supreme Court courtroom, a gated brass rail divides the room, separating the benches where members of the public can sit and watch the arguments from the area reserved for the lawyers who are presenting arguments. Inside the rail are four mahogany tables set with comfortable leather-upholstered chairs. Each place at each table is set with a writing pad and a white quill pen and ink pot. The quill pens are useless for writing, but lawyers arguing cases before the Court are allowed to keep them as souvenirs, and if any lawyer arguing at the Court for the first time has ever been so blasé as to leave without taking one of the pens, I have never heard of it.

The two tables closest to the raised bench are for the lawyers who are actually engaged in arguing the case the court is hearing, petitioners at the left-hand table, respondents on the right. Behind those tables are two identical tables for the lawyers who will argue the next case on the docket. When the Supreme Court is hearing arguments, there are no recesses taken between cases. Arguments begin in the morning as soon as the swearing in ceremony is over and continue until precisely 12:00 noon, when the Chief Justice declares the lunch recess (often in some lawyer's midsentence). Court reconvenes precisely at 1:00, and continues until 3:00, when it adjourns for the day. It is because the next argument follows immediately upon the end of its predecessor that the second set of tables is provided and counsel are required to be sitting there, ready to move up and begin their argument without delay. Thus, on the morning of January 26, I arrived well before the opening hour of 10:00 A.M., signed in with the clerk, walked through the brass rail to the front of the room, and unpacked my briefcase at the back right-hand table. John Stifler and Tom Eovaldi accompanied me, although unless I fainted dead away or became so undone by a question that I retreated to my table for help (neither seemed impossible) there was nothing more they could do to help me. At the table next to us, Richard Michael and an assistant were arranging their materials. We shook hands and wished each other well.

Precisely at 10:00 the marshal banged his gavel and everyone stood as the Justices appeared from behind the black curtain and the marshal called the Court into session: "The Honorable the Chief Justice and the Associate Justices of the Supreme Court of the United States. Oyez, oyez, oyez. All persons having business before the Honorable, the Supreme Court of the United States are admonished to draw near and give their attention, for the Court is now sitting. God save the United States and this Honorable Court. Be seated."

As soon as all the candidates had been admitted, the clerk announced the formal name of the poll-tax cases and George Gibson was invited to continue his argument. After a bit, a white light on the podium went on, signaling that Gibson had only five minutes left of his argument time. When the five minutes was up, the light turned red, signaling that his time was up.

Both sets of appellants had reserved time for rebuttal, and the last of the two rebuttal arguments was presented by an African-American lawyer who was confined to a wheelchair. He was assisted by another man, who wheeled him to the lectern and arranged his materials. After the lawyer spoke for a few minutes, the red light went on and Chief Justice Warren announced, "The case is sub-mitted," meaning that the fate of the Virginia poll tax was now in the hands of the Supreme Court. There was nothing more for the parties or their lawyers to do, the Justices would decide.

As counsel for the petitioner, it was now up to Dick Michael to make the first argument in *Pate v. Robinson*. As soon as the Chief Justice announced that the poll-tax case was submitted, the clerk read off the name of our case, and Michael gathered his materials and moved toward the lectern to begin his argument. In the meantime the man assisting the lawyer who had argued last gathered the lawyer's materials and was pushing his wheelchair away from the podium as Michael squeezed past to begin his argument. As soon as Michael reached the lectern, the Chief Justice nodded and announced, "Mr. Michael, you may begin your argument for petitioner."

Dick Michael stood stock-still, silent. From where I sat behind him, I could hear the low humming sound someone who stutters sometimes makes as he struggles to begin speaking. For some reason, Michael's ability to deliver a legal argument without stuttering had abandoned him. He stood in painful silence for what seemed to me forever, and must have seemed twice as long to him. In fact it was probably only a few seconds. Finally he was able to begin. "Mr. Chief Justice, may it please the Court. . . ." Then he was fine, and he made a good argument.

When the arguments were over, the lawyers went out to have a drink together, and Dick Michael told me what had happened. As he was moving up to the podium, concentrating on beginning his argument, he had accidentally stepped on the foot of the man who was pushing the lawyer's wheelchair. The man had turned on him furiously and said something like "You step on my foot again and I'll knock you on your ass." If it had happened to me, I'm not sure I could have ever begun to speak.

The Court did not question Michael as unremittingly as they had the lawyers in the poll-tax case, and, understandably, Michael was not quite as adept at answering questions as Thurgood Marshall or George Gibson. Still the hour passed quickly, with more time devoted to questions than to Michael's prepared argument. From the questioning, it seemed that most of the Justices were skeptical of the state's claim there was insufficient evidence Robinson was insane at the time of the crime to shift the burden to the state to prove his sanity. Most were also unimpressed by the claim that Robinson had waived the right to a determination of his sanity at the time of his trial. On the other hand, they seemed equally skeptical of the idea that the Illinois rule on proof of sanity at the time of the crime was required by the Constitution, and especially that it would be appropriate for a federal district court to retry that issue. Several of the judges who seemed generally favorable to my position on the waiver issue, however, also seemed troubled by the idea of having any court try to determine, six years later, whether Robinson had been competent to stand trial.

And then it was my turn to argue.

Although in questioning Dick Michael the Court had demonstrated an understanding of the basic facts, Michael had glossed over some of the most striking evidence of Robinson's mental illness in his answers, so I decided that while I would not repeat the facts in detail as I had in the Seventh Circuit, I would use Michael's omissions as an excuse to recite the most important facts he had failed to mention, which I did quickly and without interruption by the Court. As soon as I turned to the legal issues, however, the questioning began, much of it along the same lines as the questions that had been asked of Michael on the subject of whether my complaints about the state-court trial rose to the level of a denial of constitutional rights, and if so, what was the appropriate relief. About twenty minutes into my argument Chief Justice Warren interrupted and announced it was time for lunch.

I had been told by the clerk's office that the Robinson arguments would go over the lunch hour, and that if I wanted to take advantage of it, the Supreme Court kitchen would provide me with lunch (which I could order in advance) in a private room in the Court basement where I could eat undisturbed. I accepted, and sat barely picking at whatever I had ordered while trying to decide what I should concentrate on in the rest of my argument, based on the questions I had already been asked. In no time at all it was time to go back to the courtroom, the judges once more entered to the marshal's call, and I was back at the podium.

I can barely remember anything I said, or was asked, except for one question the Chief Justice asked, out of the blue, which seemed to have little bearing on the issues in the case. At the end of his trial, Robinson had tried to say something about some witnesses he thought his lawyer should have called, and the trial judge had cut him off and continued to sentence him. I had made no issue of this other than to cite it as a further example of the haste with which the judge conducted the trial, but Chief Justice Warren asked if I contended that Robinson had been denied his constitutionally protected right to allocution (the right to address the judge before he passes sentence). Unfortunately, I was wholly unfamiliar with the concept and had no idea what the word meant. At first I stalled, asking the Chief Justice to repeat the question as though I hadn't heard it and hoping that perhaps I had heard it wrong and would understand it the next time. I hadn't and didn't, and finally I had to simply tell the Chief Justice that I did not know what allocution was. He explained, and recognizing my embarrassment, moved on to another question. Then the red light was on, and I was given permission to finish my answer to the pending question, conclude, and it was over.

Dick Michael had reserved a minute or two for rebuttal, and then he too sat down, but instead of announcing the case was submitted, Chief Justice Warren glanced at a piece of paper one of the clerks had handed him and asked me to come back to the podium. I was delighted and excited, assuming he was going to ask another question or give me a chance to respond to a point Michael had made in his rebuttal. Instead, when I reached the lectern, he said he had been informed that I represented Mr. Robinson by appointment of the Court, and that the Court wanted to thank me for my excellent service to Mr. Robinson and the Court in the interest of justice.

I was disappointed I could not make one last argument for my client, but my family was thrilled, assuming this was an extraordinary tribute to my skill. In fact, as I found out later, it was a tribute the Chief Justice bestowed on every lawyer who argued before the Court pro bono. Nevertheless it was a nice gesture which was typical of the warmth and humanity with which Chief Justice Warren presided over the Court throughout his tenure.

Neither of the Chief Justices who have followed Warren maintained his traditional thanks to appointed lawyers, and by contrast William Rehnquist goes around the country making speeches criticizing public-service lawyers in death-penalty cases for making arguments he deems unjustified—when he is not urging Congress and the lower courts to further emasculate the writ of habeas corpus. If I made the arguments today that I made on behalf of Theodore Robinson, I would likely be the subject of Rehnquist's criticism instead of the recipient of gratitude for my efforts. Moreover, if the same case were presented to today's Court, it would have little chance of success—but on March 7, 1966, with Justices Black and Harlan dissenting, the Supreme Court granted Theodore Robinson's petition for a writ of habeas corpus, but changed the relief that had been granted in the Court of Appeals. Instead of going back to the district court for a hearing to determine Robinson's sanity at the time of the crime and for the district judge to decide if he had been denied due process by the state court's failure to conduct a hearing on his competence to stand trial, the Court itself held the failure to conduct such a hearing was a denial of due process and ordered the State of Illinois to release Robinson from custody unless it gave him a new trial within a reasonable time.

It was a more complete victory for Robinson than he had won in the Court of Appeals, especially since, as I would later realize, there was not a chance in hell that District Court Judge Julius Hoffman would have ruled for Robinson on either of the issues the Court of Appeals had remanded to him.

Back in the state court, the prosecutor soon announced he would try Robinson again. After the Supreme Court decision, Robinson had written me a long letter expressing gratitude for my help and asking me to represent him if there was a retrial. I agreed, and the Chief

Judge of the Criminal Court made the appointment. I immediately lined up a psychiatrist to review the record and examine Robinson to see if he would testify on the sanity issues. Then Robinson declared that he did not want to mount an insanity defense and would not cooperate with the psychiatrist or authorize me to assert the defense. He explained that he was afraid if the defense succeeded, it would result in his being locked up in a state mental hospital for as long or longer than he would spend in prison if he were convicted—not a wholly unreasonable fear. Even so, there was no other viable defense, and when I told him the only reasonable alternative was a negotiated plea of guilty (which probably would have resulted in only a short additional term in prison, given the years he had already served and the state's disinclination to retry a seven-year-old case), he fired me and announced he would defend himself.

Some of my friends were dismayed at what they considered a shocking display of ingratitude, but I had long since learned that a client's gratitude is a fragile reed, and no basis for taking on a pro bono case. A lawyer performs legal services for those who need but cannot afford them because it is his social and professional duty, not in the hope of enjoying the gratitude of his client. Besides, by this point I was happy to go. I had devoted an enormous amount of time to Theodore Robinson, and it was time I returned to spending more time on matters for the firm's paying clients.

Later that summer articles appeared in the Chicago newspapers reporting that Theodore Robinson, whose case had led to an important Supreme Court decision on insanity, had again been found guilty of murder and sentenced to life in prison.

At about this same time, I knew the firm's partners would be meeting to discuss the associates, and in my case the time had come for serious discussion of whether I would be asked to join the partnership in the near future. So it seemed to me that it was also time to evaluate myself. Had I become a competent courtroom lawyer in the nearly eight years since I graduated from law school? And equally important, was that what I wanted to do for the foreseeable future?

So far as appellate work was concerned, I had few doubts. I had argued successfully before the Illinois Appellate and Supreme courts and in the United States Court of Appeals. Now the *Robinson* case had given me the opportunity to argue in the Supreme Court of the United States—the chance of a lawyer's lifetime—and if I could not honestly say I had performed like a Thurgood Marshall or a George Gibson, I had survived the experience without disgracing myself or my client. That, I thought, was adequate proof of my competence as an appellate lawyer.

As a trial lawyer, particularly in jury cases, I was not so sure. I still had an enormous amount to learn about judges, jurors, and the examination of witnesses before anyone would mistake me for an expert. Indeed, as long as I tried cases, I would find myself amazed at the things I learned from each new case, and chagrined that I had not known them before.

But I had learned enough to be able to walk into a courtroom without a feeling of anxiety. And enough to believe that I would never again feel the overwhelming flood of guilt that had washed over me with the agonized scream of my client's mother when her son was sent to prison after my first trial.

I had traveled around the country finding and interviewing potential witnesses, taking and defending depositions, and examining documents and physical evidence. I had learned how to write briefs and other advocacy documents as well as impartial research memos, and how to research an issue "quick and dirty" when time constraints prevented the thorough and deliberative process employed if time and money are no impediment. I had brought in a few small clients of my own and, with Jim Sprowl's death, inherited responsibility for a few more important ones.

I had tried a half dozen or more cases to verdict in the Criminal Court and shepherded another half dozen or so to respectable plea agreements. I had tried several small- and medium-sized civil cases for clients of the firm and participated with firm partners in the trial of some major ones.

I had learned from Jim Sprowl that litigation could be conducted calmly, with polite respect for your opponent and his client, without losing anything in the way of effectiveness. And I had learned from another partner of the firm and a couple of opponents that litigation could also be conducted like a street fight, without really gaining anything. In Prentice Marshall, Tom Sullivan, and Jerry Solovy I had found, in my own firm, three lawyers who were within six years of my age and clearly on their way to becoming leaders of the trial bar in Chicago. They had become my friends as well as my teachers.

And despite the long hours, the pressure, and the moments of high anxiety, I had decided I liked what I was doing. Which required some serious reflection about what that meant.

In *One L*, Scott Turow's wonderful book about the first year of law school, he refers to the discomfort many of his classmates felt as they learned to think, act, and argue like lawyers, exchanging rules and rational argument for feelings, emotions, and deeply felt social or religious beliefs. In the book, one of the professors warns his class: "In learning rules, don't feel as if you've got to forsake a sense of moral scrutiny. The law in almost all its phases is a reflection of competing value systems. Don't get your heads turned around to the point that you feel because you're learning a rule, you've necessarily taken on the values that produced the rule in the first place."

But Turow's fellow students soon learn that while they can retain their own values for home use, if they want to succeed in law school they have to be willing to apply the rules and values of the American legal system. And that is equally true in the practice of law, especially the trial of cases.

The trial of a case is a competition, and if you plan to make your living doing it, you better have a competitive nature—an intense desire to win. That desire must be accompanied by an understanding of the rules and a willingness to play by them—a trial lawyer cannot manufacture a false document or knowingly introduce false testimony any more than a runner can trip her opponent, or a boxer hit his with a hammer. But neither can the effort and desire to win be lessened by distaste for the client or distrust of her position.

There is no question asked more frequently of lawyers than "How can you defend someone you know is guilty of a violent crime?" The answer—"Because it is not for me to decide guilt or innocence; that is the jury's job. My job is to present the best argument I can for my client"—is unsatisfactory to much of the public, and there are lawyers who insist they will only represent people they believe are innocent or causes they view as popular or just. Which seems like a noble position until you realize that it is why, in the South in Jim Crow days, African-Americans accused of a crime, or wanting to vote, could not find competent local lawyers to represent them, and people accused of leftist sympathies in the McCarthy era had the same problem.

For my part, then, there was no problem. I liked the competition, the limitations were fair and necessary, and the answer to the "guilty criminal" question seemed essential in an adversary system of justice that depends on competent and vigorous representation for both sides of a dispute. Eight years out of law school, I was happy to be a part of what I believed was the best system ever devised for the peaceful and reasonably accurate resolution of disputes.

All in all, I decided I had learned enough to be considered a competent courtroom lawyer with the potential and desire to be a better one, and that for now, that is what I wanted to do. Apparently a majority of the partners thought so too, because in July Colonel Raymond, the firm's senior partner, came into my office and told me I would be asked to join the firm the next time partners were admitted. And that is how I came to spend the next twenty years of my life enjoying the most varied, exciting, and rewarding experiences a courtroom lawyer could ever imagine.

⚜ CHAPTER 3 ⚜
LOOKING FOR JUSTICE

Lawyers like to portray themselves as valiant seekers of truth and justice. A more realistic view is expressed by the client in one of the law's hoariest jokes. Learning the judge has rendered a decision for his client, a lawyer triumphantly wires the client: "Your case was decided today. Justice was done!" To which the client replies: "Appeal at once."

In the American legal system, a lawyer's job is not to seek justice, but to win the case for his client. Indeed, the primary objective of our legal system is not to determine the truth, but to resolve disputes peacefully. Besides, in most cases where the facts are disputed, no one but the clients know for certain where the truth lies, and often they aren't really sure.

Even so, there are some situations where ambiguity ends and justice cries out for vindication. Mostly they are cases where the system has gone obviously and seriously wrong, usually because of a venal or biased judge, an incompetent lawyer, or an ignorant rule of law or bureaucracy. A great many students decide to attend law school because they want to fight injustice, and for all the cynicism engendered by their exposure to law school and the real world, most of them retain some kernel of that idealism and take pride in those rare opportunities to pursue unambiguous justice. Those are the cases we recall most clearly, and tell our children about. They are also the cases we are most likely to seek out even where little or no fee will be paid. One such case came to me as a result of *Robinson v. Pate.*

Alan Ferris Carsten* and his wife were lifelong Chicagoans living in a bungalow on the city's North Side, the same house where they had raised three sons on Ferris Carsten's modest income as a poultry distributor to the city's rapidly shrinking market of independent butchers and grocery stores. By dint of classic middle-class sacrifice and effort, the Carstens had managed to help their two youngest sons attend college, but it was the oldest, Alan Ferris Carsten Jr., who had showed the greatest promise, and whose tragedy was the reason for the call I received from the senior Mr. Carsten one day in mid-March 1966. He had read an article in the *Chicago Sun-Times* about the Supreme Court decision in the *Robinson* case, and he thought I might be able to help him with what he believed was a similar problem involving his son.

While lawyers who specialize in divorce or plaintiff's-personal-injury work are always anxious to have their latest triumph noted in the media, it is rare for lawyers whose work is primarily in business litigation to obtain a profitable new engagement from a newspaper article. Even criminal-defense lawyers find that publicity brings far more calls from indigent prisoners than paying clients with real cases. I was doubtful, but not being overburdened with clients of my own, I agreed to see Mr. Carsten the next week.

The potential client my secretary showed into my office was a short, wiry man who appeared to be in his early sixties but in fact had just turned seventy. His ill-fitting dark suit and starched white shirt were obviously not clothes he wore often, and the faint but distinctive odor of poultry that seemed to permeate his body suggested he had just changed clothes after completing his day's work. He shook my hand with the hard grip of a man whose job includes lifting and moving, apologized for being a few minutes late, told me that people called him Ferris, not Alan, and quickly launched into the reason for his visit. Ferris Carsten's problem, as he explained it, in fact had some similarity to the *Robinson* case, but as Mr. Carsten talked it soon became obvious that it was also one of those rare cases in which justice had clearly gone awry. The injustice had resulted in part from questionable lawyering and a judicial cave-in to public pressure, but primarily from a stupid and arbitrary bureaucratic regulation.

Twenty-four years earlier, in 1940, Alan Carsten Jr.* had been his father's pride and joy. He was a brilliant student with an IQ in the genius range. He was one of the stars of his high-school football team and one of the most popular young men in his class among teachers and students. Alan loved literature and philosophy and hoped to major in one of those subjects at a good college. At this time, however, college was not only something his parents could not afford, it was something people like them just didn't do. Literature and philosophy seemed a waste of time. Ferris wanted Alan to join him in the poultry business, but his son refused. Alan became morose and self-absorbed. Finally a compromise was reached for him to attend a local junior college, but the courses were dull and the reading less advanced than many of the books he had been directed to by his high-school teachers. He quarreled bitterly with his father and seemed to have withdrawn into a private world. He began neglecting his physical condition and said that he thought he was losing his sexual potency.

In the fall of 1941, a series of attacks on women had broken out on Chicago's North Side. By December, over two dozen women had reported being attacked. Most of the time the man had run away when the woman screamed or resisted, but three women had been raped, and the series of unsolved attacks generated sensational front-page stories in the Chicago newspapers. Finally, in mid-December an attacker was caught running away from an attempted rape. It was young Alan Carsten, and he was promptly identified by twenty-two other women, including the three rape victims, as the man who had attacked them. Carsten confessed. His photograph was spread across the newspapers. The family, with help from their friends, scraped together enough money to hire a criminal-defense lawyer who told them the case appeared to be hopeless, and that the best he thought he could do was negotiate a plea that might lessen the sentence.

One of the thousands of Chicagoans who saw Alan Carsten's photograph in the newspapers was psychiatrist Kurt Eissler. Dr. Eissler had been born in Vienna and graduated from the University of Vienna with degrees in medicine and psychiatry. For eighteen years he taught and practiced psychiatry at the university, becoming recognized as one of Europe's foremost experts on child psychiatry and juvenile delinquency. In 1938 he fled Vienna and the Nazis for the United States, where he obtained his M.D. and Ph.D. from the University of Illinois and was licensed to practice medicine and psychiatry. At the time of Carsten's arrest he was in the private practice of psychiatry and psychoanalysis in Chicago. Later he moved to New York, where he became one of the most prominent psychiatrists in America.

When Eissler saw Alan Carsten's photograph in the newspaper, he thought he recognized Carsten's posture as presenting the classic appearance of catatonia. Taking from his shelf Eugen Bleuler's *Textbook of Psychiatry*, one of the definitive works on schizophrenia, Eissler located a photograph of a patient in a catatonic state. The peculiar posture of the man in the textbook photograph was identical to the news photo of Alan Carsten taken during the "perp walk" staged by the police after his arrest. Kurt Eissler located the Carsten family's phone number in the telephone directory and called the house. When Ferris Carsten answered, Eissler told him that it was likely his son was suffering from a severe mental illness, and offered to examine him free of charge.

Over the next two months, Dr. Eissler personally examined Alan Carsten on thirteen separate occasions, for periods ranging from thirty minutes to an hour and a half. In the course of these examinations, Eissler concluded that Alan was a paranoid schizophrenic, whose sudden metamorphosis from ideal citizen to vicious criminal was the result of what Eissler described as an "insidious paranoid psychosis." Alan had irrationally come to fear that he was becoming sexually impotent, and had formed the delusion that he could reacquire potency by committing a rape. As a result of his extensive examination, Eissler concluded that Alan had been legally insane at the time of his crimes; that he was unable to distinguish between right and wrong and unable to conform his conduct to what is right. He also believed Alan was incompetent to understand the nature of the charges against him and assist in his own defense. So far as the future was concerned, Eissler said he could make only one statement with assurance: If Alan Carsten were placed in a large maximum-security institution like a penitentiary, there was no chance he would get better. To the contrary, Eissler predicted, he would almost surely get steadily worse. Whether Carsten could ever be "cured," even with state-of-the-art psychiatric treatment in a mental hospital, Eissler could not say, but it was the only chance for improvement in Alan's condition.

When the lawyer who was engaged to represent Alan learned of Eissler's offer to help and his preliminary conclusions, he advised the Carstens to try to obtain a second psychiatric opinion. Eissler had practiced in America for only two years, and even though Austria was known as the cradle of modern psychiatry, Eissler's thick Germanic accent might not sit well with a Chicago jury, especially in 1942. Somehow, the Carstens were able to approach one of the foremost American-born psychiatrists, Dr. Roy Grinker. Grinker was chairman of the Department of Psychiatry at the University of Chicago, a position he would soon leave for service in the wartime Army Medical Corps, where he would become world famous for his pioneering study of combat fatigue and other wartime mental diseases. Grinker, also working without fee, studied Alan's medical records and Dr. Eissler's reports, and then examined Alan himself for two hours. When he was done, he wrote a report concurring with Eissler's diagnosis in every important respect, and also concurring in Eissler's assertion that Carsten had been insane at the time of the crimes, and that prison could only make his illness worse.

Armed with the opinion of two outstanding experts, Carsten's lawyer attempted to negotiate a plea bargain providing that, in return for a plea of guilty, Alan would be sent to a mental hospital instead of prison, with an indefinite sentence that would permit his release if and when the hospital psychiatrists determined he was cured and no longer a danger to himself or others. However, faced with enormous pressure from the press and the victims' families, the prosecutors refused to make any kind of deal, and the judge would make no promise about what he would do in the absence of the prosecutors' express agreement. Of course, if the defendant pleaded guilty and saved the state the time and expense of a trial, the judge suggested, he would certainly take that into consideration in deciding on a sentence.

It is impossible to say why Carsten's lawyer decided to recommend to Carsten's family that he agree to plead guilty without any guarantee of the result—a decision known (and scorned) in the trade as a "naked plea." There may have been private off-the-record conversations that persuaded him the result would be acceptable, or winks and nods that he interpreted in the same way, or he may have just believed he had no chance of winning, and that this was the best course despite the absence of any deal or real indication of the result. Or he may have simply wanted to avoid the time and expense of a long jury trial for a client whose ability to pay a fee was already exhausted. Whatever the reason, that is what he recommended—a guilty plea, with the psychiatric testimony used in the sentencing hearing to persuade the judge to send Alan to a mental hospital rather than the penitentiary. It was an odd recommendation in a case where two eminent experts were in agreement that Alan was legally insane—but the Carstens had little choice but to follow their lawyer's advice.

On February 11, 1942, Alan Carsten pleaded guilty to three counts of rape. By prearrangement, Judge Julius Miner then conducted a sentencing hearing that lasted most of the day. Alan's family, friends, and schoolteachers testified to his intelligence and his record of impeccable conduct prior to the onset of his mental disease. They were followed to the stand by Drs. Eissler and Grinker, who testified at length to their medical findings and prognosis. It was brought to their attention that the state maintained a psychiatric unit at Menard, a prison in the southern end of the state, but the doctors emphatically denied that incarceration in Menard's psychiatric unit would provide appropriate treatment for Alan's illness because of its distance from his family and its characteristics as a maximum-security institution.

The prosecutor had read into the record a lengthy description of Alan's crimes at the time the judge accepted Alan's guilty plea, and after incorporating that into the sentencing record the prosecution called one witness, Dr. William Haines, a psychiatrist employed full time by the state to examine defendants and declare them legally sane and competent to stand trial. Dr. Haines performed as expected. He agreed that Alan Carsten was schizophrenic, but he did not agree that he was legally insane. That Alan understood the difference between right and wrong and was capable of conforming his conduct to what was right was proved, Haines declared, by the fact that he had not also attempted to rape his mother.

After listening to closing arguments, which centered on the issue of whether Alan should be committed to the penitentiary or to a mental hospital, Judge Miner retired to his chambers to consider his sentence. When he emerged, he announced that he had searched the record in vain for any evidence in mitigation of Alan Carsten's crimes. Alan was sentenced to life in prison.

Up to this point, Ferris Carsten had told me his story speaking rapidly in the too-loud voice of the slightly deaf. But when he came to his son's sentence he stopped, obviously trying to control his emotions. "I couldn't believe it," he said, when he was able to resume speaking. "I had a friend who knew the judge. He told me he was a good judge, a fair man." Carsten stopped again. "I never should have let him plead guilty. We should have asked for a jury." He stopped again. I saw no point in telling him he was right, or wondering aloud how the lawyer could have recommended anything else. I wasn't even sure, and I'm still not, how the judge had the power to order Alan Carsten sent to a mental hospital rather than a prison after a guilty plea even if he had wanted to.

Ferris Carsten continued his story. The day after his sentencing,

Alan was shipped to Joliet State Prison for evaluation. A few days later, as anticipated, he was assigned to the psychiatric division at Menard, nearly four hundred miles from his family in Chicago. There he had remained for the past twenty-four years, his condition steadily deteriorating. Within a few years, he no longer gave any sign of recognizing his own mother when the family was able to make the long trip to visit him. After five years, he hardly ever spoke a word. He had retreated into his own world, sitting for hours on end without speaking or moving. As Kurt Eissler had predicted from seeing his photograph in the newspaper, Alan was now severely catatonic.

Alan Carsten had not spoken to anyone in his family for almost nineteen years, but throughout that entire time his mother and father and two brothers had continued to make the trip to Menard to visit him whenever they could, and his father had continued to try everything he could think of to get him out of prison and into the hands of someone who might be able to help him. Now he thought I was the person who could do it.

My first question was obvious. I knew that under Illinois law at the time, anyone sentenced to a term of life in prison was entitled to be considered for parole after twenty years. Given what Ferris Carsten told me, it seemed to me the Illinois Department of Corrections would have liked nothing better than to have Alan paroled to the custody of the State Department of Mental Health. Not only did that seem to be the humane thing to do, it would rid the corrections agency of the need to take care of a man who was surely an expensive and time-consuming inmate. Why had Alan not been paroled long since?

The answer would have made Joseph Heller smile. "Because there is a rule," Ferris Carsten told me. "The rule is that no one can be paroled except from the general population of the Department of Corrections. If you are in the psychiatric division, you cannot be paroled."

In other words, unless Alan recovered from his mental disease, he could not be transferred to the general division, and thus could not be paroled; but unless he was paroled, he could not receive effective treatment for his illness, so he could never be transferred to the general division. Alan Carsten's "catch-22" was as inescapable as Yossarian's.

I said I didn't believe there could be such a stupid rule, but Ferris Carsten pulled out a letter he had received from the superintendent of the parole board saying exactly what he had just told me. I told him I was very doubtful I could help him—the guilty plea was a major obstacle to any success in the courts, and bureaucratic rules, no matter how illogical, are very difficult to change—but under the circumstances he had described, I said I would sure like to try. He should talk to his family and emphasize my strong warning about the slim chance of success, but if they wanted to go forward, and could raise a $1,000 retainer, I would try to persuade the firm to let me take the case for half my regular hourly fee. Two days later, I received a $1,000 check in the mail.

Although the guilty plea had complicated the idea of using the *Robinson* case to obtain habeas corpus relief for Alan Carsten, which is what brought his father to me in the first place, I thought there was a pretty good chance a federal court would hold that Carsten's constitutional rights had been violated by the acceptance of a guilty plea at a time when it was obvious he was not competent to enter a plea or stand trial. Unfortunately, the almost-certain result of such a ruling was that the state would attempt to retry him, he would be found incompetent to stand trial, and he would then be committed to the Illinois Security Hospital—a facility that, although run by the Department of Mental Health rather than the Department of Corrections, was little better than Menard in terms of offering any hope for improvement in Carsten's condition. Everyone I talked to at the Department of Mental Health agreed that what Alan needed was treatment in a small, specialized unit in a hospital close to his family where he could have frequent visits from them and establish some connection with the outside world. Illinois Security was a large maximum-security hospital just as far from Chicago as Menard; spending the rest of his life at Illinois

Security was not what anyone who was trying to help Alan Carsten had in mind.

Difficult as I feared it would be, I thought the best chance to do Alan any real good was to persuade the parole board to change its rule, or at least to make an exception for my client. Another avenue for achieving the same result would be a pardon or commutation of sentence from the governor, although pardoning multiple rapists was not the kind of thing politicians liked to do before breakfast.

I told the Carsten family I thought we should start by trying to persuade the parole board to grant Alan a parole, not to the free community, but to the custody of the Department of Mental Health, and they agreed. Now all I had to do was persuade Mental Health to agree to support the plan and accept Carsten, and persuade the parole board to change its rule.

I began with the Department of Mental Health, whose support would be essential, and easier to get than the parole board's. Governor Otto Kerner had recently appointed a new director of the Department of Mental Health, Dr. Harold Visotsky, a psychiatrist fully versed in modern psychiatric theory who was committed to ending the warehousing of long-term mental patients in large hospitals where almost everyone got worse instead of better.

I explained the problem first to a lawyer for the Department of Mental Health. At his suggestion, I sent Visotsky a transcript of Carsten's sentencing hearing and a description of what had followed. In a subsequent phone conversation, Visotsky declared without hesitation that Eissler and Grinker had been right: The only way Alan could be helped would be in a hospital that employed the latest treatment methods and was close enough to Alan's family to allow frequent visits and exposure to the outside world. Visotsky declared it was the job of his department to provide that kind of care to every Illinois citizen who needed it. The only question was whether Alan's condition was such that he could be safely cared for in such a facility. If he was aggressive and dangerous it might be impossible, although from my report of Alan's catatonic state it did not sound like that was a problem. He suggested I get the psychiatrist at Menard who was in charge of Alan to send the reports of Alan's conduct and treatment over the years to one of the department's consultants for evaluation. If the consultant said Alan could be treated safely in an appropriate facility, the department would agree to it and actively support the plan.

I was not surprised when my approach to the parole board was met with less enthusiasm. I knew that Alan's annual parole hearing was only a few days off, so I informed the board that I represented him and planned to request that he be paroled to the custody of the Department of Mental Health. I asked that his case be continued until the next board meeting in June to give me time to prepare and present evidence in support of my request. The board chairman, Charles Kinney, granted my request for a continuance, but made it clear the board's policy was to deny parole to anyone who was not in the general prison population. Kinney went on to say that he had reviewed Carsten's file and it did not appear there was any chance he would be able to be moved to the general division. Meanwhile, if I still wanted to make a presentation, I should appear before a subcommittee of the board on May 25 to present my evidence and arguments. The message was clear that I would be wasting my time—and the board's as well.

I had in mind a two-pronged plan for reversing Kinney's opposition. First, I knew I already had support from the Department of Mental Health, and that the department's new director was a favorite of the governor. When Otto Kerner appointed Visotsky, he made it clear that mental health was one of his priorities as governor. Second, I knew that Kerner had also appointed several new members of the parole board, who were more liberal and enlightened than the members they had replaced. They would not be anxious to parole someone who might be a danger to the community, but surely, I thought, they would be unsympathetic to a rule making it impossible for someone with a serious mental illness to get treatment. I knew Mental Health would say Alan could not be treated successfully in the prison system, and that they thought there was a chance they could improve his condition. The key was the question of danger to the community. If Mental Health said they were confident Alan could be treated in their facilities without danger it would take the parole board off the hook, even if something went wrong.

The Department of Corrections might still oppose parole—I had already gotten a whiff of resentment from the warden at Menard over the idea they were not as capable of treating Carsten as the Department of Mental Health—but I thought that could be overcome by the stark reality of Carsten's deterioration. Even so, I was careful in everything I filed to praise the efforts of the staff at Menard and make it clear the problem was not that they were incompetent, but that the nature of Alan's disease made it impossible for him to be treated in a maximum-security institution, especially one so far removed from his family.

In truth, no real treatment was going on at Menard, nor could there be. The best they could do in a maximum-security institution full of often-violent inmates was to drug them into a state of submission. When questioned, the "treatment" most often cited by the Menard staff was "hydrotherapy"—which, in plain language, meant frequent showers.

The Carstens had told me that the psychiatrist in charge of Alan's treatment, a consultant to the prison named Groves Smith, was a conscientious and caring man who seemed genuinely interested in Alan's condition, and in fact had taken them aside and told them the only hope for Alan's improvement was somehow getting him out of Menard and into an intensive treatment program closer to home. Regardless of the official position of the Department of Corrections, the Carstens thought Dr. Smith would support the request for parole. With that in mind, I requested that Dr. Smith reexamine Alan and prepare a report for me and the parole board regarding his history at Menard and his suitability for parole to the Department of Mental Health. I also asked that the report be sent to a psychiatrist representing Mental Health. At first the prison authorities balked, asserting the "confidentiality" of Alan's psychiatric records, but on this score Chairman Kinney supported me and the prison authorities gave in.

When I was first contacted by Ferris Carsten, I had talked to Dr. Roy Grinker long enough to know he would support my basic position, but now I needed something in writing to present to the parole board. Grinker, who had become director of the Institute for Psychosomatic and Psychiatric Research and Training at Michael Reese Hospital, was at a professional conference in Europe and not due back until shortly before Alan's parole hearing. Dr. Eissler had left Chicago, and I had no idea where he was or even if he was still alive, or in practice. By Friday, May 13, Dr. Smith's report had not yet come in, and the psychiatrist at the Department of Mental Health who had been recommended to do its report sounded doubtful he could do it before leaving on vacation.

Monday came and went without a call from Dr. Grinker or a report from Dr. Smith, but beginning on Tuesday, May 17, everything started to happen at once. On the good side, Dr. Grinker called and promised he would immediately write a letter supporting our position. He also told me Dr. Eissler had become one of the leading psychoanalysts in New York, and felt sure his secretary could find me an address and phone number. That same day, however, I received Dr. Smith's report, and while it supported the proposition that Carsten could not be successfully treated at Menard and made it clear that in Smith's opinion Alan should have been sent to a mental hospital rather than a prison in the first place, his report was ambiguous on the crucial issue of safety. Referring to Carsten's size and strength and his having shown sudden outbursts of anger in his early years at Menard, Smith opined that his release would involve a "calculated risk." No fool, Smith left the question of whether it was a risk worth taking to the Department of Mental Health.

Smith's report made a strong statement from the Department of Mental Health all the more important, and that same day the Mental Health psychiatrist I had been referred to called and left a message that he was now certain he could not do a report. In a near panic, I called the lawyer who was my primary contact at Mental Health to see if anyone else could render a report on such short notice. In a few minutes, the lawyer called back to say Visotsky had authorized the engagement of a Dr. Horecker, one of the department's consulting psychiatrists in southern Illinois, to review Smith's report and Alan's records and to visit Alan in person so his report would carry more weight.

The news of the Department of Mental Health's extraordinary effort to support my cause was soon followed by a call from Dr. Grinker's secretary with an address and phone number for Dr. Eissler in New York. His office said he was out of town but due back on Friday. I described the purpose of my call to his secretary and told her I would send a special-delivery letter, which should arrive at Eissler's office on Friday morning, describing the problem in detail. I emphasized the importance of his help and the extreme time pressure, but she expressed doubt he would be able to look at my letter until the next week. His absence had left him a pile of pressing matters. I could only thank her and ask that she at least mention the matter to Eissler upon his return so he would be aware of what it was about, and its urgent nature.

On Friday I spent the day drafting a petition to the board based on what I already had, which included letters written by Alan's parents and two brothers, the transcript of the sentencing hearing in 1942, Grinker's letter, and Smith's report. I also contacted the lawyer who prosecuted Carsten in 1942, and he promised to send me a letter supporting the parole.

That night, as I was having dinner with my family, the phone rang. To my amazement, it was Dr. Eissler, calling from New York. He had read my letter and was so anxious to help that he had tracked me down at home. Twenty-four years later, he said, he still remembered Alan Carsten. The case had preyed on his mind ever since, because he had always feared his inability to persuade the judge of Carsten's mental disease was somehow his fault. He was distressed, but not surprised, to learn that his prediction of what would happen if Carsten was sent to a prison had come true, and would do anything he could to help.

My letter to Eissler had described the things I wanted him to say, assuming he agreed with them: that Carsten's only hope for improvement was to receive intensive care in a modern mental-health facility, as close as possible to his home and family. Eissler said he agreed entirely, and would write a letter that weekend and send it special delivery. I was elated. I had not expected to have anything from Eissler in time for my hearing, if ever, and when I received the letter itself, I was even more pleased. In three single-spaced pages, Dr. Eissler spelled out in detail his distress at what had happened to Alan Carsten and his full support, on medical grounds, of our proposal for his parole to the custody of the Department of Mental Health. His letter could not have been a better instrument for our case.

As I worked to finalize my written submissions on Monday, I was only missing a strong statement from Dr. Horecker that Alan could be treated safely in a facility of the Department of Mental Health. Horecker was scheduled to review the records and interview Alan that morning. He had promised to write his report the same day and have it delivered to me and the parole board that night or the following morning. I knew Dr. Visotsky was supportive of my efforts and that Alan had shown no aggressive conduct for many years. Even before that, he had done nothing that was not commonly handled in the department's facilities, so I thought it unlikely that Horecker's report would be anything but favorable.

When I arrived at my office on Tuesday morning Dr. Horecker's report was on my desk. In *Catch-22,* Joseph Heller invented only one unsolvable dilemma to bedevil Yossarian, but Dr. Horecker had found a way to go Heller one better. Alan Carsten, Horecker agreed, was not currently a danger to anyone. And Horecker also agreed that Alan's condition would never improve if he remained at Menard, whereas he might in fact get better if he were to receive treatment in an appropriate facility of the Department of Mental Health. Indeed, the doctor suggested, he might even improve to the point that a psychiatrist would consider it appropriate for him to return to free society. But that, according to Horecker, was the problem. If Alan was treated, he might get better, and if he got better, at some point he might become aggressive again, and if the Department of Mental Health made a mistake and released him too soon and he then became aggressive, he might hurt someone. Thus, the good doctor concluded, "It is my considered judgment that moving Mr. Carsten to a hospital of lesser security is unwise and potentially fraught with danger to the community."

In short, we should not treat Alan because if we do, his condition might improve, and if his condition improves, we can't be certain what he will do, so it's better to leave him in his state of vegetative catatonia. It was a recommendation that perfectly complemented the rule against parole from the psychiatric division.

There was no alternative but to attack Horecker's reasoning head-on. I was already counting on the newer members of the parole board to see the injustice of the parole rule, and I could only hope to persuade them to see Horecker's recommendation in the same way. First, I called Jerry Goldberg, the lawyer who had been so helpful in dealing with the Department of Mental Health, and described Horecker's report. Goldberg was appalled and said he was certain Visotsky would be as well. Even though Horecker was one of their own consultants, I should feel free to attack him as needed.

Working quickly, I revised my written presentation to deal with Horecker's report. I argued that his belief Alan would improve if our petition was granted was the very reason it *must* be granted. To suggest that someone be denied treatment because it might improve his condition, and the Department of Mental Health might make a mistake and release him before it was safe to do so was, I argued, unjustified and "contrary to science and humanity." Just before 5:00 P.M., I hand-delivered the petition to Chairman Kinney's office in Chicago, with copies for each member of the parole board.

The "subcommittee" of the board I met with the next day at

Joliet State Prison turned out to consist of one member, its chairman. He listened politely to my presentation, but made little effort to conceal his satisfaction with Dr. Horecker's negative report. When I finished my argument, he asked a single question: Given the board's long-standing rule against parole from the psychiatric division and the fact that the Department of Mental Health's own representative had recommended against my proposal, was there really any point in presenting the case to the full board in June?

I said there was—that I had already discussed the Horecker report with a representative of the Department of Mental Health who agreed with me that the idea Alan should be denied treatment for fear he might get better was outrageous, and totally inconsistent with the philosophy of the department. I said I was certain that, despite Horecker's report, the department continued to support the parole and was willing to undertake Alan's treatment and supervision if the board granted the application. The first part was true. The second was a bit of a stretch—I didn't say the only "representative" I had spoken to was the department's lawyer—but I believed it. Goldberg had said he was sure Visotsky would agree, and he had always been right so far.

Through the legal and political grapevine, I knew that several of the newer members of the parole board were already aware of the Carsten case and were disposed to reconsider the rule against parole. A few days after my May 25 meeting with Kinney, I finally received the promised letter of support from Carsten's prosecutor and, using that as my excuse, I telephoned each board member separately to let them know the letter was coming. I also told them that if they would modify the no-parole rule I was certain the Department of Mental Health would provide written assurance that they could treat Alan without danger to the public. Several of the board members told me they agreed that the no-parole rule was illogical and inhumane, and that they continued to be interested in considering whether Alan's case would be an appropriate one for overturning it.

I waited anxiously to hear the result of the board's June 15 meeting. Finally, after a week went by with no word, I called Chairman Kinney, who told me the board had discussed the case at length on June 15 and had decided to put it over until July. Sounding somewhat disgruntled, Kinney said some of the board members were interested in reexamining the policy regarding inmates in the psychiatric division and wanted to obtain further input on the matter from a man named Arthur Huffman, who, as "State Criminologist," had ultimate responsibility for the psychiatric division and the greatest knowledge of its operation. Kinney planned to meet with Huffman to discuss the matter a week later, and I was invited to attend.

Following the Horecker disaster, I had been assured by Dr. Visotsky himself that the department would have someone else look into Carsten's case. According to Visotsky, a younger psychiatrist with a better understanding of modern treatment alternatives, especially for catatonic schizophrenics with long-term hospitalization, was more likely to support my proposal, and most certainly would reject the idea that they should be denied treatment for fear they would improve and become violent. When I learned of the proposed meeting with Huffman, I contacted Visotsky again. If possible, I needed someone who could look at the files in time to attend that meeting. Visotsky thought for a moment. Bernard Rubin, a young psychiatrist in his department, had recently obtained approval and funding to begin an experimental intensive-care unit for long-term schizophrenics. Visotsky would see if Rubin was willing to look at the file and see whether Alan was an appropriate subject for his program.

And that is how I met Bernie Rubin. I saw him for the first time in his office in downtown Chicago, where he maintained a private practice in addition to his duties with the Department of Mental Health. He had said yes to Dr. Visotsky, and I had the records of Alan Carsten's stay at Menard delivered to his office on a Friday so he could read them over the weekend. He saw patients downtown on Tuesday afternoons, and I became his last appointment of the day. Dr. Rubin was a fairly short man, perhaps 5' 8", with dark hair and a face that looked younger than the late thirties the graduation date on his diploma suggested. He greeted me with a smile and motioned me to a comfortable chair. His voice was warm and soft, but before I had really settled into the chair, he spoke angrily. His exact words are lost to me, but the substance was clear: "I can't believe anyone who calls himself a doctor could write something like this," he said, pointing at one of the papers in the file. He was talking about Dr. Horecker and his report.

Rubin went on to say that while he would like to examine Alan Carsten himself, he had no doubt he could be safely treated by the Department of Mental Health, that the progression of his disease followed the classic pattern of paranoid schizophrenics, that his chances of a full recovery were remote, but that with modern treatment methods and the ability to interact with his family there was a fair chance of significant improvement, and that he appeared, from the record, to be a perfect candidate for the new treatment program for long-hospitalized schizophrenics. I immediately fell in love with Bernie Rubin, and remained so for as long as I knew him.

A few days later, on June 29, Rubin and I drove down to Joliet to meet with Chairman Kinney and Arthur Huffman. I knew Kinney was familiar with my proposal, and Huffman said he too had read everything I had filed, so after briefly outlining the facts I introduced Dr. Rubin, who began describing the new program for treating long-term schizophrenics.

Before Rubin got more than a minute or two into his presentation, Huffman interrupted. "Have you ever examined Mr. Carsten? Have you ever even been to our facility at Menard? Do you know any of the psychiatrists we have on our staff there, or any of our consultants? Do you have any reason to think they are incompetent?" With each question, Huffman became more agitated, and after Bernie Rubin quietly said no to each of them, Huffman launched into an impassioned speech, the substance of which was that the psychiatric division at Menard was as good as anything run by the Department of Mental Health, that he had been to the department's Illinois Security Hospital across the street from Menard and, if anything, Menard's facilities were better, that he did not believe anything could be done to improve Carsten's condition, and if by some miracle he did improve, the department's own consultant had pointed out the result could be a return to violent impulses and a danger to the public.

When Huffman finished, Rubin explained that he was not impugning the skill or dedication of the staff at Menard, but that patients like Carsten simply could not be successfully treated in that kind of setting. He explained why he thought Horecker's fears were unfounded, and again described his new treatment program, but it was clear that neither Huffman nor Kinney was interested. When Rubin finished, Kinney announced that as far as he was concerned, after talking to Huffman, it would be unwise for the parole board to change its long-standing policy of paroling only prisoners who were mentally well enough to be in the general division. The first priority of the parole board, Kinney said, was to protect the public, which was tough enough when making judgments about people who were not insane. He felt sure the board would agree with him when it heard Huffman's views on the subject. I told Kinney I understood his position, but I would like to meet with the entire board when they next took up the case. Since I would be out of town at the time of the July board meeting, I would like the matter to be continued until the next meeting in September. Kinney said he doubted the board would want to do that, but he would tell them of my request. I was discouraged by the vehemence of Kinney's and Huffman's opposition, but I was pretty sure he was wrong about the views of the other board members regarding parole policy.

The full board met on July 13. A week went by before Kinney wrote to inform me of the result, which I already knew from other members of the board. According to Kinney's letter, after further review "this case has been continued to the October 1966 conference of the Illinois Parole Board in order that we might agree to a time when you could appear before the full Board in Springfield."

Behind those bland words I knew there had been a vociferous argument at the board meeting, with Kinney and Ross Randolph, the Director of Public Safety, urging the board to end the matter by denying Carsten's application and reaffirming the rule against parole from the psychiatric division, only to be overruled by a majority of the board.

The position of Kinney and Randolph was simple: If Carsten or someone else is paroled, and then escapes or is released by Mental Health and commits a terrible crime, we're going to get blamed— so why take the chance? The position of the majority differed: Let's see what the Department of Mental Health says. If they say they can help someone like Carsten and he can be treated without danger to the public, and they are willing to take on that responsibility, it would be wrong not to take the chance.

I had won the battle, but my allies on the parole board made it clear I had not yet won the war. It was crucial that the Department of Mental Health make a strong case for its ability to handle Carsten safely. The possibility of helping him was also important, but safety was the key, especially in light of the negative report from Dr. Horecker. The board members recognized the irrational consequences of Horecker's reasoning, but they were no more anxious than Kinney to someday read in a newspaper that against a psychiatrist's advice they had paroled a convicted multiple rapist who then escaped from a mental hospital and raped again.

I understood. I also thought that if anyone could satisfy the board's concerns I already had him on my side in the person of Bernie Rubin.

The board set Tuesday, October 11, for my appearance. In the interim, Bernie Rubin had gotten his pilot program up and running and taken time to make the long trip to Menard to interview Alan Carsten in person. When he returned, he reported that Alan's deterioration was so great that his concern was not safety, but whether anything could be done for him. Nevertheless, Rubin would take him into the program and do his best to help him if our parole application was granted. He wrote a long letter, which I sent to every member of the parole board, describing Alan's condition, the security precautions available in the Department of Mental Health in the (extremely unlikely) event that Alan should begin to evidence any aggressive behavior, and, in detail, the pilot program Alan would be placed in. His prediction of the possibility of improvement in Alan's catatonic condition was somewhat more optimistic than what he had told me in private.

Throughout my efforts to get Alan Carsten paroled to a mental hospital, I had impressed on the board, as the psychiatrists had impressed on me, the importance of reconnecting Alan with his family by placing him in a facility where he could receive frequent visits. Accordingly, as the October meeting approached, I decided to have Alan's father and one of his brothers come with me and present a brief statement to the board. They had already written letters, but no letter or affidavit can substitute for the testimony of a live witness. (In this age of television viewers, some "trial experts" claim a jury will pay more attention to testimony presented on a television screen than from a flesh-and-blood person sitting on the witness stand. I do not believe it.) On October 11 Ferris Carsten, his son Robert, Bernie Rubin, and I drove to Springfield, arriving well before our hearing.

Room 219 of the State Office Building, where the seven members of the parole board sat for the rare cases heard by the full board, was as bureaucratically plain as the Supreme Court chamber across the street was elaborate and rococo. Our hearing was the last of the day, affording me the chance to watch two earlier hearings. The board was largely silent during the earlier presentations and asked no questions during my opening remarks or the brief statements made by Ferris and Robert Carsten. After their statements, Kinney told each of the Carstens that the board appreciated their coming to testify and understood their concern for Alan's welfare, adding, however, that the board's primary concern had to be for the safety of the public.

As soon as Bernie Rubin began to speak, however, things

changed dramatically. Kinney began with a series of hostile questions based on the Horecker report. Soon other members of the board weighed in, some rhetorically, but mostly with questions designed to elicit real information about Dr. Rubin's pilot program and the ability of the department to safely handle Carsten if, contrary to Rubin's expectation, he did begin to demonstrate aggressive tendencies. In his soft voice, Rubin answered the questions directly and in detail. In the end, asked to assume a worst-case scenario of sexual aggression, he asserted that in the intensive daily therapy Carsten would receive, it was inconceivable that such a tendency could develop without early warnings observed by the staff. It would be a shame, Rubin said, but if worse came to worst, Carsten could be reassigned to the Illinois Security Hospital, which was every bit as secure as Menard. Rubin's answer seemed to satisfy most of the board, and for the rest of his testimony the questions primarily reflected an interest in Rubin's hopes for a breakthrough in the treatment of long-hospitalized schizophrenics, a subject that seemed close to the hearts of several members.

By the time Bernie Rubin sat down, it seemed likely that at least four of the seven board members were ready to abandon the rule against parole from the psychiatric division, and to use the case of Alan Carsten to announce the change. Kinney and one other member were still opposed, and the seventh member had asked no questions. I made a brief closing statement and the hearing was adjourned.

After the hearing Bernie Rubin returned to Chicago for a meeting the next morning, but the Carstens and I had arranged to stay overnight. At dinner I reminded my clients—and myself—that you can't be sure of anything from listening to the questions asked by judges—or parole-board members. Nevertheless, as Ferris Carsten would remind me a year later, I could not disguise my elation over the way the board reacted to our presentation.

For the next two weeks, there was silence. I called the board member who had been most helpful in the past, but he did not return my call. It seemed a terrible omen. Then, on October 27, an envelope arrived in the morning mail bearing the return address of Charles Kinney, Chairman, Parole and Pardon Board, Springfield, Illinois. It was a copy of a letter Kinney had sent the previous day to Ross Randolph, the Director of Public Safety:

Dear Director Randolph,

Please be advised that at the October 1966 conference of the Illinois Parole and Pardon board, the following action was taken in the cases of Alan Ferris Carsten:

"Definite sentence parole granted when accepted for simultaneous commitment to the Department of Mental Health."

This action was taken after a very careful review of the problem involved in this case and a full hearing on the question which was presented before the board on October 11, 1966.

Sincerely,

Charles Kinney, Chairman

Illinois Parole and Pardon Board

Several weeks later, after a few more bureaucratic knots were untied, Alan Carsten was transferred from the Menard Penitentiary to the nearby Illinois Security Hospital. From there, after a period of evaluation, he was transferred in turn to the Department of Mental Health's hospital in Tinley Park, just south of Chicago, where the pilot program was housed.

At least one member of Alan's family visited him every day that visits were permitted, and a few months later, in the spring of 1967, I received a call from his brother. That day, for the first time in twenty years, Alan had recognized his mother and called her "Mom." His condition improved gradually to the point where he could carry on a rational conversation and follow the fortunes of a favorite sports team, the Chicago Cubs. His doctors began allowing the family to visit with him outside, on the hospital grounds, and then to take him for a drive, or for lunch. On Christmas day, 1967, his two brothers picked Alan up at the hospital and took him to one of their homes, where the entire family spent the day and had Christmas dinner together for the first time since 1940. The main course was one of his father's turkeys. My family also had a Carsten turkey that day and every Christmas until Ferris Carsten retired.

A few years later Alan Carsten and a woman he met in the pilot program were married and moved into an apartment not far from the state mental hospital in Elgin, where they received regular out-patient therapy. He and his wife remained there until Alan's death.

The rule prohibiting parole from the psychiatric division was never reinstated.

At about the same time I was working on the *Robinson* case in the U.S. Supreme Court, I had become involved in another case that would take me to Washington for a Supreme Court argument in January 1968. This time, however, I would not argue myself but sit at counsel table while one of my partners presented his first argument in the nation's highest court. Our client was a man named William Witherspoon, and he resided in a cell on death row in the Cook County Jail.

In 1959 Witherspoon had killed a Chicago policeman who found him hiding in a truck after he ran away from an argument that had drawn attention from the police. The odds that someone caught after killing a Chicago cop would survive to be tried were not very good, but Witherspoon made it, only to be convicted and sentenced to death by a jury. After the usual appeals and collateral attacks on his conviction failed, Witherspoon was nearing the end of his rope when he filed a second petition for a writ of habeas corpus in the U.S. District Court for the Northern District of Illinois. Rather than dismiss the petition, which some judges would have done at this point, Judge James Parsons appointed counsel to represent Witherspoon. The lawyers he appointed were Bert Jenner, Tom Sullivan, and Jerry Solovy.

Justice is one thing, legal philosophy is another, but a lawyer's commitment to his legal philosophy can be just as powerful as his commitment to unambiguous justice. I was philosophically opposed to the death penalty, not for religious reasons, but because the scientific evidence clearly shows that it has no special deterrent effect. I do not believe state killing is good public policy unless there is the justification of deterrence, in part because it is expensive and skews the legal system, but most of all because I had seen enough to know that the criminal-justice system is imperfect, so that inevitably the state would execute innocent people. (I did not, however, imagine that such errors were nearly as frequent as DNA testing has now demonstrated beyond doubt.) Because of my interest, I had already done some research on the legal arguments that capital punishment violates the Constitution, so my offer to help with the case was accepted.

Although they had been appointed to handle a federal habeas petition, Bert, Tom, and Jerry decided to begin by filing a new collateral attack on the conviction in the state courts and to ask Judge Parsons to continue the federal petition until we completed proceedings in the state court, meanwhile staying Witherspoon's execution. The reason we gave was to be sure we had satisfied the requirement that state court remedies be exhausted before a federal court will consider an attack on a state conviction. Accordingly, our petition invoked every conceivable statutory and common law basis for overturning a state judgment, including some ancient writs that had long since been superseded or fallen into disuse.

The other purpose of this strategy was delay. If Judge Parsons would continue the federal case and stay execution, we would gain a year or more while the petition was considered in the Circuit Court of Cook County, in the Illinois Supreme Court, and finally on petition for writ of certiorari to the U.S. Supreme Court. While we had no expectation of succeeding at any step in that process, the delay would not only preserve our client's life, it would do so during a time when there was growing opposition to the death penalty in America. Both England and Canada had recently abolished or suspended the penalty, and recent polls showed that for the first time ever a plurality of Americans opposed capital punishment. A series of cases had been filed by the NAACP Inc. Fund, challenging the constitutionality of the penalty as a violation of the Eighth Amendment prohibition against cruel and unusual punishment, and there was even a chance that it would be abolished legislatively. The longer we could keep Witherspoon alive, the more likely we would be able to save his life when the case returned to federal court.

The petition we filed in the circuit court adopted the Eighth Amendment argument and asked for an evidentiary hearing at which we proposed to prove that a consensus had emerged in America that capital punishment was not appropriate in a civilized society. (It is precisely this argument that led the Supreme Court in 2002 to hold that execution of the mentally retarded violates the "cruel and unusual punishment" clause.) If it was unlikely that such a hearing would be provided in the state court, there was a real basis in the federal habeas corpus law for hoping that a hearing would be granted when the case returned to Judge Parsons.

Another issue presented by our petition related to the composition of the jury. Like every state with the death penalty, Illinois law allowed the prosecution to remove for cause any prospective juror who expressed opposition to the death penalty on moral or religious grounds. Backed by a study conducted by University of Chicago law professor Hans Zeisel, our frequent collaborator, we alleged that the exclusion of such jurors resulted in seating a jury that was "prosecution prone"—that is, more likely to rule for the prosecution on the question of guilt or innocence than a jury selected from the population at large. Selection of a prosecution-prone jury, we argued, would violate the constitutional requirement that a defendant be tried by a jury drawn from an impartial cross section of the community. We included the self-evident argument that such a jury would also favor the prosecution in the penalty phase of the trial. While it might be necessary to allow the prosecution to exclude jurors who said they would never impose the death penalty under any circumstances despite the instruction that they were required by law to consider doing so, the blanket exclusion of anyone who voiced a generalized opposition to capital punishment was too broad and deprived the defendant of an impartial cross section when the jury decided what punishment to impose.

As expected, the circuit court and Illinois supreme courts rejected our arguments. We anticipated the U.S. Supreme Court would deny certiorari; if it wanted to use our case to decide any of these issues, it seemed likely to wait until the case came up through the federal habeas corpus route. To our surprise, however, in January 1968, the Court granted cert on the jury-selection issues.

The grant of certiorari in the *Witherspoon* case had a dramatic impact on executions in America. If the Court ruled in our favor on both jury-selection issues, nearly every person on death row would have been sent there after trial by a jury selected in violation of the Constitution. Even the rare defendant who had waived a jury or pleaded guilty without a plea agreement could argue that his decision was impacted by the knowledge that if he opted for a jury trial, his jury would be selected in a manner favorable to the prosecution. Across the country, executions stopped to await the outcome of our case. If a governor or state court would not stay an execution, the appropriate federal court did. Recognizing the importance of the case, the attorneys general of death-penalty states and organizations opposed to the death penalty prepared to file amicus briefs in support of their respective positions.

The Inc. Fund, represented by law professor Anthony Amsterdam, had cases working their way up through the lower courts which raised the prosecution-prone-jury issue, as well as the cruel and unusual punishment claim. They asked our approval to file an amicus brief supporting our position, which we happily granted, and then filed a brief that said our claim that the jury was selected in a manner resulting in a prosecution-prone jury was not "ripe" for decision because there had been inadequate exploration of evidence on the subject in the courts below. Although the brief urged the Court to reverse and remand the case to the Illinois courts for an evidentiary hearing, the assertion that our constitutional claims were not ripe for decision undermined our major arguments and could have resulted in dismissal of the grant of certiorari and even the execution of our client. We were all outraged at Amsterdam's breach of faith, and Tom Sullivan, in particular, was convinced Amsterdam had taken the position he did because he wanted *his* cases to get to the Supreme Court first so he could take credit for ending the death penalty. To this day, any mention of the incident rekindles Tom's anger.

Meanwhile, Tom, Jerry, and I and several associates prepared and filed our brief on the merits. When the state's brief was filed, we convened a meeting to discuss two subjects: the reply brief, which would be due in only a few days, and who would argue the case in the Supreme Court. Although our associates probably had spent more hours on the case than the rest of us combined, Jerry, Tom, and I had also put in substantial time, and no junior associate had a chance of being selected to argue. My claim for the job was that I was more familiar with the factual basis for our theories than either Tom or Jerry, and that I had already argued and won a case in the Supreme Court. Jerry turned that argument on its head: He was the only one of the three of us who had not argued at the Court, and therefore it was his turn. Moreover, he was the person who had really been appointed to the case: He was involved in a major case before Judge Parsons when the judge called and told him he was going to appoint Jerry and include Tom and Bert if they would agree. In addition, Jerry asserted that he was the person who had come up with the jury-selection argument in the first place—a claim that Tom and I disputed, but which was probably true. Tom had three arguments: Like me he had argued at the Court, he had argued *Witherspoon* in the Illinois Supreme Court, and (perhaps most powerfully) he was senior to both of us.

The discussion was proceeding politely, but with spirit, when Bert Jenner entered the conference room to join the meeting. He had spent little or no time on the case, but we had invited him to our strategy session anyway. He listened for a few minutes as the three of us debated, and then resolved the problem. "Gentlemen," he said, "I hate to hear my partners arguing among themselves. I'll tell you what: I will argue the case." And he did.

Early in the argument, questions from some of the more liberal Justices suggested that they doubted we had made a sufficient record to justify our claim that juries from which death-penalty opponents are excluded are prone to decide for the prosecution on the issue of guilt or innocence. Bert answered their questions as best he could, and then quickly shifted the emphasis of his argument to the narrower claim that such a jury would necessarily favor the prosecution on the penalty issue, and that jurors who oppose the death penalty can be excluded only if they are shown to be unwilling to impose death in *any* case under *any* circumstances. I was disappointed that Bert had abandoned the broader argument so quickly, and asked him later why he had done so. "John," he said, "my job is to try to save Bill Witherspoon's life, not to establish some broad legal principle. Whatever else you do, you should always give the Court an opportunity to decide a case for your client on the narrowest possible ground. That's what most judges want to do."

He was right, of course, and it was advice I always tried to follow. On June 3, 1968, by a vote of six to three, the Supreme Court ruled that jury-selection procedures employed at Witherspoon's trial had denied him the right to an impartial jury in the penalty phase and ordered that Witherspoon's sentence be reduced to something less than death or that he be given a new trial.

The state agreed to reduce Witherspoon's sentence to life in prison, and similar resentencing was applied to most of the other men and women on death row across America. Four years later, Tony Amsterdam's cases finally reached the Supreme Court. In June 1972 the Court held in *Furman v. Georgia* that the death-penalty statutes and procedures then in effect violated the "cruel and unusual punishment" clause. As a result of the *Witherspoon* and *Furman* decisions, none of the four hundred–odd men and women on death rows in America when certiorari was granted in

Witherspoon in January 1968 were executed, nor were any new death-penalty sentences carried out from then until after the Supreme Court upheld newly drafted state statutes in 1976.

Bill Witherspoon had always been a model prisoner, and had also gained some prominence as a published writer. In 1981, with the support of prison officials but over the objection of the state's attorney's office, he was paroled and lived out a quiet and productive life with his sister on a farm in rural Michigan. If Witherspoon's case arose today, following the emasculation of habeas corpus by Congress and the Rehnquist Court, his petition would be summarily dismissed and he would soon be executed.

The problem with cases that offer an opportunity to pursue unambiguous justice is an awful injustice always lurks on the other side. Despite their competitive nature, trial lawyers learn to accept the inevitability of occasional defeat without rending their garments and flaying their flesh. But defeat is harder to take when a case of unambiguous justice turns out the wrong way.

Charles E. Gavin was one of those rare individuals who overcome enormous social barriers to achieve great success, while remaining humble, dedicated to service, and beloved of his fellows. Gavin was born on September 30, 1925, in Chicago Heights, Illinois, the second of six children born to Robert and Manila Gavin. Chicago Heights is a blue-collar suburb of Chicago which, even in 1925, had a substantial population of "coloreds," including the Gavin family. If growing up poor and black in Jim Crow Depression-era America was not the kind of start in life one might wish for, Charles Gavin had one huge advantage: his parents. His father owned a dry-cleaning shop where he worked sixteen hours a day, six days a week. His mother was from Mississippi, where she had attended Alcorn College and taught school before moving north with Robert. She too worked in the dry cleaners, while raising the six children and imbuing each of them with her belief in the importance of education. Through some ineluctable combination of nature and nurture, five of the six children earned college degrees (the sixth married a doctor before finishing her education), and four of them went on to postgraduate work while the oldest boy, Robert Jr., took over and expanded the dry-cleaning business. All of them, in their work or their private lives, displayed an unceasing dedication to public service.

Catherine, the oldest girl, earned a Ph.D. and served as a professor of education at Prairie State University. Marvin, the youngest boy, graduated from DePauw University and Harvard Law School. Evonne, the youngest, became a high-school principal.

And Charles, the second oldest, became a physician. After graduating from high school in 1942 at age seventeen, Charles entered the World War II army, serving for two years in a segregated unit. Upon his discharge in 1944, he entered the University of Illinois, earned his degree, and was admitted to the university's medical school. After medical school, postgraduate training in orthopedic surgery, and a residency in his specialty at Presbyterian–St. Luke's, one of Chicago's great teaching hospitals, he was offered a position on that hospital's staff. Instead, he elected to move to St. James Hospital in Chicago Heights, practicing as well at two smaller hospitals on Chicago's South Side. St. James was the largest hospital in southern Cook County and served a diverse population ranging from the wealthy white suburbs of Flossmoor, Olympia Fields, and Park Forest through the blue-collar black and ethnic populations of Glenwood, Homewood, and Chicago Heights to the all-black neighborhoods of Chicago's South Side.

Dr. Gavin threw himself into his work with skill and enormous dedication. There were white orthopedic surgeons on the staff at St. James, and it was not easy for the white suburbanites and ethnic steelworkers to believe that the best person to treat their sore backs and broken limbs was this young black doctor. But before long, through word of mouth and the recommendation of family physicians, it became an accepted fact. By 1968 Charles Gavin was doing 85 percent of the orthopedic surgery at St. James, a hospital of nearly 500 beds.

It was an enormous workload that few doctors could bear. But that was not all. The people who lived on the South Side and the poorer areas of Chicago Heights and Homewood had bad backs and broken limbs as well, and few of them had the money or insurance to pay for an orthopedic surgeon, much less for a hospital stay at St. James. County welfare and some federal funds were available, but few physicians were willing to accept the relatively complicated and meager payment arrangements, much less see patients in the overcrowded, understaffed welfare clinics and small South Side hospitals. But Dr. Gavin would, and did. It was, he thought, his obligation as a doctor, and as a man.

So, over the years, Charles Gavin became a hero, an almost angelic figure to his patients and even to the doctors, nurses, and medical administrators who worked with him. But the cost—at least, the obvious cost—was that he did nothing but work. He was a bachelor, living with his unmarried brother and sister, Catherine and Marvin, and he worked six or seven days a week, twelve to sixteen hours a day, without a vacation, every year from the time he began his practice.

But like most heroes and angels, Dr. Gavin had a flaw—or at least many people would think of it as a flaw. He was so busy treating patients he had no time, or interest, for anything else—not even essential paperwork, including billing for his services. At first no one noticed, or possibly cared. But after a while the referring physicians began to get complaints from their patients that Dr. Gavin had never sent a bill, or that he had sent one and they had paid it, but the check had not been deposited. Neither were the other doctors getting regular progress reports on the patients they referred. Finally, in 1965, his fellow doctors at St. James Hospital formed a committee to approach Dr. Gavin and insist he hire a bookkeeper to handle his paperwork.

When the bookkeeper went to work, she found that approximately 50 percent of the patients Dr. Gavin had treated in the preceding year had never received a bill for his services. She also discovered that Dr. Gavin had not filed a tax return since 1960, the year he finished his residency. If Dr. Gavin had consulted with an experienced federal income-tax lawyer at that point, he would surely have been advised to have someone go back to 1960 and, as best possible, prepare a return for each of the years he had missed, and to then contact the IRS to notify them that late returns were being filed and try to work out a civil settlement of any taxes and penalties due. Instead, the bookkeeper prepared—and Gavin filed—a return for 1965, apparently hoping the IRS would not pursue the five earlier years when no returns were filed. It was a foolish hope, especially since Gavin *had* filed returns prior to 1960, so the gap in filing was apparent, and cried out for explanation.

It took several years before the IRS got around to it, but when they did conduct an investigation, it was obvious that there was no legitimate reason for the absence of returns. In mid-1968 Dr. Gavin received word that he was under investigation and the IRS was about to charge him with misdemeanor failure to file, and perhaps felony-evasion charges as well. At first Dr. Gavin was fatalistic— what would happen would happen—he was too busy practicing medicine to worry about it. Finally, however, his brothers and sisters persuaded him to hire someone with experience in IRS matters, a well-known lawyer named Bernard Sokol. Sokol succeeded in negotiating an agreement with the government by which Gavin would plead guilty to a complaint charging three misdemeanor counts of failure to file tax returns for the years 1962, 1963, and 1964. They would not charge evasion, or failure to file in 1960 or 1961. On the issue of punishment, the government refused to agree to recommend probation, but said that while it reserved the right to suggest a period of incarceration was appropriate, it would not ask for a specific term. While a commitment not to oppose probation would have been better, Sokol correctly advised his client that given Gavin's impeccable reputation and life of service, it was unlikely a judge would send him to jail.

The complaint was filed in December 1968 and set for arraignment on January 14, 1969, at which time Gavin entered his agreed plea of guilty. A pre-sentence investigation was ordered (an investigation of the charges and the defendant's background conducted by the probation department to assist the judge in arriving at a sentence) and sentencing set for February 27.

All of this was routine, but there were two developments that did not bode well for the anticipated sentence of probation. With a sentencing date in late February, the case was entering the period of time close to April 15, when the IRS sets out every year to impress the public with the importance of filing accurate tax returns by sending a few prominent citizens to jail for evasion and, if possible, for failure to file. As a result, when the date for sentencing approached, the IRS instructed Assistant United States Attorney Richard Makarski, who was assigned to the case, to ask the judge to sentence Gavin to a period of incarceration. The prosecutor was a nice man who normally would not have opposed probation, but in tax cases the United States Attorney's office traditionally defers to the wishes of the IRS on such matters, and they did so in this instance.

Even worse, however, was the outcome of the lottery employed in the clerk's office to determine which district court judge would handle his case. When a case is filed, the clerk pulls a sticker off a sheet of paper on which the names of all of the judges are written. The names are placed on the paper in random order, and there is a name under each sticker. When the sticker is pulled and the judge identified, the clerk selects a rubber stamp bearing the judge's name and stamps it on the complaint together with the next case number, in this instance 68 CR 758, indicating that Dr. Gavin's case was the seven hundred fifty-eighth criminal case filed in the Northern District of Illinois in 1968.

The name that came up when the clerk pulled the sticker to determine the assignment of *United States v. Charles Gavin* was that of the only judge on the court who was likely to send Dr. Gavin to prison: Julius Hoffman.

Nowadays defense lawyers in criminal cases routinely file lengthy sentencing memoranda supporting their request for a lenient sentence with letters and affidavits from the defendants, family, friends, and other admirers. The pre-sentence investigation report is made available to the defense, and any negative material appearing in it is refuted or explained, as is anything that can be attacked in the prosecution's sentencing memo. In 1969, however, pre-sentence reports were not shared with the defense except by special order of court, and often the only argument about the sentence was presented orally on the day of sentencing. Although the *Gavin* case cried out for a more extensive explication of the doctor's personal virtues, that is what happened on February 27, 1969. When the arguments in aggravation and mitigation were over, Judge Hoffman sentenced Dr. Gavin to a fine of $7,500 and six months in prison on each of the three counts of failure to file, to be served concurrently. Execution of the sentence (the day he would have to report to prison) was continued to March 19 so he could get his affairs in order.

Dr. Gavin paid his fine the next day, but it was several days before the full impact of his prison sentence sunk in. No one wants to go to prison, even for a day, but there are vast differences in the way people, especially white-collar offenders, react to the prospect and the reality of incarceration. I know more than one doctor, lawyer, or businessman who worked too hard, drank too much, and exercised too little whose life was probably saved by a year or so in a minimum-security federal prison where exercise is the only outlet for a type A personality and sleep is assured by the institution's turning off the lights. Others become so depressed by the loss of freedom that they are virtually paralyzed. Not infrequently their depression becomes clinical, even suicidal, and persists long after their release. And regardless of how they react to the prison experience, I have never known a prisoner, in any prison, who wasn't desperate to get out.

Another difference among people facing prison is the way they interpret the events that led to their sentence. Some take it as the result of an oppressive and wrongheaded government or malicious God, others accept it, albeit unwillingly, as just punishment for an offense they know they committed, and still others are consumed with the embarrassment they have brought upon themselves and their families.

Within a few days after Dr. Gavin was sentenced to prison it became clear to his friends and family that he was in the last category—with a vengeance. The pride of Charles Gavin's life was his career as a doctor, the service he rendered to his fellow man, and the resulting respect he earned. Now it had all turned to ashes. He had been judged, and instead of honor and respect, he had been declared a common criminal who should be removed from society for its own protection. Had the court seen he was only guilty of a mistake, and given recognition to his value as a doctor and a human being by admitting him to probation so he could continue his work, he could live with the embarrassment and financial distress, but this was different. This was a condemnation of his character and a judgment that his work as a doctor was of no consequence. Instead of rejecting that judgment for the falsehood it was, Dr. Gavin felt he had no alternative but to accept it as true. He was devastated.

When word spread that Dr. Gavin had been sentenced to prison, his patients, friends, and colleagues in the medical community were outraged. Letters poured in to newspapers and Judge Hoffman's chambers, denouncing the ruling. And when his friends, family, and fellow doctors realized the impact the sentence was having on him, they concluded that somehow, something had to be done to keep him out of prison.

The question was what, and the options were limited and unlikely. The most direct route was to persuade Judge Hoffman to change his mind and admit Gavin to probation. As the sentencing judge, he had the power to do so up to the time the sentence was executed—that is, until Gavin entered prison. After that the trial court lost the right to consider probation, but still could reduce the sentence to time served, thus providing for immediate release. The problem was that once Judge Hoffman imposed sentence, he was notoriously unlikely to reduce it for any reason. Even pleas for mercy based on impending death from a terminal illness, a circumstance that moved many judges to allow the prisoner to spend his final days with family, were routinely rejected by Hoffman. Nor was there any realistic chance the Court of Appeals would intervene to reverse Hoffman if he refused to change his mind. Denial of probation and the length of a prison sentence within the range provided by statute were almost entirely within the discretion of the trial judge.

Bernie Sokol advised his client of the near-hopelessness of the task, but Gavin's friends and family would not be deterred. A committee of doctors was formed to coordinate the gathering of letters and petitions describing Dr. Gavin's good works and service to the community, all urging Judge Hoffman to admit him to probation. The doctors' committee used the media to urge the community to send letters to a central depository for an organized presentation to the court. In addition, petitions were gathered from every member of the medical, nursing, and administrative staffs of each hospital and clinic where Dr. Gavin practiced, as well as from the local mayors, legislators, chambers of commerce, and similar organizations. A street-corner campaign gathered thousands of signatures from members of the community who had been patients of Dr. Gavin, or simply heard of him from others. And twenty-five doctors from Chicago's South Side and south suburbs signed a petition in which each of them offered to serve one of the twenty-five weeks of Dr. Gavin's six-month prison sentence.

Despite these activities, Bernie Sokol not only remained pessimistic but seemed to discourage the idea of even trying to keep Gavin out of prison. For one thing, Sokol reported, word had reached him that some of the letters that had been sent directly to Judge Hoffman were critical of the sentence and, in Hoffman's mind, personally insulting. According to the reports, Hoffman was angry. Among his many unattractive judicial qualities, Hoffman was notoriously thin-skinned and quick to use the threat or actuality of a contempt of court citation when he felt challenged. Perhaps it would be best to back off before one of Gavin's supporters (or Sokol himself) ended up in jail. Gavin's supporters began to think it might be best to get another lawyer.

Meanwhile, although Marvin Gavin thought his brother was stoic about his situation and resigned to his punishment, some of Gavin's doctor friends saw things quite differently. What Marvin saw as stoic acceptance looked to them like loss of affect and clinical depression. At their insistence, Gavin agreed to be examined by a psychiatrist and a psychologist on the staff at St. James.

The results were disturbing. The psychiatrist, Dr. Douglas Foster, reported that Dr. Gavins's profession was so all-engrossing that it appeared to be his "sole reason to live." Subsequent to his sentencing, Dr. Foster reported, Gavin had become depressed and developed psychosomatic symptoms of acute upper gastric distress and signs of an early ulcer. Dr. Foster concluded that "the prospect of a jail sentence and the loss of medicine . . . seriously threatens this man's ego structure." If deprived of his medical practice, Foster predicted that Gavin might become psychotically ill, and even suicidal. Dr. Eugene Southwell, a clinical psychologist, administered four standard psychological tests (Rorschach, Thematic Apperception, Rotter Incomplete Sentence Blank, and Minnesota Multiphasic Personality Inventory). From the results, he too concluded that Dr. Gavin was depressed and fearful, and that his emotional equilibrium was tenuous. His whole emotional defense structure was tied to his practice of medicine, and might collapse if he were deprived of that structure.

Dr. Southwell's tests were performed on March 10, and Dr. Foster's examination on March 12. With these results, at the insistence of Dr. Gavin's friends and family, Bernard Sokol agreed to move forward with an effort to persuade Judge Hoffman to suspend his sentence and keep Gavin out of prison. Hoffman, however, was out of town on vacation, so on Friday, March 14, Sokol appeared before Judge Hubert Will, the judge who was hearing emergency motions that day, and presented a motion to reduce Dr Gavin's sentence and to continue that motion until Judge Hoffman's return. Meanwhile, the motion requested the judge to stay execution of the sentence.

In light of Sokol's extreme pessimism and reluctance to proceed, Gavin's family and supporters decided they had to get
another lawyer. They settled on my senior partner, Bert Jenner. In
the preceding five years, Bert had been constantly in the news in
connection with his participation in important cases and his
numerous civic duties, including senior counsel to the Warren
Commission to investigate the murder of President Kennedy,
member of the National Commission to Study the Causes and Pre-
vention of Violence created by President Johnson, and chair of the
ABA Committee on the Federal Judiciary.

Jenner, a Republican, had himself turned down several offers of
judicial appointments and was known to be on good terms with
both Everett Dirksen, the powerful Republican leader in the
Senate, and Charles Percy, the recently elected junior senator from
Illinois.

Jenner was out of town attending meetings but when the
urgency of the situation was explained to his secretary, she
arranged for a telephone conference which resulted in Jenner's
agreeing to come back to Chicago for a meeting on Saturday,
March 15. Then, Jenner called the office and asked me to attend
the Saturday meeting.

In addition to Bert and me, the group that assembled on Saturday morning included Dr. Gavin, his brother Marvin, his sister
Cathcrine, and two of the doctors who were active in the campaign
to keep him out of prison. Dr. Charles Gavin was a tall, thin man
with fine features and a voice so soft it was difficult to hear what
he was saying on the rare occasions when he spoke. Whether from
the depression diagnosed by the doctors or the stoicism reported
by his brother, during our entire meeting he spoke only in
response to a direct question, and then only the few words
required to answer the question without elaboration. Marvin
Gavin was similar in looks to his brother, and nearly as taciturn.
The burden of explaining the family's position thus fell primarily
on Catherine Gavin, an articulate, energetic woman whose sense of
outrage at her brother's situation seemed to far exceed his own.

The two doctors were also outraged and upset and voiced their bewilderment at the treatment their friend had received when, as they reported, they both knew other doctors who had been involved in disputes with the IRS which seemed far more serious, but which had been resolved civilly, or at worst, with a fine, pro-bation, and a requirement to perform some hours of public service. One of them found the community-service requirement especially ironic since, as he said, "Dr. Gavin does more commu-nity service in a year than all the rest of us at St. James combined."

All five of our guests had attended the hearing on Friday and reported that Judge Will had continued it until Tuesday before Judge Edwin A. Robson, who was designated to hear Judge Hoffman's cases for the next two weeks. Meanwhile, Judge Will said he would convey to Judge Hoffman the thrust of the motions so that, if he wished, he could let Judge Robson have his views on how they should be handled. It was a courtesy routinely extended to judges who were out of town, and one that Judge Hoffman insisted upon before even the most routine order was entered by another judge in one of his cases.

At that time Judge Will was probably the most liberal judge on the district court bench in Chicago, and one who might have par-ticular sympathy for Dr. Gavin as he was a longtime resident of the area surrounding the University of Chicago, a liberal white island in the sea of Chicago's black South Side, so it seemed a shame the motion to delay execution of Dr. Gavin's sentence had been put over before the far more conservative Judge Robson. In fact, how-ever, it is doubtful that even Judge Will would have changed the date for Dr. Gavin to report to prison without getting Hoffman's approval.

In their earlier phone conference, Jenner had explained to the Gavins the difficulty he anticipated in trying to persuade Judge Hoffman to change his mind, but now he did so again. Jenner pointed out there was a very good chance the Gavins would incur significant attorney's fees, to no avail. On the other hand, the sup-port for Dr. Gavin that had poured in since the sentencing, the medical reports, and new information that conclusively demonstrated that Gavin's failure to file returns was not based on any desire to avoid the payment of taxes had not been available to Judge Hoffman at the time of sentencing. Thus, the request for a stay of execution for two weeks so those new facts could be presented to the judge on his return from vacation seemed so reasonable it was difficult to imagine it would be denied. There was a possibility the community support would build to such a level in the interim that Hoffman would change his mind. There was even a chance that political influence could be marshaled to obtain a pardon or commutation of sentence for Dr. Gavin if Hoffman refused to act.

As far as Catherine Gavin was concerned, it didn't matter how slim the chances were or how much it cost. If there was any chance of keeping her brother out of prison, she wanted to risk it. The doctors agreed, and while the two brothers remained quiet, it was clear that at least on this matter, Catherine spoke for the family. We would proceed.

Early on, Bert Jenner had informed everyone at the meeting that he had to be back in Houston on Monday and Tuesday, and I would handle the appearance before Judge Robson on Tuesday morning. There was no disguising the disappointment that greeted that information, but when Jenner finished informing the Gavins of my brilliance and recognized standing as the finest young trial lawyer in the city, their anxiety was somewhat relieved. I only wished I had a tape recording of his comments for presentation to the compensation committee, the group of partners who every year established each partner's percentage share of the firm's profits for the year to come—but then, if I had such a tape, so would every other lawyer in the firm whom Bert asked to handle a matter in his absence.

In any event, it was a good cause, and I was happy to be part of it, even though I realized the rest of my weekend would be taken up with research and preparing additional papers to strengthen the argument for keeping Dr. Gavin out of prison.

Although Judge Robson was not going to decide that issue, the stronger the argument I could present in the additional papers I hoped to file, the better chance there was to obtain the crucial postponement of the sentence. What I didn't realize was that I was about to enter into a whirlwind of activity that occupied me for the next several weeks on a schedule of seven-day weeks and sixteen-hour days, much like those Dr. Gavin had followed for eight years.

Before the Gavins left, arrangements were made for me to meet on Sunday with the people who had been collecting letters of support in order to get copies and select those most likely to impress the court. On Monday the accountant who had been working on Gavin's financial records would give me his latest results. Since Judge Hoffman had expressly denied probation at the time of sentencing, Sokol had concluded it would be better to style the motion he filed on the previous Friday as a motion to reduce the sentence. However, a few hours of research revealed there might be an advantage to a renewed motion for admission to probation. The difference lay in a technicality. While a request to reduce the sentence could be made at any time, a motion for probation could be made only before Dr. Gavin was required to report to prison. Thus we could argue to Judge Robson that postponing the sentence was required not only because of concern for Dr. Gavin's mental condition, but also because denying the stay would have the effect of depriving Judge Hoffman of the opportunity to reconsider probation. There was good reason to preserve the possibility of probation, which, if granted, would provide the judge more flexibility to shape the conditions for Gavin's release. Since our immediate goal was to keep Dr. Gavin out of prison, anything that enhanced our argument seemed worth trying. Before leaving the office I prepared a supplemental motion requesting reconsideration of the denial of probation.

On Monday the accountant brought especially good news. He could now say with confidence that in 1960, the year Dr. Gavin completed his residency and began his practice, and the first year for which no tax return was filed, the amount withheld from his salary for taxes exceeded his tax liability for the year. In other words, if he *had* filed a tax return, he would have been entitled to a refund. It was an effective response to the government's suggestion at the time of sentencing that Dr. Gavin had stopped filing tax returns in order to avoid taxes when he first began earning substantial income.

Even better, the accountant said he could state with a reasonable degree of certainty that during the three years involved in the charges against Gavin, the money he was owed by the Cook County Welfare Department and the Medicare system for treating indigent patients *substantially exceeded the amounts he owed the government in unpaid taxes in those years.* The same dedication to his work that caused his failure to file tax returns had also caused him not to file the necessary documentation to collect what the government owed him. Gavin had now paid the taxes, with interest and penalties, but he had never recovered (or tried to recover) the money he was owed.

By Monday afternoon I had filed my motion and supporting documentation and sent a copy directly to Judge Robson's chambers so he could read them before the court date at 2:00 P.M. Tuesday. That morning I spent with the psychologist, the accountant, and a doctor from St. James Hospital, preparing them to testify in case Judge Robson wanted to hear them before ruling on the motion.

Edwin A. Robson was a rather formal and stiff-necked Republican who had been appointed to the federal bench by President Eisenhower. Although conservative, he was not especially ideological and had enjoyed a successful practice as a civil litigator in business cases before becoming a judge. Plump and balding, Judge Robson entered the courtroom through the door that led to his chambers and with little ceremony ascended the bench, sat down, and asked his clerk to call the next case, which was ours. A complex jury trial he had begun on Monday morning was interrupted to hear our motion, so the lawyers and clients from that case were in attendance waiting to resume their trial, and a sizable group of friends, family, potential witnesses, and reporters were there to see what happened to Dr. Gavin. I had suggested some of his friends turn out to demonstrate Dr. Gavin's strong support in the community, and I was pleased with the result.

The first order of business was the substitution of Mr. Jenner and me for Mr. Sokol as counsel, and the request for leave to file our additional motions, both of which were granted without objection, as was the request that the motions for probation and for reduction of sentence be continued for hearing before Judge Hoffman when he returned from his vacation in two weeks. In agreeing to those requests, however, the prosecutor interjected that he would object to any delay in Dr. Gavin's beginning his sentence on March 19, the next day.

In conversations on Monday, I had tried to get the prosecutor to agree to a stay. But after conferring with his boss, U.S. Attorney Thomas Foran, he reported he had been instructed to object, so his position was no surprise. Neither was I especially surprised when Judge Robson interrupted as I began to describe the new evidence we had developed to say he had conferred with Judge Hoffman, who was also opposed to any further stay of execution. However, I was surprised at the vehemence of Judge Hoffman's position, as Judge Robson described it to me, and at Robson's apparent feeling that he had no alternative but to follow Hoffman's request.

For the next fifteen or twenty minutes, I presented every argument I could think of for granting the stay—without a stay, the petition for probation would be effectively denied by the execution of judgment. The other two orthopedic surgeons on the staff of St. James Hospital were on vacation for the next two weeks, and there would be no one within forty-five miles to handle those cases if Gavin were sent to prison during that time. The psychiatrist and psychologist believed that imprisoning Gavin could have grave and irreversible consequences. None of these matters had been presented to Judge Hoffman, nor was he aware of the clear evidence now available to refute the government's suggestion that Gavin had failed to file tax returns in order to avoid paying taxes.

It was all to no avail. Judge Robson, citing strict orders he had received from Judge Hoffman, would not even grant a stay of two or three days so our materials could be sent to Judge Hoffman in Florida.

Judge Robson did have an alternative: The case was now before him, and he had a right to do whatever he thought was just and proper if he felt Judge Hoffman's directions from afar were wrong—and I was disappointed in his failure to act. Some time later, I came to have a better understanding of the dilemma Judge Robson had faced when a Court of Appeals judge told me Judge Hoffman had refused to speak to him for four years after he reversed Hoffman in an earlier case.

If Robson's refusal to order a stay was a grave disappointment, it was not such a surprise that we had not thought about what to do next. There were two possibilities. One was to file a petition for writ of mandamus in the Seventh Circuit, asking that court to order Judge Robson to hear the petition for probation himself, or stay execution until Hoffman could hear it. The second was to ask Judge Robson and, assuming he would refuse, then ask the Court of Appeals to release Gavin on bond, pending an appeal from Robson's order refusing to stay execution. Both ideas were long shots with serious theoretical problems, but we had resolved to try them if necessary, and I had already done some drafting and research before I appeared before Judge Robson.

Mandamus is a procedure by which a higher court can command a lower court to do something it has failed or refused to do. It applies only to situations that require immediate relief before there is a final, appealable order, and it is granted very rarely. One situation in which it is sometimes granted, however, is when the lower court has arbitrarily refused to grant a stay or continuance in circumstances where failing to do so will render an issue moot or gravely injure one of the parties. Arguably, that was what was happening, so immediately upon leaving Judge

Robson's court, I told the prosecutor I was going to file a petition for writ of mandamus and gave him a copy of the papers I had already drafted. I then filed the petition and an emergency motion for immediate hearing with the clerk of the Court of Appeals. It was after 3:00 P.M. and I knew the emergency judge would normally leave at 5:00. Gavin was under court order to report to the marshal's office to begin serving his sentence at 9:00 the next morning. I had told the prosecutor I was going to ask for a chance to argue the request orally before the emergency judge (a request that is almost never granted), and he joined me outside the clerk's office while we waited to see if the judge would hear argument. At about 4:30 one of the clerks came out and said the judge had denied my request for oral argument and also denied the petition for writ of mandamus.

The next step was to try to get bond pending appeal, but in the meantime, Dr. Gavin would have to report to prison the next morning. Normally, after reporting to the marshal a federal prisoner is shipped to a federal prison the same day, unless there is some reason to retain him briefly in the Chicago area for further proceedings. In a phone conference, Tom Foran agreed to have Gavin retained in the Chicago area until our effort to have him released on bond was decided.

On Wednesday morning Dr. Gavin, accompanied by Marvin and Catherine, reported to the United States marshal's office where I met them. I stayed only long enough to explain the procedures the marshal would follow in processing Dr. Gavin into the system and then took the elevator to Judge Robson's courtroom, where I intended to present a motion for bond pending appeal when court convened at 10 A.M.

As I had expected, the motion for bond pending appeal was denied by Judge Robson, who observed, with considerable justification, that it was difficult to believe that his order refusing to stay the sentence was appealable. (Only certain kinds of orders can be appealed, and refusing to postpone service of a sentence is generally not one of them.) An emergency motion for bond in the

Seventh Circuit Court of Appeals resulted in a rare conference with Chief Judge Luther Swygert in his chambers and an even rarer argument a few days later in the courtroom. Bert made the argument and Judge Swygert was clearly sympathetic to Dr. Gavin's plight, but that same afternoon he denied the motion for bond, again on the ground that there was no appealable order. The next day Dr. Gavin was transferred to the federal prison in Sandstone, Minnesota, where most white-collar prisoners from Chicago were housed.

I prepared an emergency application for bond to Thurgood Marshall, the Supreme Court Justice assigned to hear such appeals from the Seventh Circuit. Bert made a personal call to the Supreme Court clerk asking him to present Justice Marshall with Bert's plea for an opportunity to present our position in person, but several days later, after Marshall had raised our hopes by asking the solicitor general to respond to our motion, he denied both the request for oral argument and the motion for bond.

Meanwhile, a flurry of newspaper and television editorials urged Gavin's prompt release, describing again his service to patients and extraordinary reputation in the community. Bert had spoken personally to Senator Dirksen and enlisted his enthusiastic support for the idea of obtaining a presidential pardon or commutation of sentence. Senator Percy offered assistance, but Dirksen clearly wanted the credit for any success and, given his powerful position, we asked Percy to limit his involvement to a brief public statement of support for Dirksen's effort, which he agreed to graciously.

On March 26, while our petition to Justice Marshall was still pending, I flew to Washington to meet with Senator Dirksen and be available in case our request for oral argument was granted. There I spent a long and fascinating day waiting in Senator Dirksen's anteroom observing a steady flow of the most powerful politicians and lobbyists in America enter his private office. Finally, at about 4:30 in the afternoon, the senator's personal assistant, Mrs. Gomien, announced that Senator Dirksen would see me now.

She escorted me into his office, where every wall was filled with the memorabilia of his decades in public life. I had brought with me copies of nearly five thousand letters in support of Dr. Gavin and a notebook compiling the best of them. I presented the letters to Dirksen along with a petition for clemency. In a half-hour meeting, Dirksen assured me of his full support and promised to speak directly to President Nixon and Attorney General Mitchell about obtaining a presidential pardon as quickly as possible.

A few days later, Mrs. Gomien called to say the senator had indeed met with Mitchell on the matter, and that Mitchell had promised to consider it promptly and present it to the president. That same day, Senator Dirksen's press spokesman circulated the same information to the media. I thought it unlikely Dirksen would have authorized the press release if he were not confident of success.

While I was in Washington, I had also met with H. G. Moeller, the director of the Federal Bureau of Prisons, to ask that Dr. Gavin be allowed to help the medical staff at Sandstone with care of the prisoners, as had been suggested by his psychiatrist. I also met Joseph Stone, the executive director of the Federal Parole Commission, in case all else failed. Both men knew of the case and promised their support. There was a question whether Dr. Gavin's six-month sentence would fall within the usual rule providing eligibility for parole after service of one-third of the sentence, and I was relieved when Mr. Stone said he believed it did and he would push for Gavin's release at the earliest possible date.

Bert and I both thought it was unlikely Judge Hoffman would do anything to change Dr. Gavin's sentence, but the family thought there was still a chance, so on April 1, Hoffman's first day back on the bench, and the day before our scheduled hearing, I tested the waters by presenting a motion asking him to provide us with the pre-sentence investigation report. He not only denied the motion out of hand but launched into a furious condemnation of what he characterized as the "worst vilification" he had been subjected to in fifty years on the bench. There had been some criticism of his sentence in the articles calling for Gavin's release, but his characterization of it as "vilification" was only slightly less exaggerated than his claim to fifty years on the bench—although to lawyers who regularly practiced in his court it may well have seemed like fifty years.

There was no sense in giving him a chance to write an opinion justifying his sentence, which would undoubtedly include criticism of Dr. Gavin that might be harmful to the pardon effort, so the next morning Bert went to court and withdrew our motion for reduction of sentence. He told the press that with the pardon effort in full swing, he didn't want to confuse things by proceeding on two tracks at once.

As another week passed without any discernible progress on the pardon, Dr. Foster, who had written the psychiatric report on Dr. Gavin, went to Sandstone to visit him. He returned with disturbing news. After three weeks in prison, Gavin was deeply depressed. His self-esteem was shattered, as Foster had predicted. At this point, Dr. Foster thought obtaining the pardon was especially important. Whatever happened, unless something went wrong at the parole board, Gavin would be released from prison on May 19, but Foster believed Gavin needed a clear signal that society recognized his worth. For some reason, the outpouring of support from his friends, patients, and fellow doctors had not done it—a presidential pardon or commutation of sentence might.

Still, nothing anyone said or did seemed to be working. At first, Senator Dirksen remained optimistic, reporting several further discussions in which Attorney General Mitchell promised he was still working on the matter, but had to cover the necessary bases. One of the bases was U.S. Attorney Tom Foran. It was no surprise he opposed the pardon; he had to or face the real prospect that Judge Hoffman would put *him* on his enemies list, which Foran could ill afford, especially since Hoffman had just been assigned to try the famous "Chicago Eight" conspiracy case arising from the disturbances at the 1968 Democratic National Convention. Foran had agreed to stay on as U.S. attorney for long enough to try the case himself as a favor to Mayor Daley, his political sponsor. Attorney General Mitchell may have been reluctant to annoy the thin-skinned judge for the same reason. Senator Percy now joined in the effort to obtain a pardon, with Dirksen's approval. He arranged what was supposed to be a private meeting between Mitchell, the Gavin family, and some of the doctors, but at the last minute Mitchell begged off and the meeting was held with the lawyer in the Department of Justice assigned to investigate pardon requests. Dr. Gavin was due to be released on parole a few days later, and the pardon attorney, who, after all, worked for Mitchell, saw little reason to do anything but let matters take their course, despite the plea of Gavin's physicians that a pardon would be important to Gavin's recovery.

Dr. Charles Gavin was released from Sandstone prison on May 19. Reportedly, Judge Hoffman was angry, having believed that a prisoner with a six-month sentence was ineligible for parole. For some time after Gavin's release, his supporters continued to urge the Justice Department to recommend a pardon, but there was no response. After resting at home for a time, Charles Gavin returned to his medical practice. Some of his family, friends, and fellow doctors thought he was the same as before his imprisonment, others felt he was depressed, and far less sure of himself as a doctor, essentially going through the motions. Before many months had passed, it became clear that something was wrong— his energy seemed drained away. Before the end of the year he was diagnosed with inoperable lung cancer. A year later he was dead. Many of his friends were convinced there was a direct connection between Dr. Gavin's fatal illness and his conviction and prison sentence.

There was no justice in sending Dr. Gavin to prison; no justice in refusing to stay his sentence for long enough to consider the new facts we developed; no justice in failing to take those facts into account and reduce or commute his sentence; and no justice in failing to grant Dr. Gavin a pardon which might have restored his self-esteem and prolonged his life. And despite the best efforts of

Bert Jenner, one of America's best lawyers, and Everett Dirksen, one of its most powerful politicians, those injustices could not be reversed.

I had always known the legal system was imperfect—every system is—but the *Gavin* case taught me just how imperfect it could be, even in the face of unambiguous justice.

CHAPTER 4

TRIAL OF THE CENTURY

Every few years, a case comes along that captures the attention of the media and the public so completely that it becomes the latest "trial of the century." They seem to come along more often now, but for that era of social and political upheaval commonly referred to as "the '60s," the undisputed "trial of the century" was the prosecution of the eight men accused of leading the antiwar and civil-rights protests at the 1968 Democratic National Convention in Chicago. The "Chicago Eight" conspiracy case was not only the most highly publicized trial of the era, it was among the most polarizing cases in American history. To the establishment in Chicago and much of the country, the conspiracy defendants and their chief defense lawyer, Bill Kunstler, were the most reviled participants of any case I can recall. But to most of the country's younger and more liberal population, that distinction went to the defendants' archenemy and nemesis, Judge Julius Hoffman, with the two prosecutors, U.S. Attorney Tom Foran and his assistant, Dick Schultz, running close seconds.

According to what Abbie Hoffman told me later, when he and fellow "Yippie" (Youth International Party) leader Jerry Rubin met Students for a Democratic Society leader Tom Hayden and National Mobilization Committee to End the War in Vietnam field coordinator Rennie Davis in Grant Park on Saturday, August 24, 1968, a shouting match ensued. Although there were serious tactical and philosophical disputes, and considerable distrust, between the Yippies on the one hand and Hayden and Davis on the other, months earlier the men had agreed that their respective groups would join forces at the Democratic National Convention to protest the Vietnam War. Each group had promised the others, and the press, that they would bring thousands of supporters to Chicago to join in the protests. It was the day before the convention was to open, a rally had been planned for the park that evening, and neither group had produced more than a few hundred people. It was a disaster each group blamed on the other.

Then the Chicago police rescued them. That night the police enforced Mayor Daley's order to clear the park by 11:00 P.M. with a minimum of violence, but the next night they used waves of tear gas and began joyously beating, kicking, and arresting everyone in sight, including members of the press and bystanders.

In the days that followed, the press coverage, the number of protesters, and the violence multiplied each day until by the end of the convention the war in the streets was the whole story. As the demonstrators chanted, the whole world was in fact watching, and poor Hubert Humphrey's candidacy was dead on arrival. Worse yet, from Mayor Daley's perspective, the national press and many of his fellow Democrats were blaming him and his police for the colossal mess.

When it was over and Richard Nixon was elected, Daley set out to get his revenge. At first the Justice Department, still headed by Attorney General Ramsey Clark, refused to authorize prosecution of the protesters; but after Nixon was inaugurated and John Mitchell took over at Justice, the climate changed. William Campbell, a longtime Daley ally and chief judge of the local U.S. district court, convened a grand jury. Holdover U.S. Attorney Tom Foran promptly persuaded it to return indictments against eight men for allegedly conspiring to incite the riots. Six of them were also charged with crossing state lines with the intent to incite a riot, and the other two were charged with planning to bomb the underground parking garage in Grant Park. The recently enacted statute on which the indictment was based was the government's answer to the increasing incidence of demonstrations against the war and racial discrimination. Commonly called the "Rap Brown law," its passage was most directly attributed to a violent encounter in the wake of a speech in Maryland by black power advocate H. Rap Brown.

Other than the fact that they were all males and opposed to the war in southeast Asia, it was a diverse group of men who found themselves joined as defendants. David Dellinger, the defendant named first in the indictment, was a fifty-four-year-old Yale graduate and pacifist who had devoted his entire adult life to radical, nonviolent activism against war, racism, and poverty. A man of undaunted courage and unwavering (if sometimes unrealistic) principle, Dellinger had twice served time in prison during the Second World War, first for refusing to register for the draft, declining even to claim an exemption he was entitled to as a student at the Union Theological Seminary, and a second time (in a bizarre failure of the courts to apply the double-jeopardy clause) for thereafter refusing to report for a pre-induction physical.

As an activist supporter of civil rights, Dellinger became a friend and associate of Martin Luther King Jr. and was instrumental in persuading King to also become involved in the anti–Vietnam War movement. Dellinger was a founder and cochairman of the National Mobilization Committee to End the War in Vietnam— commonly known as the MOBE—a broad-based consortium of antiwar groups that was the guiding force for most of the major antiwar demonstrations from the late 1960s until the war finally ended.

Rennie Davis, the second-named defendant, was a twenty-nine-year-old ex–4H Club member who had attended Oberlin College in Ohio, where he became an antiwar activist and early member of Students for a Democratic Society. After working for SDS for several years he was hired by MOBE in 1967 as its national field coordinator. In that capacity he participated in efforts by MOBE to obtain permits to conduct antiwar demonstrations at the 1968 Democratic National Convention.

Tom Hayden, next in line in the list of defendants, was also twenty-nine, a graduate of the University of Michigan, and, like Davis, an early member and leader of SDS, and an active opponent of the war. After graduating from college Hayden had been a civil-rights worker with the Student Nonviolent Coordinating Committee in Albany, Georgia, and then headed an antipoverty agency in Newark, New Jersey. Of the defendants, Hayden and Davis were the most alike, and had known each other the longest through their work with SDS.

Next in the defense lineup were Abbie Hoffman and Jerry Rubin, the "Yippies," who also opposed the war, but had abandoned ordinary political activity for an activism based on a "youth culture" featuring sex, drugs, and rock and roll. The Yippies delivered their political messages through guerrilla theater and outlandish humorous pranks. Although friends and fellow "leaders" of their self-proclaimed "Youth International Party," Hoffman and Rubin were quite different in personality. Rubin was intense, almost dour, and his humor seemed angry, while Hoffman (a mostly manic manic-depressive) was joyously, irrepressibly funny.

Next came John Froines and Lee Weiner, both young college professors whose alleged scheme to bomb the Grant Park garage turned out to be a figment of either the overactive imagination or self-serving perjury of a government informant.

Finally came Bobby Seale, chairman of the Black Panther Party, who had been in Chicago for only a few hours to give a speech that was originally to be given by Stokely Carmichael or his wife, South African singer Miriam Makeba. Seale had no prior contact with any of the other defendants, and his speech, which was full of the usual Panther rhetoric about the need for blacks to take up arms and defend themselves against the racist pigs, was the antithesis of David Dellinger's message.

Seale's speech was virtually a carbon copy of speeches Black Panther leaders were making all over the country and had no impact whatsoever on the conflicts with police that marked the week of the convention. Nevertheless, and despite his lack of connection with the other defendants and any conspiracy, real or imagined, between them, Seale's inclusion in the indictment was apparently considered strategically important by the prosecutors. As much as Chicago jurors, at least the older ones, were likely to dislike the long-haired yippies and SDSers, nothing they had done or said was really threatening. Bobby Seale, with his talk of guns and pigs, was a different story, and the prosecution probably hoped that damage from Seale's rhetoric would rub off on the others.

The conspiracy indictment was returned in February 1969. Indictments are "returned" before the chief judge of the U.S. district court where the grand jury sits—meaning simply that after the grand jury has authorized the charges the prosecutor has prepared, the prosecutor informs the chief judge and a proceeding is scheduled at which the grand jury formally presents ("returns") the indictment to the judge. Normally, the chief judge has someone from his staff deliver the indictment to the court clerk's office, where it is filed and assigned to a judge for trial. The assignment is by random lot from among all the judges of the district.

So far as the record shows, it was in this way that case number 69 CR 180 (the 180th criminal indictment filed in the U.S. District Court for the Northern District of Illinois in 1969) came to be assigned—first to Chief Judge Campbell, and then, when Campbell disqualified himself, to the Honorable Julius Hoffman. But after the conspiracy case was over, a friend of mine who had been a senior lawyer in the Department of Justice in 1969 told me a different story which he had been told by a lawyer friend in the office of U.S. Attorney Foran. In fact, the story goes, when the indictment was returned, Chief Judge Campbell assigned it to himself, presumably in order to do everything in his power to procure the defendants' conviction. When Tom Foran found out about the assignment, he supposedly called Campbell and told him it was a bad idea for him to preside over the case given his close identification with Mayor Daley and his reported role in pressing for a grand jury investigation over the objection of Ramsey Clark. According to the story, Campbell acceded to Foran's suggestion that the case should be reassigned, and said he would "take care of it." Thereupon the case was assigned to Judge Hoffman, the most pro-prosecution judge in the district. According to my friend's source, Foran did not know for certain, but suspected the assignment to Judge Hoffman was procured outside the random-selection procedure. (Dick Schultz, Foran's primary assistant during the trial and subsequent law partner, doubts the story, saying he believes Campbell decided on his own to disqualify himself and that Foran never suggested he had any doubts about the regularity of the reassignment.)

I don't know whether the story is true, but I'm certain my friend accurately reported what he was told, and would not have repeated it unless he believed it himself. However it came about, the assignment of the Conspiracy Eight case to Julius Hoffman brought together one of the most disastrous combinations of defendants, lawyers, and judge in the history of American jurisprudence.

It did not take long after the Conspiracy indictment was assigned to Julius Hoffman for the defendants and their lawyers to begin to understand what they were facing. Three lawyers had signed on to represent various of the defendants at trial. Bill Kunstler was a New York lawyer whose practice was, by choice, primarily devoted to cases involving civil rights and other "liberal" issues. Together with Arthur Kinoy, a Rutgers University law professor and Morton Stavis, a Newark, New Jersey, lawyer, Kunstler had founded the Center for Constitutional Rights, a public-interest law firm in New York. Kunstler was its chief counsel and had served as the trial lawyer in several important cases involving civil rights and political dissent. Leonard Weinglass, a young Yale Law School graduate, was brought into the case by Tom Hayden, who had become his friend, client, and political mentor in Newark, where Weinglass had a state court criminal-defense practice. The third lawyer on the defense team, and by far the most experienced in the defense of criminal cases, was Charles Garry. Garry, whose offices were in San Francisco, had represented

Bobby Seale and other leaders of the Black Panther Party with extraordinary success.

In addition to the three trial lawyers, the defense procured the services of four outstanding younger lawyers to assist in presenting pretrial defense motions involving issues in which they had special expertise. Each of them was a recent graduate of a top law school and would go on to an outstanding legal career. Michael Tigar had just left his position with Williams & Connolly in Washington for a professorship at UCLA. He would become a nationally recognized law professor while continuing to defend criminal cases, including his recent brilliant defense of Terry Nichols in the Oklahoma City bombing case. Michael Kennedy and Dennis Roberts were practicing in California, where Roberts would remain and establish a successful civil-litigation practice while Kennedy moved to New York and became one of the country's top trial lawyers in high-profile criminal and civil cases. Gerald Lefcourt had already begun practicing in New York City and remained there to become another top criminal-defense lawyer and a recent president of the National Association of Criminal Defense Lawyers. Whenever any of the defendants' lawyers appeared before Judge Hoffman to argue their motions he treated them with ill-concealed disdain, and one by one denied their motions.

Then, a month before the case was scheduled to go to trial, the defense suffered an even worse blow. Charles Garry, the only lawyer Bobby Seale knew or trusted, suffered a serious gallbladder attack while on trial in another case. His doctors insisted his gallbladder be removed without delay. The operation would require a lengthy period of recovery that made it impossible for him to begin trial of the conspiracy case on September 24. The defense notified Tom Foran of the problem and on August 27 presented a motion to continue the case until November 15, when it was expected Garry would be recovered enough to participate. It was a request most prosecutors would have readily agreed to, at least in the absence of some doubt about the validity of the medical claim, but the government opposed it and the judge denied it.

Garry postponed his operation for long enough to come to Chicago himself to urge the judge to reconsider the continuance or in the alternative to sever Bobby Seale's case for later trial. Again the judge refused. All of the defendants asserted Garry was their "lead trial lawyer" and that denial of a continuance deprived them of their Sixth Amendment right to counsel of their choice, but Judge Hoffman declared, with his usual sarcasm, that there was no such thing as a "lead counsel" in the federal rules. A lawyer is a lawyer in my court, Hoffman asserted, and the defendants had plenty of them without Charles Garry. As for Seale, Hoffman pointed out that two local lawyers and the pretrial lawyers had filed appearances for all of the defendants, including Seale. When the defense responded that it was always clear that none of those lawyers was going to participate in the trial, Hoffman responded that there was also no such thing as a limited appearance in the Federal rules of criminal procedure.

While unfair, Hoffman's intransigence may not have been in error with respect to the other defendants. But it had always been clear that Seale's lawyer was Garry, so his claim presented the prosecutors with a real problem, and they knew it. Thus the stage was set for some of the most extraordinary events ever to occur in an American court. It began with the four young lawyers who had helped with the pretrial motions. Each of them had filed an appearance for the defendants in order to be permitted to argue the motions, and while it was indeed clear they were never intended to have a role in the trial, as September 24 approached, the prosecutors and judge continued to insist the answer to Bobby Seale's Sixth Amendment claim was those appearances. Accordingly, following the judge's refusal to continue the case, the pretrial lawyers sent telegrams to the court and prosecutor specifically stating they would not participate in the trial and were withdrawing their appearances. Tom Foran fired back a telegram of his own saying they could not withdraw without court permission, and if they failed to show up for the trial, he would seek an order compelling them to appear.

Inside the defendants' camp there were differences of opinion. Seale had decided that if he had to go to trial without Garry, he would defend himself. Whether that was Seale's idea or Garry's is unclear, but Garry told Seale he had that right if he so chose. Whatever else might be said about it, it would certainly dramatize and perhaps strengthen the Sixth Amendment claim. Kunstler, however, felt that Seale's defending himself would destroy the solidarity of the defense and might injure the chances of an acquittal for all the defendants. Seale and Garry (in touch by telephone) remained adamant that Seale would be represented by Garry or no one. There the matter stood when *United States v. David Dellinger et al.* was called for trial on Wednesday, September 24, 1969.

One of the Chicago lawyers who had acted as local counsel told the court Kunstler and Weinglass had filed appearances for all eight defendants and would be acting as trial counsel. Judge Hoffman asked Kunstler if that was true, and he said it was—explaining that Weinglass would be representing four defendants, and he would represent the other four (including Seale). However, he went on to say, "All the defendants take the position that they are not fully represented in court because of Mr. Garry's absence."

Standing next to Kunstler, Weinglass was shocked, and confused. He had participated in the conversations about the representation of Bobby Seale and to his knowledge Garry and Seale had never budged from the position that no one but Garry was authorized to represent Seale. Now Kunstler had told the court he had filed an appearance to act as trial counsel for Seale. Regardless of his statement that all the defendants claimed a Sixth Amendment violation from the absence of Garry, by filing the appearance Kunstler had compromised Seale's individual claim.

Before Weinglass could decide what to do, however, the judge and prosecutor reacted in a manner that was either the product of a prior discussion between them or a striking example of two prosecutorial minds in perfect synchrony. Their response to Kunstler's statement set in motion a series of events shocking to lawyers across the country, foreshadowed Judge Hoffman's blatant proprosecution conduct for the rest of the trial, and persuaded the defendants and their lawyers, if any doubt remained, that they were facing a judge who would go to any length to help put them in prison. But surprisingly, their reaction also suggested that neither the judge nor the prosecutor had digested the fact that Bill Kunstler's appearance for Seale had altered, if not fully alleviated, the problem they now heavy-handedly set out to solve.

Upon hearing Kunstler say the defendants still claimed a Sixth Amendment violation, Judge Hoffman first made the specious assertion that because Supreme Court Justice Thurgood Marshall had refused to order him to grant the request for a continuance, Marshall had resolved the Garry issue against the defendants. Then, as if on cue, Hoffman turned to Foran and asked him to comment. Foran was ready. After asserting that nine attorneys had filed appearances for the defendants, none of which had been formally withdrawn, Foran unveiled his plan: Hold the pretrial lawyers hostage until the defendants agreed to waive their Sixth Amendment claims. Referring to the telegrams he had received from the pretrial lawyers, Foran described his response telling the lawyers that their telegrams were not a proper withdrawal and he would ask the court to order their appearance in court for the trial. Then came the fastball:

> MR. FORAN: Your Honor, I now move that this court order the appearance in court of Michael J. Kennedy, Michael E. Tigar and Dennis J. Roberts. It has been the law in the Federal Court for over a hundred years . . . that an appearance once filed cannot be withdrawn without the consent of the Court. . . .
>
> By the way, your Honor, I would like to add one further statement, that if the defendants are prepared at this time to represent to this court that they are satisfied with their counsel in this case who are present here . . . *and will waive any claim that their Sixth Amendment rights are abridged, then we would ask*

the Court not to issue an order to have [the lawyers] *brought in before this court immediately.* (emphasis supplied) [3]

Kunstler erupted in protest, denouncing what he characterized as the government's hostage scheme, but Judge Hoffman, on cue, endorsed the scheme and went Foran one better:

THE COURT: There will be an order on [the pretrial lawyers] to attend here as expeditiously as possible, and I direct, Mr. Clerk, the issuance of bench warrants for the apprehension of those lawyers who are obligated in law to be here.

It is doubtful that Foran intended or expected Judge Hoffman to issue bench warrants, a judicial order directing the United States marshal to immediately take a person into custody. Such orders are normally used only when a bail-skipping defendant has failed to appear for trial. Foran had asked for an order on the lawyers to appear, and there was no basis for issuing bench warrants unless the order was entered and they disobeyed; but, as would often occur during the trial, Hoffman could not resist the more dramatic and draconian approach of having the lawyers taken into custody. If, as Dick Schultz now says, he and Foran were surprised and somewhat unhappy about the bench warrants, they made no protest and the clerk had no alternative but to issue them.

Word spread to the four lawyers. In Los Angeles, Michael Tigar hired a lawyer and headed to the federal courthouse to file a petition asserting that the incarceration order violated the Constitution. When he and his lawyer went to the clerk's office to file the petition and ask for an immediate hearing, a U.S. marshal approached and asked which of them was Michael Tigar. The lawyer shoved the petition at the clerk and said, "I want this filed

---

[3] All quotations of trial proceedings are from Judy Clavir and John Spitzer, ed., *The Conspiracy Trial* (Bobbs-Merrill, 1970).

now!" The clerk stamped it filed, and Tigar identified himself. He was placed in custody. The three men proceeded to Judge Plagerson's courtroom where the judge interrupted what he was doing to hear the petition. A local assistant U.S. attorney argued in support of the bench warrant, and when everyone had their say the judge said, in substance, I think he's wrong, but I can't second-guess another District Court judge. He suggested that if Tigar promised to go to Chicago voluntarily, he would order the marshal to let him go on his own. Tigar refused, fearing it would be taken as acceptance of the proposition that he represented Seale. Well, then, the judge said, they'll have to take you back.

The marshal agreed to forgo handcuffs. Tigar asked to call his wife before they left Los Angeles to let her know what was happening, but the request was refused because, the marshal explained, it had been against regulations to let a prisoner make such a call ever since Baby Face Nelson made a call and arranged to be rescued while the marshals were transporting him across the country. A second "guard" was enlisted, and the three of them caught the red-eye to Chicago. Tigar was placed in the center seat and whenever he had to go to the bathroom one of the guards accompanied him. They arrived at dawn and Tigar was placed in the Federal Building lockup, where he watched the sun rising over Lake Michigan and boats beginning to move around the harbor and out into the lake.

It was the '60s, and one of the courses Tigar was teaching at UCLA was called "Repression of Dissent in America." A class was scheduled the day after he was arrested. Students were greeted with a sign on the door: "Repression of Dissent in America will not meet today. Professor Tigar is in jail."

In San Francisco, where Kennedy and Roberts practiced law, then–U. S. Attorney Cecil Poole called Kennedy and informed him of the warrant. Kennedy told Roberts and the two of them agreed to meet Poole. The three of them went to a judge. Neither Poole nor the judge thought the warrant was valid, but Kennedy and Roberts said they would go to Chicago anyway, although they made it clear they would not agree to represent Bobby Seale. The judge agreed to that solution. In New York, when Gerry Lefcourt heard of the warrant, he also went to court. An agreement was reached that he would go to Chicago voluntarily and report to Judge Hoffman's courtroom. However, when he arrived at the Federal Building on Friday morning, a marshal recognized him as he entered the lobby and took him into custody. He joined Tigar in the lockup.

Back in the courtroom, after ordering the bench warrants, Judge Hoffman was about to move on to other matters when Len Weinglass, who had watched these events unfold with increasing amazement, concluded he had to do something to preserve Bobby Seale's position that he had not authorized anyone but Charles Garry to represent him. For his trouble, he was, for the first of many times, ordered to sit down without making his argument:

MR. WEINGLASS: If the Court please, there is a defendant in court, Mr. Bobby Seale, who is sitting here. He is entitled to counsel. As of now he does not have counsel.

THE COURT: That is not a fact, as it appears in the record.

MR. WEINGLASS: Mr. Birnbaum and Mr. Bass [local counsel] have withdrawn from the case as trial counsel. Mr. Seale is not represented here in court.

THE COURT: Mr. Weinglass, I direct you to sit down.

MR. WEINGLASS: If the Court please, I would like to know—

THE COURT: I would like you to sit down or I will ask the marshal to escort you to your chair.

MR. WEINGLASS: I will sit down, but I do so under protest.

What Weinglass wanted to know was whether, in fact, Seale had authorized Kunstler to file an appearance for him, and if, as Weinglass believed, the answer was no, to have that on the record. Judge Hoffman cut him off, but it would not be long before Seale raised the point himself, claiming he had never authorized Kunstler to appear for him and demanding the right to represent himself in Garry's absence.

Thus began the conflict between Bobby Seale and Judge Hoffman which ended in the spectacle of Seale bound and gagged in the courtroom, still struggling to be heard through the ever-tighter and more painful gags the judge ordered the marshals to apply to the defiant black leader. Thus also began the determination of the other defendants and their lawyers to defy the efforts of a viciously biased judge to maintain order in the courtroom while he railroaded them into prison. Once again the whole world was watching, but this time the victim was not a presidential candidate, but the very legitimacy of the American judicial system in the eyes of much of America.

Thus also began my first connection with the conspiracy case, as an indirect result of a case Bert Jenner and Tom Sullivan had handled several years earlier for Dr. Jeremiah Stamler, a prominent Chicago heart researcher who had been supoenaed to appear before the House Un-American Activities Committee. Dr. Stamler was also a friend of Arthur Kinoy, and *Stamler v. Willis*, the case Kinoy, Jenner, and Sullivan put together for him, protected him from testifying, saved his job, and defeated efforts to prosecute him for contempt of Congress. Many believe the *Stamler* case and a statistical survey prepared for it by University of Chicago law professor Hans Zeisel was the primary reason HUAC was finally disbanded by Congress. Zeisel's study showed that in all the years of its operation, HUAC had destroyed many lives, but had failed to produce a single piece of legislation. If the committee had uncovered any "un-American" activities in its long and notorious history, they were only those of the committee itself.

In the meantime, despite the considerable gulf between their

political views, Tom Sullivan and Arthur Kinoy had become friends
and admirers of each other's legal skills. Thus, in the spring of
1969, when Kinoy's close friend and fellow "old left" lawyer Bill
Kunstler agreed to join the defense team for the conspiracy case,
Kinoy had called Sullivan and asked if the defense could use the
library and other facilities of Jenner & Block as a base for doing
legal research while in Chicago. With Bert Jenner's assent, Tom
agreed. Then, when Kinoy learned of Michael Tigar's and Gerald
Lefcourt's arrests, he called Sullivan and asked him to represent
them. And when I learned about it, I volunteered to help. I was no
pacifist, yippie, or movement leftist, but I was appalled by what was
happening in the conspiracy case. I believed in our legal system—
it was my life's work—and I wanted to defend it. In this case, I had
no question about who it needed to be defended against—it was
the judge, not the defendants. I also knew the way for a lawyer in
a large law firm to become involved in a case of his own choice was
to volunteer—quickly—before the normal assignment system
could operate.

Tom Sullivan welcomed me. By that time he had already contacted Tom Foran and told him he would be representing the
arrested lawyers. Foran and Sullivan had known each other profes-
sionally for years and, if not friends, they held each other in mutual
respect. Prior to the conspiracy case Foran had been a good U.S.
attorney. Surely something could be worked out. Foran suggested
a meeting in his office during the noon recess of the trial on Friday.
Whatever came out of the meeting, the matter would be taken up
with the judge at four o'clock, the end of the trial day.

In the large office maintained for the United States Attorney in
the Federal Building, Bill Kuntsler, Len Weinglass, Tom Sullivan,
and I sat across from Tom Foran's large mahogany desk. Foran sat
behind the desk, with Dick Schultz next to him. Sullivan and
Foran argued their respective positions back and forth, with occasional interjections from the rest of us. I have been assured, Sullivan said, that the defendants will consent to and specifically waive
any claim of prejudice arising from the withdrawal of Messrs. Tigar

and Lefcourt and the other two pretrial lawyers; they will not, however, waive their claims arising from the absence of Charles Garry. The government, Foran replied, insists that unless the defendants waive their Garry claim, the pretrial lawyers who filed appearances for the defendants must remain and defend them—or take such consequences as Judge Hoffman may impose—which, we all knew, was likely to be imprisonment for the duration of the trial unless a higher court intervened.

There was really no middle ground between the two positions, and thus nothing to negotiate about—the two sides simply repeated their positions, with whatever arguments they could summon to justify them. In truth, there were no legitimate arguments for the government's effort to coerce the defendants into trading their rights for the freedom of the pretrial lawyers. Either the refusal to continue the case so Garry could participate for Seale was reversible error, or it was not. Either Kunstler's appearance for Seale solved the problem, or it did not. Adding one or more of the pretrial lawyers to a team Seale refused to accept was not going to change the outcome of that argument.

Tom had written a statement spelling out our position which he offered to make in court and have each of the defendants affirm it in any way the court or prosecutor requested. Foran again said no, standing and gathering up his papers to indicate the meeting was over. Kunstler and Weinglass left to return to the courtroom. It was understood we would convene again at 4:00 P.M. when the judge would take up the matter. Foran, Schultz, Tom, and I gathered our papers and left together. Standing in the elevator hallway, waiting for an elevator, Tom Foran looked at Schultz, shrugged his shoulders, and turned to Tom and me. "OK," he said, "I'll go along if the judge will."

After the prosecution completed its direct examination of the government's first witness at about four o'clock that afternoon, the judge announced he would return to the issue of the two pretrial lawyers in custody. After a brief recess to get Tigar and Lefcourt down from the lockup, Tom Sullivan told Judge Hoffman that all of the defendants would consent to the withdrawal of the pretrial lawyers and waive any claim based on their absence, without, however, waiving their claim of prejudice from the absence of Charles Garry. Tom Foran remained silent. After a moment, the judge interjected:

THE COURT: . . . I don't want to participate in a bargaining session. . . . We have two men here who have flaunted the authority of the Court. I have the court to protect, but I am inclined to give sympathetic consideration to any agreement you might work out with the United States Attorney. It should be understood that the alternative is that these men must know that they must remain in custody if there isn't a resolution of the issues here.

Sullivan looked at Foran. "Your Honor," he said, "I believe that the Government and Mr. Kunstler and Mr. Weinglass and I have reached an agreement, subject of course, to Your Honor's views." Taking up the slip of paper, which he had read at the end of the meeting in Foran's office, he read it to the judge. Once again, Foran remained silent. He did not object, but neither did he confirm that he had agreed to the solution if the court would approve it. Judge Hoffman scowled and bobbed his head in anger:

THE COURT: What is the position of the defendants in respect to who their lawyers are now?

MR. SULLIVAN: Your Honor, it is difficult for me to speak for these defendants because I don't represent them. I think Mr. Kunstler has to make that statement.

THE COURT: If he is going to say the same thing he said before, he needn't waste my time or his.

MR. SULLIVAN: I tried my best anyhow.

THE COURT: You are doing the best you can for these lawyers who are in difficulty. Let them be remanded to the custody of the United States Marshal without bail.

MR. SULLIVAN: If the Court please—

THE COURT (Interrupting): I don't bail a lawyer contempter. [sic]

Furious, Sullivan asked facetiously if the lawyers were to be held for the rest of their lives, the Court having set no term. With clenched teeth, Hoffman responded that he would impose sentence on Monday morning. He banged his gavel and was off the bench and through the door to his chambers before anyone could speak again.

Over the weekend the lawyers would be housed in the Cook County Jail, and there was little doubt that unless something changed, Hoffman would keep them there for a long time.

It was nearly five o'clock on Friday afternoon. We told Foran we were going to try to obtain bail from the Court of Appeals and asked him to have the marshals hold Tigar and Lefcourt in the lockup while we made the effort, rather than shipping them to the county jail. Foran agreed, but warned they had to be moved in an hour or so, as they could not remain in the lockup overnight. Tom and I raced to our office a block from the courthouse. Tom's secretary was a niece of one of the judges of the Court of Appeals, and with her help we tried to reach him by phone, but he was nowhere to be found. Next we tried Walter Cummings, the designated emergency judge. Cummings had left the courthouse, but somehow Tom located him at a black-tie party in the home of a prominent Chicago socialite. Cummings himself was a member of an old Chicago banking family and lived in an exclusive apartment building on Chicago's Gold Coast.

Hoffman's arrest of the two lawyers had already generated

wide coverage in the media, and when Tom explained to Judge Cummings that Judge Hoffman had now remanded the lawyers to jail without bail, there was a moment of silence on the telephone. "Oh, Julius," Judge Cummings finally muttered in a voice mixed with sadness and exasperation. Cummings asked if Tom would promise to produce the two lawyers in court on Monday morning. Tom said yes, and the judge said to send an order granting the lawyers release on their own recognizance to his apartment. He would meet us there and sign it.

I agreed to carry the order to Judge Cummings. When we reached Foran to tell him what had happened, he said he would send a lawyer from his office to go with me and say the government objected to the order but would make no argument—thereby trying to avoid offending Judge Hoffman without appearing unreasonable to Judge Cummings. Cummings met Assistant U. S. Attorney Mike Nash and me and signed the order. As he handed the signed order back to me, he sighed. "Well," he said, "until a few months ago Julius hadn't spoken to me for four years because I reversed him in another case. I suppose it will be another four years before he speaks to me again."

Back at the Federal Building, a couple of marshals had remained beyond the end of their shifts to process the lawyers' release. As soon as the processing was completed, Gerry Lefcourt raced to the airport to catch the last plane back to New York and Tigar caught the red-eye to California.

Thirty-two years later, Gerry Lefcourt still vividly recalls that day:

"Sometime after I was taken to the lockup, Mike Tigar and I were taken down to the courtroom. The judge ordered us to represent Bobby Seale, and we both refused. I told the judge I had done nothing to prepare to represent Seale, and in fact had barely met him. So the judge said we were in contempt of court and would be held in custody. Something was said about taking the matter up again at the end of the day, and they took Mike and me back to the lockup. The trial had started, and at the noon recess they brought Jerry Rubin and Bobby Seale into the lockup—Jerry was in custody finishing up a short state-court sentence arising from the convention, and Bobby was being held in connection with a murder charge in Connecticut. I remember that opening statements were going on and I said to Bobby if he was serious about representing himself, he might want to stand up after the others were done and make an opening statement—it was his turn—and that afternoon he tried to do that, and Hoffman refused to let him, and that's when everything started between Bobby and Judge Hoffman. *and of right to appear as one's own attorney.*

"Then in the late afternoon they brought us back to court and we had that session which ended with the judge saying he didn't bail contemptuous lawyers. I remember that phrase. They took us back to the lockup and Bill Kunstler came up to the lockup and said there was nothing he could do. All the Court of Appeals judges had left, so it looked like we were stuck over the weekend. And then he asked if he could borrow the keys to my car and my apartment in New York. I don't think I knew you guys were still trying to get us out, but I said no anyway.

"So Jerry and Mike and I sat in the lockup and sang songs— 'You get a little drunk and land in jail' and stuff, and I was frankly scared as hell, but I didn't want anyone to know it. I was twenty-six years old, only two years out of law school, with no money and no real job and it looked like I was going to jail and maybe lose my law license before I had hardly used it.

"Then someone told us the Court of Appeals had granted us bail, and we were released, subject to our promise to appear back in Hoffman's courtroom on Monday.

"So I caught the last plane back to New York, and when I arrived I had a phone call from my client Abbie Hoffman, who said, 'We got to have a press conference tomorrow morning,' and I said, 'What press conference? What about?' And he said he'd figure it out, and he'd already called the press and scheduled the conference for my office. So the press came, and Abbie was talking about what an outrage it was, what they had done to me and the other lawyers, and that lawyers from all over the country were coming, and should come, to Chicago to protest . . . [that] there was going to be a big lawyers' protest, and so on. And I was very nervous and worried, because I figured Judge Hoffman would see this press conference and it would make it even worse for me—as far as I knew he was still going to sentence me for contempt on Monday morning, unless I agreed to represent Bobby Seale, which I knew I just couldn't do and wouldn't do. So I was very careful what I said, but Abbie went on and on, and the video of the press conference got played over and over that weekend. By then the New York press had turned against the prosecution, and when I got on the first plane Monday morning there was a whole bunch of lawyers on the plane, headed to Chicago to demonstrate— including Charles Nesson and two other guys from Harvard with a petition signed by the entire Harvard Law School faculty protesting the judge's conduct."

Over the weekend, Tom Foran had agreed to meet again on Monday morning, before the opening of court, to try to find a mutually agreeable solution to the pretrial lawyer issue. When we arrived at court, over one hundred lawyers from all over the country were demonstrating around the courthouse. Chief Judge Campbell had entered an order prohibiting any demonstrations inside the building, but several dozen lawyers carried the demonstration into the first-floor lobby. Campbell donned his judicial robes and, with his law clerk and a marshal in tow, descended to the lobby and announced that anyone who did not immediately leave the building would be held in contempt of court. Someone from the back of the crowd yelled, "Fuck you, Campbell, it's a public building!" A few of the lawyers exited, but most of them stayed put. After a minute, Campbell and his entourage retreated back to his chambers.

In Foran's office, he said he had decided to recommend letting the lawyers withdraw and was (somehow) confident Hoffman would go along. He was right. As soon as the case was called, Foran suggested letting the lawyers withdraw and the judge indicated agreement. "Are the two lawyers who were not here Friday here now?" the judge asked. Michael Kennedy announced that they were, and launched into a speech about how he was there of his own volition to represent his brother lawyers, not because of the judge's warrant, which, he said with relish, had been quashed. Michael Tigar (who remains Kennedy's close friend) recently described his feelings to me when Kennedy continued in that vein. "Here I am, out on bail and back in court thinking the judge is probably going to put me back in jail again, and then it sounds like maybe he's gonna let me off, and this madman Kennedy is trying to piss him off. And I figure this judge is hanging by a string anyway and may go off at any minute. So Lefcourt and I start nudging him and kicking him trying to make him shut up, but he just keeps talking!"

Kennedy recalls it the same way: "They were both kicking me, but I wouldn't shut up. We were all nuts in those days." Somehow, for perhaps the only time in the trial, Judge Hoffman refused to take the bait and stuck to the plan. The pretrial lawyers could go home.

The saga of the arrested lawyers was over, but the seeds sown by the incident would grow throughout the trial. Judge Hoffman's conduct not only convinced the defendants and their lawyers of his gross bias, it convinced much of the national media as well. The *Chicago Tribune* dutifully continued to support the prosecution and berate the defendants and their lawyers at every turn, but it was virtually alone among major national media. The effort to use the pretrial lawyers to coerce Bobby Seale to accept Kunstler's representation also focused attention on Seale's complaint about the refusal to grant him a continuance so he could be represented by his own lawyer. When Hoffman also refused to allow him to represent himself, and ultimately had him bound and gagged in the courtroom for trying to do so, the media understood the context and sided with Seale. Thus judge and prosecution performed the near-miracle of persuading at least some of America's white establishment to sympathize with the chairman of the Black Panther Party.

In addition, the events of the first few days of the trial may have triggered the decision of some of the defendants—Abbie Hoffman in particular—to bring his street-theater approach to political persuasion into the courtroom. Contrary to the prosecution claim that the defendants came to Chicago with the intent of disrupting the trial, thirty-two years later the remaining defendants and lawyers insist their original hope was for a quick trial and a favorable verdict so they could return to their efforts to "make a revolution." According to Gerry Lefcourt, however, when Judge Hoffman ordered the pretrial lawyers arrested, and ordinary, nonpolitical lawyers from around the country protested, Abbie Hoffman immediately saw the game had changed. With much of the eastern press now convinced that the judge and prosecutor were unfair, they had an opportunity to put the American justice system itself on trial as part of their effort to turn young people against the establishment. At the same time, after Judge Hoffman rushed through jury selection in a few hours, refusing to ask any questions to seriously probe the possible bias of jurors against the defendants, a Northwestern law professor who was advising the defense opined that the jury selection was so flawed as to practically guarantee an appellate-court reversal if the defendants were convicted.

"You mean," Abbie Hoffman asked, his eyes sparkling, "this whole trial could just be a practice run?" When the answer was yes, Hoffman's attitude changed in another way. Not only could the defendants put the judicial system on trial outside the courtroom, they could respond to the judge's bias inside the courtroom as well; and if doing so offended some of the jurors, it was just a practice run anyway.

Beginning with such relatively innocent demonstrations as a kiss blown to the jurors and a failure to stand when the judge entered the courtroom, Abbie and Jerry Rubin brought into the court some of the same tactics they had used to bedevil authority for years. The police and Defense Department officials had reacted with amusing seriousness to Hoffman's claim he was going to lead protesters in "levitating the Pentagon" during peace demonstrations in Washington, and Mayor Daley had ordered extra police protection of Chicago's main waterworks when Hoffman claimed he was going to "turn on" Chicagoans and the delegates to the Democratic National Convention by putting LSD into the water supply, but Abbie had never had as easy a foil as Julius Hoffman. The more he was pushed, the more autocratic and transparently biased he became, until by the end of the trial one of the defendants could assert, with considerable justification, that Julius Hoffman had done more to radicalize young Americans than the defendants had ever dreamed of. Or, as Michael Kennedy put it to me thirty-two years later, "That Julius Hoffman was assigned to try that case restored my belief in the humor of the gods. We couldn't have done it without him."

The great irony of the debacle caused by the arrest of the pretrial lawyers and the subsequent refusal to allow Bobby Seale to represent himself is that there was no sensible prosecutorial reason for it. When Bill Kunstler filed his appearance as trial counsel for Bobby Seale on the first day of the trial, he solved the government's Sixth Amendment problem, at least to the extent that trying to coerce the pretrial lawyers to participate would have solved it. And if, as seems to be the case, Kunstler had never been authorized by Seale to represent him at trial, the same was surely true of the pretrial lawyers. Seale, advised by Garry, would have made that clear and demanded his right to represent himself, just as he did with regard to Kunstler. Neither the prosecutor nor the judge, however, seemed to recognize those facts on September 24, and instead stubbornly continued with a strategy that cost them dearly.

Of all the mistakes made even by experienced trial lawyers the most common is failure to adjust to changing circumstances in the heat of battle. Time and again, lawyers plow ahead with questions they had planned to ask on cross-examination even though a witness's previous answer has rendered the planned questions unnecessary, or even dangerous. Concentrating on their planned attack, it is as though they had been rendered blind and deaf. Military *insut should stp*.

histories suggest that generals often have the same problem. It cost the lives of thousands of Union soldiers at Fredericksburg, and as many or more American lives in a German forest eighty years later.

By Friday Tom Foran had realized his mistake and tried to abandon the plan, but it was too late to prevent the fallout. And then, to make matters worse, he greatly exacerbated the problem by continuing to resist Bobby Seale's insistence on his right to discharge Kunstler and represent himself. No prosecutor ever wants to let a defendant represent himself—it is too likely to lead to mistakes requiring a mistrial—but the law was quite clear that Seale had that right, and Seale himself made it clear he was not going to stop asserting it. It was not until Judge Hoffman had Seale bound and gagged in the courtroom that Foran seems to have recognized the disastrous road he and the judge were embarked on. A few days later, Seale was severed from the case. As a parting gift, Hoffman found him guilty of sixteen counts of contempt of court and sentenced him to a total of four years in prison.

Seale's conviction

Although my own involvement had ended, for the time being, when the pretrial lawyers were released and permitted to withdraw, I continued to follow the progress of the trial, which frequently occupied the front pages of newspapers in Chicago and around the country. While outrage at the judge's conduct, especially regarding Bobby Seale, grew in most places, in Chicago the public was deeply divided. Liberals and opponents of the war were sympathetic to the defendants, even though few shared their more extreme political views. Most lawyers who understood what was going on were appalled by the perversion of our legal system, regardless of their political persuasion. On the other hand, supporters of the war, anti-hippie cultural conservatives, and members of the business and political establishment were equally appalled by what they saw as a threat to the country and civilization itself. Many Chicagoans received their only information about events in the courtroom from the *Tribune*, which made the judge and prosecutors sound like Horatio at the bridge, fighting to preserve the American way of life against assault by a band of evil, Communist-inspired conspirators.

For several years I had been one of the authors of the script for a gridiron show the Chicago Bar Association put on at Christmas. Traditionally, its targets were prominent judges, lawyers, and politicians and the satire ranged from gentle to biting. As the conspiracy trial progressed I had come to think of it as something out of *Alice in Wonderland*. I seized on the trial conducted by the Queen of Hearts as a setting for one of the satirical sketches. With a black lawyer playing Bobby Seale bound and gagged in the foreground, I played the Judge, dressed as the Queen, shouting "Off with his head!" every time Seale grunted or a defense lawyer spoke.

The skit was not calculated to please Judge Hoffman or his defenders, but I never imagined it would create a major controversy. Before the week of performances were over the *Tribune* had editorialized against the skit, and me personally, three times, as had the local all-news radio station. The *Sun-Times* in turn had twice editorially defended our "free speech" rights. Chief Judge Campbell persuaded all the judges of the district court (except for Hoffman) to sign a letter denouncing the skit as a violation of a local court rule (which it wasn't) and had the letter served personally by U.S. marshals on each member of the board of managers of the bar association and the four of us who were in charge of the show. We refused to remove it. Never have so many trees died over an amateur skit in a gridiron show.

It had been clear for months that when the trial was over Judge Hoffman intended to cite some or all of the defendants and their lawyers for contempt of court. It seemed unlikely—too outrageous even for Julius Hoffman—that he planned to rule summarily on the citations himself rather than refer them to another judge, as the law required. By now, however, the defense camp knew there was no way of predicting what Hoffman would do to see the defendants behind bars, and when a few comments suggested he might even take up the contempt issue while the jury was deliberating its verdict, Arthur Kinoy called and asked that we be prepared to make the appropriate objections and motions for bail, in case the judge put Kunstler and Weinglass in jail before they could do so. We agreed.

During the week of February 9, 1970, it became apparent the case would probably go to the jury on Saturday, February 14. Tom had plans to be out of town that weekend, so I agreed to attend court on Saturday in case the judge proceeded with the contempt citations.

By Saturday morning, word on the grapevine was that the judge would in fact begin pronouncing the contempt citations as soon as he finished instructing the jury. When I arrived, the courtroom was already packed with press, members of the defendants' families, support staff for both sides, a coterie of "establishment" citizens selected by Judge Hoffman, and a handful of observers from the long line of ordinary citizens who waited every day to fill the few remaining seats. When I reached the courtroom door, bypassing the citizens' line, a marshal guarding the door refused to let me in unless the prosecutor or judge vouched for my claim to be there in a professional capacity. Another marshal recognized me and vouched for my integrity. I walked up to the defense table, told Kunstler and Weinglass I was there, said hello to the defendants, crossed to the prosecution table to tell Tom Foran why I was there, and returned to a seat in the public area. As I did so, I recognized that one row of seats was filled with leaders of the Illinois and Chicago bar associations, including the man who had been president of the Chicago Bar Association during the gridiron show controversy. He was a political liberal who was somewhat supportive during that controversy, but when he saw me, he blanched. "What the hell are you doing here?" he asked. When I told him, he swore. "You said back in December you didn't represent these people."

"I didn't then, but I do now," I replied. He shook his head, and declared I was crazy.

A few minutes later, the clerk banged the gavel, Judge

Hoffman took the bench, called for the jury, and delivered his instructions. When he finished, he directed a marshal to escort the jury to the jury room to begin their deliberations, commenting that he now had some other matters to take up with counsel and the parties.

After reading from a prepared document which attempted to provide a factual and legal justification for the contempt citations to come, Judge Hoffman recited thirty-two separate contempt charges against David Dellinger. When he finished, he started to impose sentence but caught himself, realizing he was required to provide Dellinger and his lawyer an opportunity to be heard before passing sentence. After rejecting Kunstler's argument that the law required a jury trial before a different judge on charges of criminal contempt, Hoffman called on Dellinger to speak on his own behalf if he so desired.

He did.

Speaking quietly, but with great emotion, Dellinger began with the two great issues that brought him to Chicago in the summer of 1968; the war in Vietnam and racism. His effort to speak about those issues during the trial had resulted in several of the contempt citations against him. Judge Hoffman had not wanted to hear it then, and didn't want to hear it now. He tried to keep Dellinger from speaking, but Dellinger persisted:

> MR. DELLINGER: Now I want to point out first of all that the first two contempts cited against me concerned . . . the war against Vietnam, and racism in this country, the two issues this country refuses to solve, refuses to take seriously.

> THE COURT (interrupting): ... I don't want you to talk politics.

> MR. DELLINGER: You see, that's one of the reasons I have needed to stand up and speak anyway, because you have tried to keep what you call politics, which means the truth, out of this courtroom, just as the prosecution has.

THE COURT: I will ask you to sit down.

MR. DELLINGER: Therefore it is necessary—

THE COURT: I won't let you go on any further.

MR. DELLINGER: You want us to be like good Germans supporting the evils of our decade and then when we refused to be
good Germans and came to Chicago and demonstrated, now
you want us to be like good Jews, going quietly and politely to
the concentration camps while you and this court suppress
freedom and the truth. And the fact is that I am not prepared to
do that. You want us to stay in our place like black people were
supposed to stay in their place—

THE COURT: Mr. Marshal, I will ask you to have Mr. Dellinger
sit down.

Everyone knew that the marshals, who had been charged with
trying to maintain order in the courtroom throughout the trial,
had enormous respect for David Dellinger. He had always treated
them with respect and done everything he could to make life
easier for men who were only trying to do their jobs while
caught between a vicious judge and the determinedly unruly and
disrespectful defendants. At the judge's order to seat him
forcibly, they moved toward Dellinger, but were reluctant to lay
hands on him.

Dellinger continued, his voice now growing desperate:

MR. DELLINGER:—like poor people were supposed to stay in
their place, like people without formal education are supposed
to stay in their place, like women are supposed to stay in their
place—

THE COURT: I will ask you to sit down.

MR. DELLINGER: Like children are supposed to stay in their place, like lawyers are supposed to stay in their places. It is a travesty on justice and if you had any sense at all you would know that the record that you read condemns you and not us.

THE COURT: All right.

MR. DELLINGER: And it will be one of thousands and thousands of rallying points for a new generation of Americans who will not put up with tyranny, will not put up with a facade of democracy without the reality.

THE COURT: Mr. Marshal, will you please ask him to keep quiet?

THE MARSHAL: Be quiet, Mr. Dellinger.

MR. DELLINGER: I sat here and heard that man Mr. Foran say evil, terrible, dishonest things that even he could not believe in—I heard him say that and you expect me to be quiet and accept that without speaking up.

People no longer will be quiet. People are going to speak up. I am an old man and I am just speaking feebly and not too well, but I reflect the spirit that will echo—

THE COURT: Take him out!

MR. DELLINGER: —throughout the world—

(Applause)

MR. DELLINGER:—comes from my children who came yesterday—

(complete disorder in the courtroom)

No one in the courtroom will ever forget what followed. When the judge ordered Dellinger removed, two of the marshals finally grabbed him and started pulling him toward the door to the lockup as he continued trying to speak. His daughter Michelle, who was thirteen at the time, was in the second row of spectators. She stood up and screamed, then shouted, "Leave my dad alone!" Her sister Natasha also began screaming, and several marshals—there must have been at least twenty in the courtroom—plowed into the audience and jumped on the two girls.

Dellinger saw what was happening. Shouting, "Leave my daughters alone!" he somehow shucked two marshals off his back and rushed to his daughters, who were now on the floor between the benches with marshals on top of them, trying to drag them away. He tried to pull the marshals off of his children, joined now by Abbie Hoffman and John Froines.

More marshals joined the fray. A spectator leapt over two rows of benches onto the back of one of the marshals. Everyone—the audience, the press, the defendants and their lawyers—was screaming or shouting or sobbing. Bill Kunstler broke down completely. Tears streaming down his face, he collapsed on the lectern. His voice racked with emotion, he begged the judge: "My life has come to nothing. . . . You destroyed me and everybody else. Put me in jail now, for God's sake, and get me out of this place. Come to mine now, Judge, please. Please. I beg you. Do me, too. I don't want to be out."

Meanwhile, the marshals finally succeeded in dragging Michelle and Natasha Dellinger out of the courtroom, along with a dozen or so other supporters of the defendants. Jerry Rubin shouted "Heil Hitler!" at Judge Hoffman again and again. David Dellinger was dragged back to his seat, and suddenly the courtroom was eerily quiet. Dellinger spoke one last time, his voice breaking the silence. "Well, you preserved law and order here, Judge. The day will come when you take every one of us."

Through it all, I was sitting two rows behind the Dellinger children, clutching the back of the bench in front of me, trying to keep from jumping into the melee and getting thrown out of the courtroom myself.

When the turmoil finally ended, Judge Hoffman sentenced Dellinger to a total of two years, five months, and sixteen days in prison: a term arrived at by accumulating individual sentences ranging from one day for failure to rise when the judge entered the courtroom to six months for trying to read the names of the war dead and asking for a moment of silence on Vietnam Moratorium Day.

When he finished with Dellinger and had him taken away, refusing bail, Judge Hoffman continued through the rest of the day, and into Sunday, imposing prison sentences on the other six defendants ranging from over two years for Rennie Davis and Jerry Rubin to just over two months for Lee Weiner. Each defendant was silenced by Hoffman before he could finish speaking, and each was taken into custody without bond as soon as his sentence was announced. Although no outburst of the intensity of the Dellinger incident followed, the efforts of each defendant to speak were greeted with applause or cries of approval, and his removal into custody with tears of despair from his family.

Finally, when the last defendant was removed from the courtroom, the judge came to the lawyers. He began with Bill Kunstler, and with special vitriol in his voice, his head bobbing furiously, he declared Kunstler guilty of twenty-four counts of contempt. When the judge was done, Kuntsler defended his conduct, ending with an eloquent plea to other lawyers not to be deterred by his punishment from vigorously defending other unpopular defendants in the years to come:

"Stand firm, remain true to those ideals of the law which even if openly violated here, are true and glorious goals, and, above all, never desert those principles of equality, justice, and freedom without which life has little if any meaning."

Kuntsler's speech was greeted by thunderous applause, not just from the defendants' supporters, but from much of the press and general audience, including at least one of the specially invited leaders of the bar who was sitting immediately in front of me. Angrily, Judge Hoffman ordered the marshals to remove everyone who had applauded from the courtroom, an order which, if strictly observed, would have left it nearly empty. Fortunately for me, the marshals settled for a few token expulsions. Julius Hoffman then proceeded to sentence Bill Kunstler to more than four years in prison. As he read the sentence, I moved from the audience to the podium to make the necessary motions; but when he finished reading his sentences for each count, he declared that execution of the sentence would be delayed until May so Kuntsler could represent the defendants in posttrial motions if they were convicted.

A short while later, Len Weinglass was sentenced to more than two years in prison on fourteen counts, nearly all of which involved Weinglass's effort to argue a legal point after the judge had ruled against the defendants without allowing argument. Weinglass too was allowed to remain free until May. Each lawyer was permitted to state his own challenge to Hoffman's right to hold him in contempt, and his own fruitless motion for bond, so in the end my attendance was unnecessary. Even so, heart-wrenching as they were, I would not have missed those two days for anything.

Like the reaction to the trial as a whole, the public reaction to the contempt sentences was intense—and intensely divided. On both coasts, sympathy overwhelmingly favored the defendants. In New York the national board of the ACLU immediately condemned the contempt citations and sentences as an unconstitutional use of judicial power in violation of due process. In Los Angeles over 7,000 people attended an early Sunday-morning rally for the defendants on the UCLA campus. Similar rallies occurred spontaneously on numerous other college campuses. New York Mayor John Lindsay called the trial a "tawdry parody" of justice, and warned against repression and whittling away of constitutional rights. Meeting in Atlanta, a committee of the American Bar Association voted to investigate the contempt citations, calling Judge Hoffman's conduct patently "injudicious."

In Chicago, however, the reaction was quite different. While the tabloid *Sun-Times* printed an editorial questioning the severity of the contempt citations, especially without a jury trial, the state's Republican senator and the president of the Illinois Bar Association strongly supported Judge Hoffman and called for an investigation to determine if Kunstler should be disbarred. The *Tribune* produced a series of editorials denouncing the defendants and their lawyers in the strongest terms, and announced a reader's poll had produced an 83 percent majority approving the judge's conduct of the trial.

If it is doubtful that public opinion in Chicago was as overwhelming as the *Tribune* poll suggested, there is no doubt that the "establishment"—as represented by the Daley wing of the Democratic Party and Chicago's big-business Republicans—supported Judge Hoffman and despised the defendants and their trial lawyers with unflagging intensity.

Thus, when Sam Block, enjoying a drink with friends and clients after a day of skiing in Aspen, Colorado, saw a report on the evening news that Tom Sullivan and John Tucker of Jenner & Block had filed an appearance on behalf of the men held in contempt of court, he almost fell off his bar stool. That night he called Tom and me, urging us not to proceed with the case for fear it would offend the firm's clients and disastrously affect our business. Sam was one of the most liberal members of the firm, but given the passions running in Chicago, he was genuinely concerned about client reactions, and about me in particular. Given the earlier controversy over the gridiron show, he was afraid my representing the defendants now would confirm the prior criticism and injure my career.

However, Bert Jenner was unswerving in his belief that lawyers should represent anyone who needs them and never refuse a client because he or she is unpopular. His first decision was that Tom and the firm should continue the representation, but in light of my special situation, I should withdraw. By this time, having sat through the contempt hearings, I was committed to the case and decided to try to change Bert's mind. Knowing he was also a champion of the firm as a true partnership (except in matters involving his own prerogatives), I argued that if the firm was involved, I was involved as well, regardless of whether I worked on the case. I had done nothing unethical in the gridiron show, and there was nothing unethical in my now representing the defendants. If the firm wanted to withdraw from the case for fear that the unpopularity of the defendants would antagonize clients, that was one thing (a thing, I knew, that Jenner would never admit to), but if the firm was involved I had as much right, and duty, to work on the case as any partner.

It worked—and to his credit, Sam Block, who was a great lawyer and good friend, never held it against me that I went around him to persuade Jenner.

As far as I am aware, with the exception of Judge Hoffman himself, no judge ever treated me badly because of the conspiracy case. Neither do I believe that any client or potential client went elsewhere because of the firm's connection with the case, despite the emotions surrounding it. Years later, when I handled several high-profile cases for men who were alleged leaders of the Chicago Mafia, some friends expressed similar concerns that it would cost me clients. So far as I know, it did not. While lawyers rarely get clients through newspaper publicity, I think it is equally rare for a lawyer to lose clients by representing someone who is unpopular. The only clients who ever mentioned my "mob" cases seemed to think that if a Mafia boss hired me, I must be good.

Once the contempt hearings ended on February 15, we faced the question of seeking bond in the Court of Appeals. While normally we would have immediately filed an emergency motion in the Seventh Circuit, Tom and I strongly advised waiting a few days until the emotions stirred by the contempt rulings calmed down. It was hard to believe there was any valid basis for denying bail, but Judge Hoffman had justified his ruling by asserting the defendants were "dangerous." With protest demonstrations that could turn violent occurring almost every day, we thought it wise to wait before asking the Court of Appeals to take the unpopular step of ordering the defendants released. The defendants, who were the ones sitting in jail, agreed reluctantly.

We also decided the motion for bond pending appeal was not the place for a virulent attack on the judge's conduct of the trial. Hoffman's bias and misconduct would be an important part of the argument for reversing the contempt citations, but for now there was no reason to make it even more controversial for the court to release the defendants by attacking the judge. While others would take primary responsibility for writing the appellate brief on the merits, Tom and I took the lead on the bond motion and handled it as we saw fit. As local lawyers known to the court, we hoped our appearance in the case would soften any bias against the defendants which some of the Court of Appeals judges might share with the general public.

Three days after the contempt hearings, the jury returned a verdict on the criminal charges. Each of the defendants was acquitted of the conspiracy charge, but the five who were also charged with crossing state lines with the intent to start a riot were convicted of that charge. John Froines and Lee Weiner were acquitted of all charges. Two days later, Judge Hoffman sentenced the five who had been convicted to five years in prison— the maximum allowable sentence—and again denied bail pending appeal.

The next day we filed our motion for bond pending appeal from both the contempt and criminal convictions, and a week later, on Saturday, February 28, the Court ruled. In a unanimous order the Court held there was no basis for Judge Hoffman's claim that the defendants were dangerous or that an appeal would be frivolous. Therefore the defendants were entitled to immediate release on reasonable bail. Adding emphasis to their decision, the Court provided that their order be delivered to defense counsel by hand so the defendants could be released that same day. Also on the same day, the Court announced that its most conservative member, a former Republican attorney general of Illinois, had retired from active status on the Court and therefore had not participated in the decision. Everyone understood that by avoiding participation, the judge had agreed to preserve the unanimity of an unpopular decision without having to join it. It was a conscientious act that complemented that of the judges who ordered the defendants' release.

A magistrate set bond at $15,000 for Froines and Weiner and $25,000 for the rest of the defendants. Tom Sullivan removed the required 10 percent of the total from a savings-and-loan account where it had been deposited by a supporter of the defendants, and delivered it to the magistrate, who then signed an order releasing the defendants. Early that afternoon, the seven men were transferred from the county jail back to the federal lockup, where I met them to oversee the processing necessary for their release. Once out, the seven held one more press conference as a group, vowing to continue fighting to stop the war and end racism in America. Listening to their rhetoric, I was amused to recall that a short time earlier, when I appeared at the lockup to confirm that they would soon be free, their exclamations of anticipation and appreciation contained no revolutionary rhetoric but centered primarily on expressions of solidarity with Abbie Hoffman's joyous shout: "Tonight we all get laid!"

Over the following months, I attended several strategy sessions on the contempt appeals with a group of prominent law-school professors including Tony Amsterdam, Alan Dershowitz, Charlie Nesson, and Mike Tigar, and a couple of lawyers I recruited from two other "respectable" Chicago law firms in an effort to demonstrate to the Court of Appeals that "real" lawyers—not just left-wing ideologues—supported reversal of the contempt citations. Given the length of the record and the extraordinary number of separate charges that had to be analyzed, especially in the contempt case, briefing took a great deal of time on both the contempt appeal and the appeal of the convictions. Most of the work was done by Morton Stavis, Kunstler's law partner, with assistance from a group of law students and younger lawyers. When the briefs were completed, the court set aside two full days for argument, starting with the criminal appeal on February 8, 1971, and continuing on February 9 with the appeal from the contempt citations.

Three months later, the court reversed both the contempt case against Bobby Seale and that against the remaining defendants and the two lawyers. A retrial was ordered before a new judge and a jury, unless the new judge decided at the outset that in the event of any guilty findings the total sentence would not exceed six months, in which case a jury was unnecessary. The court dismissed many of the citations outright, as insufficient as a matter of law, and defined the elements of contempt in a way that made it probable a new judge would find for the defendants on most of the remaining charges.

A decision on the criminal convictions of Dellinger, Davis, Hayden, Hoffman, and Rubin took longer, but in late November 1971, the court announced those convictions had also been reversed and the case remanded for a new trial. A number of errors were cited as requiring reversal, including the inadequate voir dire examination of prospective jurors which the defense had predicted before the first witness was called and, to the great satisfaction of all impartial observers, the repeated prejudicial misconduct of both the trial judge and the prosecution. In this category, the first of many examples cited by the court was the jailing of the pretrial lawyers.

Even before the contempt decisions were rendered, Jim Thompson, the new U.S. attorney in Chicago, announced he intended to dismiss the criminal charges against Seale. Then, after a reportedly heated argument with his predecessor and some superiors in the Justice Department, Thompson announced he would also decline to retry the other defendants on the criminal charges, although he would defend some of the contempt citations. Thereafter, all of the judges of the Northern District of Illinois having disqualified themselves, Edward Gignoux, a respected trial judge from Maine, was appointed to retry the remaining contempt cases.

His first act was to announce he would not impose a sentence in excess of six months on any defendant. Next he dismissed the vast majority of remaining citations as insufficient as a matter of law. Finally, after hearing evidence and arguments on the citations left, he dismissed most and held that the time already served by the defendants in the two weeks before they were granted bail was adequate punishment for those he upheld. In the case of the few citations he upheld against the lawyers, he found no jail time was appropriate. Thus ended the great conspiracy trial—the paradigmatic legal event of the 1960s.

Looking back from a distance of over thirty years, it is difficult to imagine how important the case seemed at the time, not only to the participants, but to the huge numbers of Americans, liberal and conservative alike, who never set foot in the courtroom and whose understanding of what happened was dictated entirely by which newspaper or magazine they read or what commentator they trusted.

For those who were convinced that the unruly, longhaired, pot-smoking generation of free-love fornicators and disloyal detractors of racial segregation and unfettered capitalism were destroying America, the Conspiracy 8 and their lawyers were Exhibit A. As the *Tribune* put it editorially; "No one can calculate the harm that these convicted men's leadership has done the unity of the country, the morale and loyalty of its citizens, or the strength of its orderly institutions."

In speeches given after the end of the trial, Tom Foran, normally a reasonable and moderate man, was so caught up by the case that his claims were as hyperbolic as the *Tribune*'s. "The defendants, he warned listeners, are "freaking fags" who are out to "steal your children." And thirty-two years later, unmollified by perspective or the passage of time and apparently still unable to distinguish between political rhetoric and violence, Dick Schultz asserts that the defendants were out to "overthrow" the government and destroy our country, and that their prosecution was "essential" to prevent it.

Ironically, the defendants themselves shared the *Tribune*'s view, if not Schultz's, albeit from a different perspective. In the speeches they gave at the time of sentencing, and in the days that followed, they freely predicted that outrage at the conduct of the trial would radicalize America's youth and bring hundreds of thousands of new recruits to their social revolution.

Meanwhile, many who saw the prosecution as an egregious effort to destroy the First Amendment right of free speech and political dissent—a government-sanctioned follow-up to the efforts of the Chicago police to achieve the same purpose with their nightsticks in 1968—engaged in their own doomsday hysteria. The "movement" defense lawyers, in particular, were certain that the protective dike of the Constitution was leaking badly and that their fingers and thumbs in the breach were all that prevented its collapse. My own effort to get involved in the case by volunteering to help Tom Sullivan was motivated not by agreement with the extreme views of some of the defendants (although I shared their opposition to the war and racism) but by a desire to resist what I saw as Judge Hoffman's abuse of a legal system I believed in. Even so, by the time Bill Kunstler had been sentenced to over four years in prison for his effort to defend his clients, I found myself nodding in grim-faced agreement and determination when he asserted that if his punishment served to deter other lawyers from vigorously defending their clients, "then my punishment will have effects of such terrifying consequences that I dread to contemplate the future . . . course of this country."

If I was not as pessimistic about the future of constitutional government as Bill Kunstler, I was deeply disturbed by the perversion of justice I had observed, and even more so by the blind eye turned to it by so many people I knew and had respected. And if I was not as ready for revolution as Abbie Hoffman or Tom Hayden, my opposition to racism and the war in Vietnam became stronger and more urgent in the face of the transparent effort to turn back the tide on those issues that the conspiracy prosecution represented.

❈   ❈   ❈

In retrospect, of course, neither the defendants' cataclysmic predictions nor my more modest fears were realized. The defendants were freed, first on bail and then altogether, and continued pursuing their activities, but American society did not collapse as a result (except in the minds of latter-day commentators Bill Bennett, Pat Buchanan, and Jerry Falwell). The patently unfair trial did radicalize a lot of young (and old) people and undoubtedly added to the strength of the antiwar and civil-rights movements; but it hardly led to the broader cultural and political revolution the defendants promoted and predicted. (And ironically, if, as many believe, the convention demonstrations were decisive in giving Richard Nixon his presidential victory over Hubert Humphrey, the defendants' activities may well have extended the war and delayed racial progress.)

As for suppressing political dissent and deterring lawyers from vigorous advocacy on behalf of their clients, the concerns raised by the conspiracy prosecution and Judge Hoffman's conduct were soon alleviated by the Seventh Circuit reversals. Indeed, because of those reversals, the overall impact of the case may have been to discourage other judges and prosecutors from oppressive courtroom conduct and misuse of the law to silence legitimate dissent.

But if the conspiracy trial was not the transcendent event it seemed at the time, neither was it without significance. All over America, much of the establishment was in fact feeling beleaguered by the changes occurring around them; and had the outcome of the *Chicago Eight* case remained where Julius Hoffman left it when he adjourned *United States v. Dellinger et al.* for the last time, it is quite possible other judges and prosecutors would have seen the case as an invitation to strike back at the counterculture and peace movement. Indeed, when one observes what the "war on drugs" has done to eviscerate the Fourth Amendment to the Constitution, with the consent of the courts, it is not hard to imagine what might have happened to the First Amendment if the courts had been equally compliant in the face of the Conspiracy prosecution and others like it.

Soon we will know whether our courts will now stalwartly defend our fundamental rights guaranteed by the due-process clause—or compliantly endorse the government's effort to undermine those rights in the name of today's "war on terrorism."

CHAPTER 5

FORESTS, TREES, AND THE FRUITS OF EXPERIENCE

I t is a common criticism that some trial lawyers, especially from large law firms, "can't see the forest for the trees," and thus become lost in individual facts and issues instead of getting to the heart of a case. It is a legitimate concern, but it doesn't tell the whole story.

The most important thing a trial lawyer does is develop a logical theory of the case that can be supported by the evidence. In the "forest and trees" analogy, the theory of the case is the "forest." If you don't keep your eye on the forest and become lost in a host of minor legal issues and factual disputes, you are not likely to win (unless your opponent is equally lost). But if your theory of the case is the forest and the individual facts and issues are the trees, you had better pay close attention to both. Just as the shape of a forest depends on the trees that make it up, a logical theory depends on the provable facts and legal precedent you can marshal to support it. Unless you have found, recognized, and selected the important "trees," you cannot present an attractive "forest."

In short, details are important, and sometimes the most important ones are not easy to recognize. Two very different cases provide good examples of the importance a single detail can play in the construction of a persuasive theory. One was a murder case; the other was a civil action for Madison Square Garden against Muhammad Ali when he was heavyweight champion of the world.

Don Harris was a relatively new associate in the firm who had joined the committee that provided lawyers for indigent criminal defendants. I hadn't tried a pro bono criminal case for a couple of years but in the late summer of 1967 I accepted an assignment to defend a murder case with Don as my co-counsel. The defendant was a man named Robert Manley*, who, according to the indictment, was also known as "Prince 6X."

I assumed the "X" meant that Manley was a Black Muslim. Not long after receiving the assignment, Don and I went out to the county jail to interview our new client. After signing in and asking that Manley be brought to one of the cubicles where attorneys interviewed their clients, we waited for a guard to admit us to the jail proper and escort us to an interview booth. Normally we had to wait awhile for the prisoner to be brought to the interview room, so I was surprised to find Manley already sitting on the prisoner's side of the cubicle when we arrived. He was a young, dark-skinned African-American about six feet tall, with a prominent knife scar on his upper right cheek. His arms appeared roughly the circumference of an elephant's leg, all muscle.

I knew from information supplied by the prosecutor that Manley was twenty-four years old and already had two adult felony convictions, both for armed robbery. He had spent four of the six previous years in prison, and I soon learned how he managed to have a guard bring him to the interview booth so quickly. Manley had been in jail since early summer; he had fired his public defender and asked for a "bar association lawyer." He was housed on the tier of the jail Warden Jack Johnson set aside for inmates he classified as Black Muslims, although some of them, including Manley, had no real connection to the Nation of Islam. After Manley was there awhile, Johnson concluded he was the toughest man on this, the toughest tier of the jail. When the prisoner who had been the tier's "barn boss" was shipped out, Johnson designated Manley to replace him. With far too few guards to enforce order in the jail's overcrowded tiers, Johnson essentially allowed the inmates to police themselves, within certain limits. The barn boss and a few lieutenants he selected were the enforcers. In return they had certain privileges. Apparently, one of the privileges Manley enjoyed as barn boss of the Muslim tier was expedited service from the guards.

When I introduced myself, calling my new client "Mr. Manley," he scowled. "My name ain't Manley, it's Prince 6X."

"Well," I said, "I saw that on the indictment, but I'm planning to ask the judge to strike it. It's not a name that's likely to help you with a jury, especially since the prosecutor will use as many challenges as necessary to make sure the jury's all white."

My client scowled again, insisting that Prince 6X was his name and he didn't give a damn what anybody thought of it. I said as far as I was concerned, he could call himself anything he wanted; but as his lawyer I was telling him he'd have a better chance of winning his case if we called him Mr. Manley in court. Prince 6X scowled again, hesitated, and offered a compromise. "OK, in court it's Manley, but everyplace else you call me by my real name." Prince 6X Manley is a practical man, I thought, and we're going to get along fine. Which we did.

The state's case against Robert Manley (the judge, somewhat to my surprise, granted my motion to strike the name Prince 6X from the indictment) was straightforward and strong, though not impossible to defend. According to the arrest report, Manley, only six weeks out of prison, was sitting with a group of men on the front steps of a building on Chicago's Southwest Side. It was a warm, sunny Saturday afternoon in spring, and the men were talking, drinking beer, smoking pot, and verbally harassing passersby. Manley was visiting a man he met in prison—otherwise he was a stranger to the neighborhood and to the other men on the steps.

At some point a young man walked by and someone on the steps yelled an insult. The young man flashed a middle finger at the step sitters, shouted an insult of his own, and kept walking. Someone ran down from the steps and attacked him. There was a brief struggle and the young man slumped to the street, bleeding from a knife wound in his chest. The attacker and most of the men on the steps ran off. Someone called the police, an ambulance arrived, and the victim was transported to the nearest hospital, where he lingered in a coma for several days and then died.

Three weeks later, Manley was arrested on a tip from an unnamed informant. At the time of his arrest, he had in his pocket a switchblade knife with a thin four-inch blade and a small amount of pot. The knife was examined by the crime lab for blood, but none was detected. Manley was taken to a police station and placed in a lineup. Most of the men on the steps who could be found denied seeing who attacked the victim, but a young woman from the neighborhood identified Manley as the killer, as did one of the men who originally denied seeing anything. A couple of other witnesses placed Manley on the steps that day, but said they didn't see the attack.

I began the interview with Prince 6X as I always did, by telling him I was not going to ask whether he was guilty or innocent, but instead would tell him as much as I knew about the state's case and then ask him some specific questions about the facts. If he didn't want to answer a question, he should say so; but if he did answer, it was important he tell me the truth. By the time the interview was over, my client had admitted being on the steps with his friend on the day of the murder, admitted seeing the attack, but emphatically denied attacking or even approaching the victim (thus saving me the necessity of explaining "self-defense" before going any further).

Prince 6X had seen the attacker, but didn't know who he was. He had run away after the attack because he knew that with his record, he would be a suspect. Besides, everyone on the steps was smoking weed, and he was on parole. He had not returned to the neighborhood or seen his friend again, but he was surprised when he was arrested because he had heard someone else was charged with the crime.

The public defender who initially represented my client had filed the standard pretrial motions, including a "Brady motion" asking for the production of any evidence that was exculpatory or helpful to the defendant. The state's response denied the existence of such material. A standard request for the inspection of physical evidence and any scientific reports had yielded the switchblade knife and a crime-lab report showing the knife had tested negative for human blood. It seemed to me the fact that someone else was arrested for the crime, if it was true, should have been disclosed as Brady material, so I resolved to file a supplemental motion asking specifically for any reports relating to any other person who had been arrested or identified as a suspect.

A week or so later, before I filed my supplemental motions, a plain manila envelope arrived in the mail with no return address or identification of the sender. At first, when I inspected its contents, I couldn't figure out what it was about. There was a police report of two or three pages that described the arrest of a young man I had never heard of on a charge of assault with a deadly weapon. The report went on to reveal that a search of the apartment where the young man lived with his mother had (not surprisingly) turned up several knives in a kitchen drawer, one of which was sent to the crime lab for analysis. A second document in the envelope was a crime-lab report describing the knife and reporting that a trace of blood on the knife was too small to determine if it was human or animal.

It took me several minutes and a rereading of the police report to realize that the date of the report was the day after the murder charged to my client and that the name of the victim was the same. The charge was assault with a deadly weapon rather than murder because the victim had not died of his wound until several days later.

My first reaction was to go ahead with the supplemental Brady motion, attaching the material I had received, accusing the state of failing to fulfill its Brady obligations in its initial response, and demanding access to all additional reports and information about the charges against the first suspect. But on reflection, I decided to wait. I now had information about a person who, for some reason, had once been arrested for the crime now attributed to my client, and as far as I knew, neither the prosecutor nor the police knew I had that information. The element of surprise might well be more valuable than anything else in the police files, which in the end had resulted in the dismissal of charges. At least it seemed smarter to do some further investigating before tipping my hand.

The friend from prison who Manley was visiting agreed to talk to me, but stuck to his story that he didn't know who had committed the assault. He did, however, give me the names of others who were on the steps, and I recognized one as the person who was initially arrested. They were all friends from the same neighborhood. The man who identified Manley as the killer after first telling the police he didn't see the attack also talked to me, explaining that at first he didn't want to be involved, but his conscience had finally compelled him to tell the truth. From watching and listening to him, it seemed unlikely that conscience had anything to do with it. Using the list of names I obtained from Manley's friend, I determined the man would identify most of the others on the scene, including the person who was arrested. I couldn't locate the female witness, but I discovered she too lived in the neighborhood.

I now had the basis for a tentative theory of defense, if not much to support it. The theory was that the witnesses were accusing Manley of the crime to protect one of their friends—possibly the man arrested originally. Manley was the fall guy because he was the only stranger present when the murder happened. An advantage to the theory was that the prosecutor—if he knew about the prior arrest—didn't know I knew about it and might be caught by surprise when I brought the existence of a real second suspect to the attention of the jury.

There was another witness I wanted to talk to before the trial: the sergeant who wrote most of the police reports in the case, including the one mailed to me anonymously. The sergeant was a veteran homicide investigator who was in charge of the case from the time the crime was first reported to the police. My desire to interview him was based on the need to find out anything I didn't already know about the investigation and the possibility of using him as a witness to bring out the arrest of the other suspect before the jury.

Somewhat to my surprise, the sergeant agreed to meet me at his apartment one afternoon when he was off duty. In preparation for the meeting, I reread all the police reports I had obtained concerning the investigation. I had read the reports I received in the plain brown envelope before, but as I reread the crime-lab analysis of the knife taken from the first suspect's kitchen, I stopped short. There—in the description of the knife—I recognized a powerful piece of evidence I could use to support my theory of defense. It was a tree that made the forest of my defense much stronger, and I had read the document that contained it at least three times before I recognized it.

Sergeant Jackson* was a polite, plainspoken black man of about forty. He had spent the last eleven years in homicide. He was summoned to the scene of the crime by the beat officer who responded to the first call and arrived at about the same time as the ambulance. The paramedics had cut away the victim's blood-soaked shirt revealing a single knife wound in his chest. They tried to stop the bleeding and raced the victim to a nearby hospital, but from what he saw the sergeant was pretty sure the man was beyond help. In response to my question, he confirmed that in eleven years on the homicide squad he had seen a lot of knife wounds—how many he couldn't say, but it was certainly more than a hundred.

I had asked the sergeant to have his case reports with him, but he declined to do so. He said, however, that he recalled the case pretty well, and if I had any of his reports, I could show them to him and he would answer questions about them. I started by asking him to tell me everything he remembered about the case. During his recitation, he volunteered that another suspect was arrested originally based on what someone in the neighborhood told an informant. The information could never be confirmed, and the suspect was released and then cleared when the witnesses against Manley came forward.

After Sergeant Jackson described what he could recall about the investigation, I thanked him for his time and prepared to leave. I told him I assumed he would be called as a witness by the state, but just in case he wasn't and I decided there was something I wanted to ask him, I was going to give him a subpoena to appear at the trial. I pointed out that the subpoena called for him to bring with him any police reports he had prepared during the investigation and said I would let him know as soon as possible whether I really required his appearance.

The case of *People v. Robert Manley* came to trial before Judge Thomas McMillan on a Monday morning in early December 1967. Jury selection took most of the day, followed by opening statements. The next day the prosecutor began his case, starting with the "life and death" witness—an anachronistic "requirement" that the state prove the victim was once alive and is now dead. Its only real purpose is to provide a pretext for the state to call one of the victim's relatives as a witness to gain sympathy from the jury. After I released the victim's sobbing mother from the stand with no questions and a look of sympathy, the state called its traditional second witness, a coroner's pathologist who testified to the cause of death. In most cases, like this one, there is no dispute about the cause of death, but the pathologist is called anyway so the prosecutor can offer in evidence grotesque photographs of the victim taken during the autopsy. No matter how strenuously defense counsel objects and offers to stipulate to the cause of death, at least some of the photographs are usually admitted and passed around to the jury. I made the obligatory objections, knowing they would be overruled but hoping that some of the jurors would understand that the first two witnesses had nothing to do with any issue in the case, but were simply an effort by the prosecutor to manipulate the jury's emotions.

The prosecution next called Sergeant Jackson, who described his visit to the scene, the lineup at which Manley was identified, his arrest, and the discovery of the switchblade knife, which was received in evidence over my objection that there was nothing to tie it to the crime. I asked a few questions to show that everyone the sergeant questioned except for Manley were friends and lived in the same neighborhood, and then told the judge I had subpoenaed the sergeant as a hostile witness for the defense case and at that time would ask him some questions beyond the scope of his direct examination. (The rule that in cross-examining a witness one can ask only about matters covered on the witness's direct examination has pretty much disappeared in federal court trials and increasingly in state courts as well, but in 1967 it was still alive and well in Illinois. Generally, the rule favors the side presenting the witness, but in this case I was happy to use it as an excuse for postponing my questions about the other suspect until the defense case, when I thought it would be most effective.)

Next the state called the man who first said he didn't know who committed the crime and then changed his story to accuse Manley. On cross-examination, Don Harris brought out the witness's change of story, the deal he made to avoid prosecution on a marijuana charge in exchange for his testimony, and his friendship with everyone at the scene except Manley. The state's last witness would be the young woman who also identified Manley as the killer. In pretrial proceedings I told the judge I had not been able to interview her because the state refused to give me her address, claiming she was afraid one of Manley's friends would kill her. Rather than order the prosecutor to give me her address, the judge said he would give me a chance to talk with her just before she testified.

It was now almost noon on Wednesday and the judge adjourned for lunch, saying I could use the time to interview the woman in his chambers if she was willing to talk to me. The prosecutor, he said, should introduce Don and me and tell the witness it was up to her whether she answered our questions or not, and then leave us alone. I suspect the judge was as confident as I was that the prosecutor had long since advised her not to talk to me, but it was a charade he devised to avoid the possibility an appellate court would find error in not requiring the state to give me her address so I could try to interview her before trial. For my part, I thought it was worthwhile to meet her and observe her demeanor, even if she didn't answer my questions.

She didn't, but she did something even better. Felicia* was a small, slightly built African-American girl who looked even younger than her fifteen years. She spoke so softly that Don and I could barely hear her, and she was obviously uncomfortable with the trial setting and her role in it. After the prosecutor left, I told her I just wanted to ask her a few questions about what she had seen on the day of the murder. When she said she didn't want to answer any questions, I told her it would take only a few minutes, and all I wanted was for her to tell me what she knew so that Mr. Manley could have a fair trial. When she again demurred, I said it didn't seem fair—she had talked to the police and the prosecutor and told them what happened, and all I wanted was for her to tell me the same thing.

"I didn't talk to no prosecutor," Felicia said, raising her voice for the first time.

"Well," I said, "I mean Mr. Jones, the man who was just here. You talked to him and answered his questions about what you saw, didn't you?"

"I never told nobody," she insisted.

Carefully, I asked her about everyone she might or must have talked to. Someone else in the prosecutor's office? An investigator? A policeman? Specifically Sergeant Jackson? Someone on the ambulance crew? Each time she insisted she had not told anyone what she had seen. Finally, I asked how it was, then, that she had come to court. "A policeman brought me. He came to my door this morning and carried me down here." She didn't know why. Don and I thanked her and went for a quick sandwich, a little incredulous at receiving another major break for our case.

After lunch, Felicia testified on direct examination that she had been standing by the stairs and had seen Robert Manley stab the victim. When she was turned over for cross-examination, I reminded her of our conversation over the lunch hour and she repeated, under oath, her story that she had never told anyone

TRIAL AND ERROR · 177

what she knew until her appearance on the witness stand. Several of the jurors rolled their eyes. The prosecutor sat in stunned silence. He should have stood up on his own and informed the court and jury that in fact he and the police had talked to Felicia, but when he didn't, I addressed the judge. "Your Honor," I said, "at this time I will request the prosecutor to stipulate that prior to her testimony here the witness did in fact talk to him and answer his questions, and that the testimony she just gave to the contrary was false." The judge called a sidebar conference, berated me (justifiably) for making my speech in the presence of the jury and, in effect, told the prosecutor he could either work out a stipulation or be called as a witness. The prosecutor agreed to stipulate. The state then rested.

For some reason, witnesses, especially unsophisticated ones, often have the idea it is improper to talk to a lawyer and be "prepared" to testify, and as a result, unless warned, they may lie about it. It is the oldest cross-examination tactic in the book to ask a witness about her preparation and try to create the impression her testimony was fed to her by the lawyer, but no one expects the witness to lie about having had the conversation—the first thing a lawyer tells a witness during preparation is that there is nothing wrong with what they are doing, so for heaven's sake don't lie if the other lawyer asks about it. Her lies were an unexpected break that injured the credibility of the state's most important witness. Either the prosecutor had failed to prepare her for the question, or she was untrainable.

When the state rests in a criminal trial, the defense routinely moves for a directed verdict of acquittal, claiming the state has failed to prove an essential element of the charges and/or that the evidence is insufficient as a matter of law to prove the charges beyond a reasonable doubt. The court usually denies the motion outright or takes it under advisement while the defense puts on its case. My routine motion was routinely denied, and after reading the stipulation about the young lady's falsehood I called Sergeant Jackson as a witness.

My first series of questions probably caused the judge and the prosecutor to wonder about my competence or my sanity. In essence, I established in considerable detail the sergeant's many years of service and his knowledge and expertise as an investigator of homicide cases, especially cases involving knife wounds. Next I had him describe his examination of the victim's wound at the crime scene, and his conclusion that it would be fatal.

A few more questions established that everyone the police questioned at the scene had denied knowing who stabbed the victim and that all of them lived in the neighborhood and most belonged to a local youth gang, while Manley was an outsider to both the neighborhood and the gang. Then I asked if the investigation had turned up any suspects other than Mr. Manley.

Sergeant Jackson said he couldn't recall. "Well," I asked, "do you recall a young man named Dwayne Richmond*? The sergeant hesitated as though he was trying to think. Finally, acting as if the name had suddenly rung a bell in his mind, he said yes, he did. And yes, he now recalled that Richmond had been a suspect before the two eyewitnesses came forward and solved the case with their identification of Manley.

I had more important things in mind than the sergeant's gratuitous interjection about the eyewitnesses solving the crime, and let it go.

"In fact," I continued, "on the day after the crime, Dwayne Richmond was arrested and held on a charge of aggravated assault, wasn't he?"

"I believe he was," the sergeant responded.

"Well, you don't just *believe* he was, you *know* he was, don't you?" I persisted. And the sergeant, looking a little sheepish, said yes, and yes again to my suggestion that he himself had made the arrest and written a report about it, and (after looking) that he had a copy of the report among the documents he had brought with him in response to my subpoena.

Next I established that Richmond had been arrested at his house, and that a search had turned up several knives. "Well,

Sergeant, did you send any of those knives to the crime lab for analysis?" I asked.

He looked at his report. "One of them," he said.

I paused and lowered my voice to signal the jury that something important was about to happen. "Did any of the knives have obvious bloodstains on them." He said no. "I take it that you selected the one you sent to the crime lab because you thought it might have been used in the stabbing?"

"Yes."

"It was consistent with the wound you had observed?"

"That's right."

"Did you then receive a report back from the crime lab providing an analysis of that knife?"

"I'm sure I did."

"Do you have that report with you?"

The sergeant thumbed through his reports. "I don't see it," he said finally.

I turned to the judge. "Your Honor," I said, sounding furious, "the state has not produced this report despite the pretrial order that I be given a copy of any scientific report obtained by the state in the course of investigating this murder. I ask that the state be ordered to produce it for me immediately."

The judge sent the jury back to the jury room and asked the prosecutor if he had produced the report. The prosecutor said he didn't think so, and didn't recall ever seeing it. The sergeant still couldn't find it among his documents, but felt sure he had gotten one—the crime lab would not have failed to respond to his request. The prosecutor was ordered to go to his office and search his file. He reported back that he had found nothing in his file, but had called the crime lab. They had a record of something that sounded like the report we were after and were sending it to the courtroom by messenger. It would take about a half hour.

The judge was unhappy, and in a hurry. "Finish your examination of this witness while we wait," he told me.

"I have nothing more, except for what may be suggested by the report," I said.

"All right, then, while we wait we'll have the prosecutor ask any questions he has so far. Bring in the jury."

When the jury was seated, the prosecutor proceeded to use the opportunity to have Sergeant Jackson repeat his testimony about the emergence of witnesses who identified Manley and say that evidence had caused him to clear the first suspect and charge Manley. As he was finishing, a man entered the courtroom carrying an envelope, bearing the report we were after. The judge removed the report from the envelope, looked at it, and handed it to me. I looked at it and broke into a broad smile, as if I had just discovered King Tut's tomb. The jury looked on, intensely curious.

After marking the report as Manley Exhibit 1 and showing it to the prosecutor, I handed it to Sergeant Jackson and asked if he recognized it as the report he received from the crime lab about the knife from Richmond's kitchen. He said it was, and it was received in evidence without objection.

"The knife described in that report is the one you selected from among several knives you found in the apartment?" I asked.

"Yes."

"Did the crime lab find any blood on the knife?"

"Just a trace."

"Was there enough to determine whether it was human blood?"

"No."

I thanked the sergeant and sat down. The prosecutor had no further questions.

Robert Manley could not possibly testify. He didn't really have anything to say anyway—he had no alibi—but in any event, if he testified the jury would learn about his extensive prior record, which would be devastating. At the same time, I hated for the jury not to hear him deny the murder—some jurors naturally assume that if a defendant doesn't testify, he must be guilty. I had decided the day before to try out a little skit to present to the jury at this point, and when I went through it with Manley in the lockup he did his part well, so I decided to do it.

The skit went like this: When I finished with the sergeant, I told the judge that I thought I would rest, but wanted to consult briefly with my client. The judge asked if I wanted a recess, and I said no. I bent over and whispered to Manley. He looked angry and gestured that he wanted to take the stand. "There's no case," I mouthed silently, dismissing the state's evidence with a look and a gesture. He resisted, pointing first to himself and then the witness stand. I repeated my "no case" gesture, and Manley shrugged as if accepting my advice reluctantly. "Your Honor," I announced, "the defense rests." There was no rebuttal.

It was midafternoon, and the judge sent the jury home while we spent the rest of the day arguing over jury instructions.

On Friday morning, we finished the instruction conference and the prosecutor gave his closing argument. He had a simple, straightforward case based on the two eyewitnesses who had identified Manley as the killer, and that is the way he argued it. I couldn't tell if he had figured out the use I was planning to make of the "other suspect" and the lab report, as he made little mention of it other than to point out I myself had brought out the sergeant's experience as a homicide investigator and that it was the sergeant who, based on the evidence, released the first suspect and charged Manley with the murder. When he was arrested, the prosecutor went on, what did they find in his possession? A switchblade knife! He brandished it.

During the prosecutor's argument, I had ripped a clean sheet of paper from my lined yellow pad and removed a ruler from my briefcase. With the crime-lab report in front of me and using the ruler to get the right proportions, I drew a knife of the same size and shape as the one described in the report. When the prosecutor's argument was over, I asked for a moment before starting my argument, picked up Manley's switchblade from the prosecutors' table and, placing it on the paper from the yellow pad, traced its outline. The jurors could not see what I had drawn during the prosecutor's argument but they watched me tracing the switchblade knife. They were curious.

I began the closing argument by describing my theory of the case, disparaging the testimony of the state's witnesses based on their inconsistent statements and lies and assigning a motive to their false testimony which repeated my theory of the case—they were protecting a friend by accusing the one person at the scene who was not from the neighborhood.

Those facts alone, I contended, left the prosecution short of its obligation to prove its case beyond a reasonable doubt. But there is another fact, I said, a fact the prosecutor failed to mention, which affirmatively demonstrates that Robert Manley is not guilty. Reminding the jury of Sergeant Jackson's experience and expertise, and the fact he had personally observed the single knife wound that killed the victim, I recalled that the very next day Jackson had arrested Dwayne Richmond, searched his apartment, and selected from among several knives the one he thought might have caused the fatal wound. "In the jury room," I said, "you will have the crime-lab report about that knife, Manley Exhibit 1, in evidence. When you read the report, you will see it describes the knife as a butcher knife, and gives its dimensions. Using those dimensions, I have drawn a picture of it."

With that, I displayed my drawing to the jury while reading the dimensions from the crime-lab report and using the ruler to show that the drawing was accurate. Then I pointed out the much smaller tracing of the knife taken from Manley. "Throughout this trial," I said, "the prosecutor has tried to convince you the knife taken from Mr. Manley was the knife which killed the victim and that Mr. Manley's possession of the knife is evidence of his guilt. But in fact, it is the exact opposite. When Sergeant Jackson went through that kitchen drawer and selected the one knife he thought was consistent with the fatal wound he observed on the victim's body, he selected a fourteen-inch butcher knife with a blade ten inches long and an inch and a half wide. Common sense tells you, and you can see for yourself from this drawing, that the fatal wound Sergeant Jackson observed and believed was consistent with a knife of that size could not have been made by a knife as small as the one taken from Mr. Manley. If we had not been fortunate enough to obtain the lab report giving us this information in the middle of this trial, we would never have been able to demonstrate, as this drawing demonstrates, that the state's effort to persuade you the victim was killed by Mr. Manley's knife is a fraud."

I asked them to return the only verdict possible on the basis of the evidence—a verdict of not guilty—and sat down.

In rebuttal, the prosecutor said a small knife could make a big wound, and even if the knife taken from Manley wasn't the murder weapon, it didn't mean he wasn't guilty; he may have had another knife. The only important evidence was the testimony of the eyewitnesses.

The judge gave his instructions and the jury retired to consider its verdict. It was time for the lunch recess. There was a tradition among defense lawyers trying cases at the Criminal Court building that you waited for your verdict while drinking and telling war stories with the other lawyers who were doing the same thing at Jean's Restaurant, a block north of the courthouse on California Avenue. I told the judge I could be reached there when the jury came back. He said he thought it might take a while, and I should come back to the courtroom at 5:00 if no verdict had been reached—he would call in the jury send them home for the night.

Although I hadn't tried a case in the Criminal Court building for several years, I'd eaten lunch at Jean's for the last four days and the staff had come to recognize me. Don and I packed up our briefcases, stopped off at the lockup to wish Prince 6X luck, and headed for the restaurant. As we walked in, someone saw me and called out from behind the counter, "Hey, Tucker, the court just called. Your jury's back."

I couldn't believe it. The jury hadn't been out a half hour, barely time to select a foreman and take a quick preliminary vote, if that's what they decided to do before starting to discuss the evidence. The received wisdom is that a quick verdict is a guilty verdict, and I just didn't think we'd done that badly. When we got to the courtroom the judge was waiting impatiently on the bench. The prosecutor wasn't there, but another assistant state's attorney who was trying the next case on the judge's calendar was in the room—the judge had skipped lunch and started the next case as soon as our jury retired and we cleared the courtroom. "OK," the judge said, "get the defendant and bring in the jury." He denied the assistant state's attorney's request that he wait even a few minutes so the man who had spend the last five days prosecuting the case could be present when the verdict was returned.

In came Robert Manley, followed quickly by the jury. "Have you reached a verdict?" the judge asked.

"We have, Your honor," the foreman responded. He was a middle-aged white man who worked as a salesman. We had almost used one of our challenges to keep him off the jury, but decided someone else was worse.

"Hand it to the clerk." The clerk took the verdict form and passed it to the judge. "Mr. Manley," the judge said. "Please stand up to receive the verdict." (I think the judge had seen that in a movie—I'd never seen it before.) Manley stood up, and I stood up with him. The judge unfolded the verdict form and read: "We the jury find the defendant Robert Manley not guilty."

I cannot say for certain how the trial of Robert Manley would have turned out without the comparison between the two knives, but I do know from the jurors that the knife comparison was responsible for the unanimous first-ballot acquittal reached only twenty minutes after the jury retired to deliberate. My theory of the case, that the witnesses were identifying Manley, the stranger, out of loyalty to or fear of their neighbor, was essential. But the description of the knife in the crime-lab report—a single tree among all the trees in the forest of evidence—provided crucial support for that theory.

When I received that anonymous packet in the mail, I immediately recognized the value of a second suspect—every defense lawyer loves to have someone else to blame for the crime—and I even recognized that the trace of blood on the knife might help create reasonable doubt that my client and not the original suspect had committed the crime. But it took me at least three readings of the crime-lab report to put together the fact that the police were touting my client's four-inch knife as the murder weapon with the description of the butcher knife—and recognize the importance of the discrepancy between those facts to my defense. You don't want to get bogged down in details, but you had better know them and understand which ones are most important.

Trying cases for a large law firm in a big city doesn't look much like *The Practice* or *L.A. Law*. Major clients are substantial corporations and the cases, while involving large sums of money, are often dull, take forever, and almost always settle before trial. Since the kind of cases I enjoyed were those that might actually go to trial, and since such cases were relatively hard to come by, I kept my eyes open for them and volunteered to handle them when possible.

Over the years I tried quite a few cases for Wes Hall, who was the firm's senior corporate specialist, so I was not surprised when Wes called one day in early 1977 and asked me to handle a case for one of his clients on an emergency basis. He said he thought I would find it interesting. It was, and it turned out to provide another example of the importance an individual fact can play in painting the overall picture you present to a judge or jury.

The case had come to Wes from Simpson Thacher & Bartlett, a prominent New York law firm, and the client was the giant conglomerate Gulf+Western Industries. I soon learned why Wes thought the case would be interesting. One of Gulf+Western's subsidiaries was about to file a lawsuit in the federal court in Chicago. The plaintiff was Madison Square Garden Boxing, Inc. and the defendant, world heavyweight boxing champion, Muhammad Ali.

At the time, Muhammad Ali was the most famous man in the

world. After regaining the heavyweight title with his "rope-a-dope" victory over George Foreman in the "Rumble-in-the-Jungle" in Zaire and defending it in his third fight with Joe Frazier, the "Thrilla-in-Manila," widely considered the greatest heavyweight prizefight in modern history, Ali had fought and defeated several lesser opponents. Then, after a close and difficult defense against Ken Norton in September 1976, Ali announced his retirement from the ring.

The Norton fight showed Ali's skills were beginning to deteriorate, but he was still The Greatest—and the only major draw in boxing. Madison Square Garden had promoted the Ali-Norton fight and Teddy Brenner, the Garden's longtime matchmaker, aware that boxing retirements are often temporary, kept close contact with Ali and his manager, Herbert Muhammad.

In November 1976, Brenner was in Palm Springs, California, negotiating with the managers of Ken Norton and the current "white hope," Duane Bobick, for a fight the next spring. During the negotiations, Brenner heard a rumor that Ali might fight again, after all. He took Bobick's manager aside and mentioned the rumor, suggesting he might be able to arrange a fight between Bobick and Ali that would be more lucrative for everyone. Bobick's manager jumped at the idea. An agreement for the Bobick-Norton fight was signed with the understanding that if Ali agreed to fight Bobick, Norton would step aside in return for getting the first fight against Bobick, if he took the title. Brenner called Herbert Muhammad and suggested he would come to Chicago where Herbert lived to discuss a fight between Ali and Bobick. Herbert said to come ahead, and Brenner took the next plane. In Chicago he met with Charles Lomax, who was Herbert Muhammad's lawyer and held his power of attorney.

An agreement was soon reached for Ali to fight Bobick for $2,500,000 plus expenses. Lomax prepared a letter of intent summarizing the deal. Normally, only Herbert's agreement and signature were required to seal an Ali fight, but Herbert had been criticized in the press for allegedly pressuring Ali to keep fighting to earn more money for the Nation of Islam. (Herbert Muhammad was the son of Nation of Islam founder Elijah Muhammad.) Herbert told Brenner he wanted it clear that whether Ali fought was up to him, so Brenner should take the letter to Houston, where Ali was making a movie. Ali could then decide for himself if he wanted to sign it and fight again. Herbert would inform Ali that Brenner was coming. Brenner dutifully hopped the next plane to Houston, where Ali did sign the letter of intent. Brenner flew back to New York with the signed letter and he and another Madison Square Garden officer made plans to return to California to conclude the agreement for Norton's withdrawal from the Bobick fight.

Meanwhile, a Garden lawyer turned the letter of intent into a formal agreement on the usual long-form boxing contract. There was one provision in the letter of intent, however, that the lawyer thought should be changed. It provided that Madison Square Garden would pay Ali $125,000 for training expenses on or before November 25. It was now November 22, the business with Norton in California had to be concluded before a formal agreement with Ali could be signed, and November 25 was Thanksgiving, when no bank transfers could be made. The Garden lawyer was afraid it would be impossible to make the transfer on time. The contract was prepared leaving blanks for the date of execution of the contract and payment of the training money. According to Brenner, he then called Lomax, told him he now had prepared a formal contract for the fight on the same terms as the letter of intent, except for the concern about the payment date. Lomax said, "No problem, just make it sometime the following week." Brenner and two other Garden executives then flew back to Palm Springs to conclude the agreement with Norton. Brenner carried the Ali-Bobick contract with him.

On November 24 the Norton agreement was signed. Brenner called Herbert Muhammad with the news, told him he had the Ali agreement with him, and offered to take the red-eye to Chicago so Herbert could see it. But Herbert said not to bother, just take it direct to Houston for Ali to sign. Brenner said the airplane schedule had him arriving in Houston very early in the morning— around 6:00 A.M.—and Herbert said that was all right, he would let Ali know Brenner was coming.

Accordingly, early on Thanksgiving morning, Brenner met with Ali, who signed the contract. Brenner, who had been on the road with little sleep for over a week, mistakenly filled in the blank space for the date of signing as November 24 instead of 25. In the blank space for the date of paying the training expenses, he placed November 29, the following Monday. When he finished his business with Ali, Brenner phoned Herbert Muhammad in Chicago, told him Ali had signed the contract, and again offered to bring it directly to Chicago. Herbert said not to bother—he was spending the day with his family and Brenner should go back to New York and mail him a copy. Brenner did so, satisfied that his exhausting odyssey had paid off with another profitable fight for Madison Square Garden.

On Friday November 26, the Garden announced the fight to the world and began promotion. On Monday the agreed-upon sum of $125,000 for Ali's training expenses was wired to an account Lomax had set up on Friday to receive those funds. Almost immediately, however, rumors began circulating that Ali would not fight, and a few days later Ali confirmed them, announcing he had again decided to retire. Although his retirement was a breach of the Bobick fight contract, Brenner knew there was no way to force Ali to fight if he didn't want to, so the Garden quickly revived the prior plan for a Norton-Bobick fight. At Brenner's request, Ali helped the promotion by telephonically joining a press conference announcing the fight. Not long thereafter, rumors began again. Ali was not retired after all; he was going to fight an unnamed challenger in a fight to be promoted by Don King, the Garden's most successful competitor in the boxing business.

Furious, Madison Square Garden decided to sue for the money it had lost by cancellation of the Ali-Bobick fight, and to enjoin Ali from fighting anyone else until he lived up to his agreement to fight in the Garden.

The lawyer in charge of the case for Madison Square Garden Boxing was Jack Guzzetta, a Simpson Thacher partner who was something of a character in his own right, but nothing compared to the witnesses who would testify—a cast of boxing characters straight from a Damon Runyon story, including Brenner, King, Herbert Muhammad, and Ali himself. Guzzetta had interviewed the Garden witnesses and prepared a complaint. He planned to ask the judge for an immediate trial so the issues could be decided in time to avoid additional financial injury to the parties.

There was good reason to try the case promptly, but no one really expected that Guzzetta's request to start the trial only two weeks after the complaint was filed would be adopted. There had been none of the usual pretrial discovery which makes big-firm, big-case litigation last so long and cost so much. Guzzetta was a former prosecutor and loved to play the cowboy who could ride into town and try any case quick and dirty. I suspect his suggestion was as much a gesture to his self-image as something that he actually expected would happen. However, John Crowley, the judge to whom the case was assigned, was also a former prosecutor, criminal-defense lawyer, and fight fan who liked the fact the case was in his court, and liked the idea of trying it quickly instead of spending the next year watching the parties masturbate over discovery disputes and pretrial motions. He said he would clear his calendar to try the case on Guzzetta's schedule if the defendant would agree. Whether because of the real financial risk of getting ready for a fight that might not occur, or because they just weren't about to be out-cowboyed by Guzzetta and the judge, to everyone's surprise, Ali's lawyers from the Chicago firm Sidley & Austin agreed.

Guzzetta went back to New York, gathered up his young wife and a couple of Simpson Thacher associates, and returned to Chicago, where he and his entourage booked two large suites in the city's most expensive hotel. They arrived from the airport in a long stretch limousine on Sunday evening. Over the next week and a half, the lawyers worked night and day to prepare for trial. After a few days, I took a room of my own in the hotel rather than lose a precious hour of sleep commuting from home.

The two sides agreed to exchange trial briefs setting forth their theories of the case and the evidence they expected to produce at trial. In their trial brief, Ali's lawyers revealed two primary theories of defense. First: There was no valid contract because a contract with Ali was not valid unless it was signed or approved by his manager, Herbert Muhammad. Second: Madison Square Garden had abandoned the contract by its conduct in going ahead with the Norton-Bobick fight and accepting Ali's return of the training money in January.

The validity of the abandonment defense was essentially a question of law, there being no dispute about what happened after Ali's second "retirement," but the facts relating to the first defense were hotly disputed. Ali claimed that not only had Herbert Muhammad not signed the Ali-Bobick contract, neither Mr. Muhammad nor Mr. Lomax had ever seen it or known and approved its terms. According to the defendant's trial brief, Herbert Muhammad and Lomax would so testify. In addition, Ali would say that when he signed the contract he told Teddy Brenner, and Brenner acknowledged, that the contract would be valid only if Herbert approved it thereafter. Don King would testify Ali had told him the same thing when he obtained Ali's signature on a contract the same day Ali signed the Garden contract.

The defendant's reference to King's testimony confirmed the report Brenner had heard that Ali was going to fight again, but for King. As it turned out, shortly after Brenner obtained Ali's signature on the Bobick contract on November 25, Don King had appeared at Ali's door with a contract for Ali to fight a white boxer named Mike Schutte, whom King characterized as the South African champion. As King would later testify, "I was in Houston chasing the same rumor Teddy was chasing, that perhaps The Legend would come back out of retirement and fight again. As you know, he retires every other week." When Ali told King he had just signed an agreement with Brenner to fight Bobick, King pressed ahead: "I said, 'Well, I got his guy who is a much easier opponent than Bobick. . . . You can use this guy and you can really be fighting the best of two worlds. You know, you can really strike a blow against oppression [in South Africa].' So Muhammad got excited about this and he said, 'Well, I'll fight both of them.' "

Ali had signed King's agreement, supposedly telling King, "You must get Herbert Muhammad's signature on it for it to be valid, the same as I told Teddy Brenner." King then flew to Chicago where he met Lomax. In King's presence, Lomax had some of the pages of the Ali-Schutte agreement retyped to reflect revisions he wanted, including the addition of a section referring to the Ali-Bobick agreement and setting alternative dates for an Ali-Schutte fight, depending on whether the Ali-Bobick fight went forward. Lomax, with power of attorney, then signed Herbert Muhammad's name to the revised agreement. Included in the documents that the defendant produced during the frenzied days of trial preparation was a copy of the revised agreement Don King had obtained for Ali to fight Mike Schutte.

For its part, Madison Square Garden did not much dispute the claim that custom in the industry required that a boxing contract be approved by the fighter's manager, but insisted that both Herbert Muhammad, and Charles Lomax acting on Herbert's behalf, knew the terms of the Ali-Bobick contract and had approved it. Teddy Brenner would testify he had told Lomax the material terms of the contract were the same as the letter of intent, which Lomax had drawn himself with Herbert Muhammad's approval. The only exception was the later date for payment of the training money, which Lomax agreed to. Moreover, Brenner had told Herbert Muhammad the same thing when he called him after Ali signed, and when he offered to bring the contract to Herbert in Chicago. Herbert had told him it was unnecessary, indicating to Brenner his approval of those terms.

With that dispute and the credibility of the competing witnesses at issue, on Wednesday, March 23, 1977, the trial of *Madison*

Square Garden Boxing, Inc. v. Muhammad Ali commenced in a federal courtroom packed with reporters and spectators.

The spectators were there to see Muhammad Ali in the flesh, and if I had not been a lawyer in the case, I might have been one of them. I too was a fan of Ali's and had watched many of his fights on television. Even so, I was not prepared for the sight of the champion when he first appeared in the courtroom. He was 6'2" tall and about 220 pounds, vital statistics not unusual among my friends and acquaintances, but he appeared enormous. He looked to be the size of a 6'7" 350-pound defensive end on a professional football team. To this day, I can't understand it, unless it was an optical illusion caused by his reputation and accomplishments.

If the spectators had come to see what Ali looked like in the flesh, the show that kept everyone amused, and often in uproarious laughter for the next two days, came from the witness stand, and especially from the two promoters, Teddy Brenner and Don King. Neither of them was about to let the solemnity of the courtroom interfere with their irrepressible personalities and penchant for storytelling and self-promotion. On direct examination they stayed fairly close to the script they had rehearsed with the lawyers, but on cross they were unstoppable, rarely allowing their answers to remain long in the neighborhood of the question they were asked. At first, the lawyers tried to keep them under control, as a good cross-examiner learns to do, but it being a bench trial where the irrelevant and prejudicial could be simply treated as such by the judge, it soon seemed easier and probably less time-consuming to simply lie back and enjoy the show. Brenner, with his Brooklyn accent and great sense of timing, had the audience laughing throughout his cross-examination by Henry Mason, Ali's lawyer, but Don King was the champ in this contest:

> GUZZETTA: . . . are you functioning simultaneously as both a promoter and a manager?

> KING: No, I was a manager first. I was a manager first and I had a

fighter that I bought. I learned my first lesson about how cruel and cold the boxing game can be, not the game per se, but the people that are in the game. Every fighter across the nation lives to fight in the Garden.

Every manager wants to take his fighter to the Garden. The Garden indeed was the temple of boxing. New York was the Mecca. . . .

I had a fighter named Ernie Shavers. Ernie Shavers was contracted with Ted Brenner and myself to fight in Madison Square Garden, the high point in my boxing career as coming into the game as a manager of a fighter.

I brought my fighter to Madison Square Garden. He had a one-round knockout of Jimmy Ellis. He was supposed to fight Jerry Quarry. Unfortunately, Jerry Quarry . . . didn't fight on the day he was supposed to fight. So they put a substitute in named Jimmy Ellis, which was a former WBA World Champion.

Ernie Shavers knocked out Jimmy Ellis. When he knocks him out with one punch, Teddy Brenner jumps all over me and tells me how great I am, I'm going to be a member of the Garden, we are all one big happy family, I've got a fighter with a punch like Joe Louis, nobody has been on the scene in the history of boxing like that since Joe Louis.

We reschedule the fight for December 14th with Shavers and Quarry. This is the big fight. Quarry is the white hope. Shavers is coming out of obscurity. He has got a knockout punch. This is my first experience coming to the Garden. Again, I'm totally indoctrinated by Teddy Brenner.

When Shavers goes into the ring to fight Jerry Quarry on December 14th, Jerry Quarry knocks out Shavers in the first round.

Now, I'm walking through the hall and I speak to Teddy Brenner and he walks by me. He doesn't even speak.

The next morning I goes into Teddy Brenner's office. He is reading a paper, you know, and I'm really despondent, dejected, my dreams and aspirations have been shattered.

I say, "Teddy, you know, what do I do to revive my fighter?"
"Who is your fighter?"
I say, "Teddy, my fighter is Ernie."
"Ernie," he says, "Ernie who?"
I say, "Ernie Shavers, the one the people in New York love him. You told me the people in New York love him."
"That was yesterday. They don't love him today. Get out of here."
You know, that was my first experience.

By this time, the audience was laughing so hard you could barely hear Don King trying to continue. Finally Judge Crowley, who had himself bent over double behind the bench, interrupted: "Pardon me, Mr. King. All right, ladies and gentlemen, I realize that many things Mr. King says may strike someone as humorous, but we are trying a lawsuit here, and we'll try it with closed doors if we have to."

It was a little unfair to the spectators. If everyone who was laughing had been excluded from the courtroom, the trial would have to go on without lawyers, the other witnesses, the judge's staff—and the judge himself. But the judge had a point: There was a serious case to be tried, and serious questions of credibility to be resolved regarding whether Lomax or Herbert Muhammad had known and approved the terms of the contract Ali had signed for Teddy Brenner on Thanksgiving morning. The last defense witness would be Charles Lomax. In dividing trial responsibilities, Jack Guzzetta and I had agreed that I would cross-examine Lomax. I had reason to hope my cross-examination would provide the judge with a basis for resolving the credibility issue in our favor.

The basis for that hope had occurred to me only a day or two before the case went to trial as I examined, for probably the fourth time, the agreement Don King had obtained for a fight between Ali and Schutte. I knew the agreement had been partially revised by Mr. Lomax after King obtained Ali's signature on it, and I could see the agreement made specific reference to the Ali-Bobick fight on one of the pages Lomax had revised. On its face, the document proved Lomax knew about the Ali-Bobick fight, but that was not quite the issue. Lomax and Herbert Muhammad didn't deny that they knew and approved of the letter of intent signed on November 18, and they admitted their knowing Brenner had gone back to Houston and obtained Ali's signature on a formal contract for the fight. What they claimed was they had not seen that contract or been informed of its terms, and therefore had not approved it, as custom and usage required. The defense could argue that the mere reference to an Ali-Bobick fight in the Schutte agreement did not disprove their claimed ignorance of the terms of the November 24 contract.

What I finally realized was that the Lomax revisions to the Schutte agreement proved Lomax *had* to have known the terms of the Bobick contract. For one thing, the signature of Herbert Muhammad on the Schutte agreement was dated November 24, probably an effort to make it conform to the erroneous November 24 date on the Bobick contract. But of greater significance was the provision of the Schutte agreement that if "the promoters [of the Bobick fight] have not made the initial deposit of $125,000 required by that contract by the close of banking hours on Monday, November 29, 1976," the Schutte fight would be moved forward and take place in the time period set aside for the Ali-Bobick fight.

There was only one significant difference between the terms of the November 18 letter of intent and the November 24 contract between Ali and Madison Square Garden: the change in the date for paying the training money from November 25 to November 29. The only place that date appeared was in the contract Ali had signed for Brenner. That Lomax had inserted the November 29 date into the Schutte contract when he revised it proved he knew and approved of the only change between the Ali-Bobick contract and the letter of intent he himself had drafted ten days earlier.

Before confronting Lomax with the proof that he knew and approved of the November 29 date when he revised the Schutte agreement, I wanted to close the door to any argument that what Lomax knew and approved was not binding on Herbert Muhammad as Ali's manager. I needed to do it before Lomax saw where I was going, lest he fall on his sword and claim that for some reason in this case he had acted in Herbert's name without authority. Staying far away from the Schutte agreement, I used other contracts Lomax had negotiated for Ali, and the suggestion that Lomax might have exceeded his authority in those transactions, to encourage him to defend the broad reach of his power of attorney and the care he took to obtain Herbert Muhammad's prior approval of the terms of any business agreement Lomax prepared for him. Thus committed, Lomax had nowhere to go when I finally confronted him with the November 29 date he had inserted in the Schutte agreement. Realizing it was apparent that he had taken the date from the Bobick agreement he claimed not to have seen or approved, a distressed look crossed Lomax's face. "I think I know where you're going," Lomax blurted. But I was already there.

Judge Crowley immediately understood the significance of the date. It was the point he relied on when two weeks later he found for the Garden on the issue of the validity of the contract. Unfortunately, at the same time, he found for Ali on the legal issue of abandonment. Ali had won, but the factual findings and debatable legal ruling gave the Garden a strong basis for appeal. It was a decision that provided both sides with an incentive to settle their differences, and they promptly did so. Ali would first fight for Don King in May and make his next fight for the Garden in September.

A few months after the Ali case was over, one of my partners reported that in a conversation with Judge Crowley, the judge said he was using the transcript of my cross-examination of Charles Lomax in a trial-practice course he was teaching at a local law school. Crowley had said: "John picked up a shovel and started digging a hole while Lomax stood off to the side, looking on. When he was done with the hole, John asked Lomax to come and see what he had done, and when Lomax did, standing on the edge of the hole peering down, John gave him a little nudge and shoved him in."

It wasn't really that good a cross—the hard part had been recognizing the significance of one little date in a big stack of documents—but I thought Judge Crowley's description of the structure was perfect. It is a rare case when a cross-examiner has the material to mount a dramatic, head-on attack on a witness in the manner of a TV prosecutor. More often, if there is a point to be made, it requires sneaking up on the witness or surrounding him with seemingly benign and indisputable facts to cut off the escape routes he may find if confronted with an uncomfortable fact at the start.

Despite Judge Crowley's effort to control it, there was a lot of laughter during the Ali trial, all or most of it spontaneously provoked by the witnesses, not by design of the lawyers, and the nature of the case was such that it had no impact on the result. Over the years, however, I came to realize that in other settings, courtroom humor can be important.

Starting in the early seventies, I taught trial technique to practicing lawyers under the auspices of the National Institute of Trial Advocacy and the Illinois Bar Association. I had not thought much about humor as a strategy until I was teaching a course together with a leading plaintiff's personal-injury lawyer who declared to the class that a plaintiff's lawyer should *never* laugh, tell a joke, ask a humorous question, or otherwise suggest there was anything funny about a case he was trying. "Your client is injured," he said. "He was injured by the defendant's negligence, and his injury is serious. His pain and suffering are terrible. *You must never suggest there is anything funny about it!*"

When I thought about it, I realized he was right, and that his theory had application to a lot more than the plaintiff's side of a personal-injury case. For example, if a personal-injury plaintiff really has been seriously hurt, it is probably as inappropriate for the defense to try to inject humor into the case as it would be for the plaintiff's lawyer. A jury is not likely to look kindly on a lawyer makes jokes in a case where someone has been paralyzed. On ther hand, if the circumstances of the accident are somewhat humorous—as they often are—and the injury is considerably less serious than the plaintiff is making it out to be—which is also not unusual—treating the plaintiff's claims with some humor could be helpful to the defense.

I didn't try personal-injury cases, but I thought the same principle would apply to other kinds of cases. Certainly the reason plaintiff's lawyers should avoid humor would apply to prosecutors in criminal cases, and without really thinking about it I had instinctively understood that in most of the street-crime cases I tried in the Criminal Court of Cook County, the same principle would apply to defense lawyers. When someone has been raped, murdered, assaulted, burglarized, or robbed on the street, the defense lawyer must make it clear he doesn't condone the crime. There's nothing funny about it—he sympathizes with the victim, but his client didn't do it.

On the other hand, I thought, there may be other kinds of cases, both civil and criminal, where getting the jury to laugh might be a good tactic.

At about the same time I was teaching the course where the subject of courtroom humor came up I was defending a civil case in which the Federal Savings and Loan Insurance Corporation was claiming my client had defrauded a savings and loan by bribing the lender's president and obtaining an inflated appraisal of the property that secured the loan. The plaintiff's star witness was a loan broker who admitted soliciting a payment of $300,000 from my client and, with the client's knowledge, paying it to the savings-and-loan president. While cross-examining the broker, I inadvertently drew a huge laugh from the jury when, in high dudgeon, I pointed in the direction of one of the other lawyers in the case while accusing the witness of giving her an answer that was directly contrary to the answer he had just given me. As it happened, the lawyer I thought I was pointing toward had stepped out of the courtroom behind my back, so I was pointing dramatically into thin air. When I realized why the jury was laughing, I made some crack that drew another laugh, and when I thought about it that night, I decided getting the jury to laugh— however inadvertently—was a good thing under the circumstances. The judge was a grumpy, pro-government man who had sternly rebuked the jury for laughing and me for instigating it the second time; the loan-broker witness was a scumbag; the plaintiff's lead attorney was unduly self-righteous, and the FSLIC was not likely to draw much serious sympathy from the jury the way a defrauded individual might. The next day I got the jury to laugh again a couple of times while finishing my cross of the broker and examining the plaintiff's valuation expert, who had made an obvious mistake in his appraisal. I can't say for certain that it helped, but I was pretty sure the humor didn't hurt when the jury decided to award the plaintiff only a fraction of what it claimed to have lost.

The most humorous thing I ever saw in a trial occurred in a federal criminal prosecution of five men accused of running a sports bookmaking operation for the Chicago mob and threatening violence against a customer who failed to pay his losses. I had been hired to represent the lead defendant in the case, "Rocky" Infelice, the alleged boss of a "crew" that, among other things, accepted layoff bets and collected "street taxes" from independent bookmakers in Chicago and its northern suburbs. (Layoff bets are bets one bookmaker makes with another. A "street tax" is the fee an independent bookmaker has to pay the mob for the privilege of doing business. If he doesn't pay, he's likely to be put out of business, either by withdrawal of the protection afforded by a favorable relationship with local law enforcement, or worse.)

The case was prosecuted by lawyers from the "strike force," the special unit of the Justice Department established by Robert Kennedy to investigate and prosecute cases against "organized crime," meaning the Italian Mafia. The prosecution case consisted almost entirely of the testimony of a small-time bookie and recordings he made of conversations with the defendants on a "body wire" supplied by the FBI. In addition to my client, the defendants included three members of his "crew." Lou Marino and Salvatore

(Solly) DeLaurentis were full-timers. The third, referred to by his lawyer only as "poor Chuckie," was a "mope" who served as a kind of part-time gofer and messenger boy for the others. Each was represented by one of Chicago's best criminal-defense lawyers.

The government's star witness—we'll call him Stan—owned a used-car lot and booked bets on the side, going around to taverns and taking small bets on football games from the customers. He had made a connection with DeLaurentis through the mope, and for three weeks running had laid off several thousand dollars in bets with the defendants. Each week those bets, on balance, had been winners, and he had been paid what he was owed.

The fourth week Stan bet again, but this time the bets he made were net losers, to the tune of several thousand dollars. When the time came to settle up, however, Stan said he was short and needed time to get the money. This went on for several days until someone suggested to Stan that the people he owed money to were not people to mess around with, whereupon Stan promptly went to the FBI and, in return for their protection, agreed to wear the wire. Several additional meetings were held in which Stan was urged by DeLaurentis, Marino, and finally Infelice himself to find a way to meet his obligations. (Stan was even introduced to the operator of a small loan company who offered to make him a high-interest loan. For his trouble, this man became the fifth defendant in the indictment.)

In one of his last meetings with any of the defendants, Stan met Marino for lunch at a restaurant. Once again he had promised to bring the money, but didn't. Lou Marino was a man whose bulk, visage, and demeanor were well calculated to impress a reluctant deadbeat with the seriousness of his obligation. When Stan again claimed poverty, Marino sought to explain the depth of his unhappiness with a long and increasingly agitated stream of expletives, featuring repeated variations on the common four-letter word for sexual intercourse and colorful descriptions of the way in which he proposed to perform that act upon Stan's person if Stan did not pay his just debts by the end of the day, all of which was duly recorded on the hidden tape recorder. At one point, according to Stan (the tape could only pick up the noise of something clattering on the table), Marino picked up a table knife and suggested by words and gestures that in the course of the described events he intended to supplement his God-given tools with a similar instrument.

No one ever touched Stan, but the statute required only a *threat* of violence, and it was hard to argue that his lunchtime tête-à-tête with Marino did not qualify. It was the government's best evidence, and the lead prosecutor decided to tell the jury about it in her opening statement. Not only to tell them *about* it, but to quote Mr. Marino's comments verbatim. The prosecutor, Gay Hugo, was some six feet tall, a slim, strikingly beautiful blonde who eschewed the drab mannish business styles adopted by some female lawyers for stylish, colorful, perfectly fitted suits and dresses. After apologizing for the language, she recited Marino's speech in full, with force and emphasis equivalent to his own. When she finished, the courtroom was deadly silent. It was a difficult enough case to defend, but now, I thought, with Marino's outburst ringing in the jurors' ears, the prosecutor had dug a hole it would be difficult for any of us to climb out of. But I had not envisioned the devious and creative mind of my co-counsel, Sandy Volpe.

Although Rocky Infelice had been alluded to and, according to the government, pointed out to Stan as the boss, he had met Stan only twice and the conversation in the only recorded meeting contained no threatening words. It even contained language from which I could argue that Rocky had no responsibility for Marino's outburst and was interested in Stan's debt only because Marino and DeLaurentis owed money to him. Without doing anything to prejudice them, my plan was to separate Rocky from the other defendants as far as possible and try to let him fade into the woodwork. Accordingly, I had exercised my prerogative as counsel for the lead defendant to situate my opening statement in an inconspicuous slot near the end of the lineup. My recollection is that the first defense opening was given by Pat Tuite for Lou Marino. Pat, as always, did a fine job of making the best of a bad situation, apologizing for his client's language and Italian temper while explaining it by reference to Stan's perfidy in taking money three weeks in a row when it was owed him and then refusing to pay when he lost. Pat emphasized the fact that even on an occasion when Marino and Stan were alone in an empty parking lot, Marino had not so much as touched him, nor had anyone else in the period of several weeks that Stan continued to welsh on his debt despite numerous promises to pay.

Sandy Volpe was next. While playing much the same tune as Tuite, he paced around the courtroom, always addressing the jury but meanwhile circling the prosecutors' table, now behind the table, now between it and the jury, occasionally stopping for a minute to emphasize a point. Physically, Sandy was Gay Hugo's opposite. He was no more than five feet six inches tall, stockily built, with a rumpled suit and a perpetual grin to go with a devilish glint in his eyes. If you had known what was in his mind, you would have noticed that whenever his perambulations took him past where the prosecutor was sitting, upright and expressionless at her table on the side next to the jury, Sandy's head was almost exactly level with hers. He had been speaking for some time when he reached the subject of Lou Marino's outburst. It was, he said, understandable that Lou was angry in light of Stan's conduct; but on behalf of his client Solly, who was admittedly Lou's friend, he had to apologize again for the language. It was inexcusable, and he was sorry that the jury had to listen to it, and that Ms. Hugo had to repeat it to them. Sandy had stopped. He stood between the prosecution table and the jury, right next to where Gay Hugo sat, their heads on a level, and as he said he was sorry she had to repeat Marino's words, he had turned and looked at her. Then, his own eyes sparkling brighter than ever, he looked into hers and spoke to her directly, his voice full of longing: "But Jesus, Gay, I love it when you talk dirty."

The courtroom erupted. All of the jurors were laughing, some howling so hard there were tears rolling down their cheeks. The judge was laughing. The defendants and the other lawyers were laughing—none of us had known what was coming. (I'm not sure Sandy did, either.) Even the second prosecutor in the case and the FBI agent in charge of the investigation were laughing. Only Gay Hugo was even trying not to laugh.

If Stan had been a more sympathetic victim, it might not have worked. It might even have backfired. If he had actually been hurt, if he hadn't collected his winnings for three weeks and then failed to pay the first time he lost, if he hadn't lied so often on cross-examination that he even damaged the credibility of the tape recordings, the defendants, or at least Marino, probably would have been convicted. But Sandy had miraculously dug us out of the hole we were in, and the prosecutors never recovered. A couple of the jurors at first voted to convict, but in due time they were persuaded to join the majority and find everyone not guilty.

The jury returned its verdict midafternoon and the defense lawyers adjourned to a nearby bar to celebrate. The defendants had invited us to join them later for dinner at Gianotti's, an excellent Italian restaurant which had been described during the trial as the site of numerous meetings between the defendants. The government had even put photographs of the restaurant and a diagram of its interior into evidence, and the testimony of an FBI agent that it was the regular meeting place of most of Chicago's top bookies had apparently titillated the jurors. As the defendants and lawyers sat at a large table in a room off the main dining room, someone recognized a woman who walked by and peered in. It was one of the jurors. We immediately invited her to join us, and it turned out she was not alone. Six of the twelve jurors had come to the restaurant together to see it for themselves. More chairs were found, room was made at the table, food and drinks were ordered, and for an hour or more the ex-jurors ate, drank, laughed, and told trial stories with the acquitted defendants and their lawyers. The government's attempt to portray the defendants as monsters had failed miserably, starting, I had no doubt, with the laughter Sandy Volpe had precipitated in his opening statement. (In retrospect, I also wondered what kind of investigation might have been triggered if one of the FBI agents who routinely conducted surveillance at the restaurant had seen the party that went on that night.)

CHAPTER 6

POLITICS, PATRONAGE, AND PAYING CLIENTS

A popular tactic of candidates for public office is to run against politics. "I am not a politician," the candidate announces, while striving mightily to become or remain one. And next to not being a politician, a politician's favorite claim is that he or she is not a lawyer.

The rationale for this odd assertion that one is without either experience or relevant training for the office he seeks stems from the low standing of politicians and lawyers in public-opinion polls. Fortunately, when it comes to actually electing someone to an important office, the voters are usually smarter than their own reported opinions. Most competent incumbents are reelected if they choose to run, most higher offices are won by someone with experience in a lower one, the term-limit craze appears to be fading, and a huge percentage of officeholders are lawyers.

Politics is dominated by lawyers, and almost every lawyer is interested in politics, for the obvious reason that by training and experience, lawyers know and care more than anyone else about the laws that politicians make and administer.

In Chicago, if you were interested in politics in the period between the late 1950s and mid-1970s, you were, by definition, an ally or opponent of Richard J. Daley. Until his death on December 20, 1976, Daley was the most famous and powerful mayor in America. Despite his short, round physique, his fractured syntax, and his thick "Chicawgo" accent, face to face he was a man of enormous presence and personal magnetism. He had absolute control of the last big-city political machine and, through it, every aspect of Chicago government. No political sparrow fell in Chicago or Cook County without Mayor Daley's notice and attention.

Daley's control of the city had many positive consequences, but it led to some serious negatives as well. One was the poor quality and political enslavement of the elected state-court judges in Cook County. As a result, a fair number of lawyers belonged to a loosely organized group of liberal Republicans and reform Democrats who were the main, albeit pathetically weak, political opposition to the Daley machine. I was one of them, although initially my role was minor and sporadic, consisting primarily of precinct work, poll watching, and a position on the board of the Chicago Council of Lawyers, an "alternative" bar association which, unlike the Daley–co-opted Chicago Bar Association, provided honest and often harsh evaluations of judges and judicial candidates.

Then, in 1970, reform lawyers won a surprising victory in the United States Court of Appeals for the Seventh Circuit in *Shakman v. Democratic Organization of Cook County.* A series of Supreme Court cases had held that firing public-school teachers because of their political views or activities was a violation of the First Amendment. Citing those cases, the Seventh Circuit upheld a complaint alleging the patronage practices of the Daley machine violated the rights of opposition candidates by raising a publicly financed army of workers to support machine candidates.

The next step was to see if the courts would apply the same principles to a case brought by ordinary patronage workers terminated for political reasons. If government employees could not be fired (or hired) based on political support for the officeholder who controlled their jobs, the power of the Daley machine and other patronage-based political organizations across the country would be sharply diminished.

An opportunity to find out came quickly. The Daley machine's control of Chicago offices was virtually complete, but in Cook

County, which included several heavily Republican suburbs, Republicans occasionally won a countywide office. In 1970, the office of Cook County sheriff was held by Republican Joseph Woods. Then in November 1970, Woods lost his bid for re-election to Democrat Richard Elrod, a city lawyer who had tackled one of the participants in the SDS "Days of Rage" riots in 1969. In doing so Elrod had suffered an injury to his spine that rendered him partially paralyzed, but politically potent.

Elrod took office on December 7, 1970, and immediately began the traditional process of terminating any employee who was neither civil service–protected nor willing to agree to support the Democratic organization in the future. A few weeks later, I received a call from the ACLU asking if I would represent the fired employees in a case claiming that their termination violated the First Amendment. I was a liberal Democrat and had no reason to believe the patronage employees Woods hired when he was elected in 1966 had been any better than the ones Elrod would replace them with, but the principle was important. I agreed to take the case.

Within a few days, I interviewed the fired employees who agreed to serve as named plaintiffs and representatives of a class of employees for whom the case would be filed.

Frank Vargas began work as a juvenile-court bailiff in October 1969 with Republican political sponsorship. When Elrod took over, Vargas's supervisor was replaced by a Democratic appointee who told Vargas he would be fired if he did not obtain responsorship from a Democrat, which would require him to join the Democratic organization and provide financial support and precinct work for Democratic candidates. A few weeks later, he was summarily discharged. The new supervisor told him it was no reflection on his work. The supervisor had been told to replace him with someone with Democratic political sponsorship. The supervisor said he had orders to replace twenty-two others in the same department.

Frank Buckley had been a process server since 1967. His

supervisor was also replaced after Elrod took office and told Buckley he would have to get Democratic sponsorship if he wanted to keep his job. Sometime later, a Democratic precinct captain he knew approached him and said he would get him Democratic sponsorship if he would agree to switch parties and work a precinct for the Democratic organization. Buckley declined, and at the time I interviewed him was expecting to be fired any day.

John Burns was a supervisor of process servers. Because of his position, he had personal knowledge of the political purge that took place after Elrod took office. The *Shakman* decision had come down before Elrod became sheriff, and Woods had posted a letter in the office describing the decision and suggesting that patronage firing by Elrod would be illegal. When the firings began, Burns brought the letter to Elrod's attention and asked about it. Elrod said he had no intention of changing the "system" and didn't believe he had to. About this time, a Mr. Carvis was hired as the sheriff's patronage supervisor. Carvis had Burns prepare a list of the employees in the process division, indicating the order in which they could be replaced with new, inexperienced employees with the least disruption to the work of the office. Burns did so, and Carvis then checked the list, removed the names of employees who had obtained Democratic responsorship, and began replacing employees on the list. One man who was fired was rehired a few days later, when he obtained the necessary responsorship from a Democrat.

At some point, the replacements were coming so fast that Burns went to Elrod and said it was disrupting the work of the office. Elrod said he was under pressure from "the man on the fifth floor" to move fast to provide jobs for "our people." In Chicago political parlance, everyone knew "the man on the fifth floor" was Mayor Richard J. Daley, whose office was on the fifth floor of City Hall. Shortly thereafter, with most of the process servers replaced by Democrats, Burns himself was fired and replaced by the secretary of one of the Democratic ward organizations.

With these facts in hand, I prepared a complaint naming Elrod,

Daley, and the Cook County Democratic Organization (of which Daley was chairman) as defendants and charging them with conspiring to violate the plaintiffs' First Amendment rights. Since the replacement process was continuing and several employees still on the payroll (including Buckley) had been threatened with discharge unless they agreed to switch parties, I also prepared a motion for preliminary injunction asking the Court to enjoin further patronage firings pending final determination of the case. The complaint was verified (sworn to) by Burns, Vargas, and Buckley.

When all the pleadings were ready, I turned them over to my docket clerk for filing with the U.S. District Court. That afternoon stamped copies of the pleadings were returned to me in the interoffice mail. The name of the judge to whom the case was randomly assigned was stamped on the face of the complaint. It was Julius Hoffman. To add to the irony, when an appearance was filed for the defendants a few days later, the lawyer who appeared for Mayor Daley and the Cook County Democratic Organization was Tom Foran. No one was much surprised when Judge Hoffman denied my motion for preliminary injunction. I promptly filed a notice of appeal.

The defendants next filed a motion to dismiss the complaint for failure to state a cause of action. Before Judge Hoffman could rule on it, the case was reassigned by lottery to fill the docket of a newly appointed district-court judge. The transfer of *Burns v. Elrod* to a new judge marked the end of the remarkable string of interesting cases that brought me to the courtroom of Judge Julius Hoffman.

Given the unusual personal antipathy between Julius Hoffman and me, it seems appropriate to say a few words about the relationship between trial lawyers and judges. Obviously, it is better for a lawyer never to have the kind of adversarial relationship with a judge that I had with Julius Hoffman, and I never had such a conflict with any other judge. Even so, there is a tension between the role of lawyer and judge which courtroom lawyers cannot ignore.

There are smart judges and judges who are not so smart, decisive judges and some who are painfully indecisive, honest judges and a few who are dishonest, and judges with all levels of that elusive but essential characteristic called "judicial temperament." Wherever they land on those scales, the majority of judges try hard to decide cases fairly and in accordance with the law as they understand it. Those who are as temperamentally unsuited for the job as Julius Hoffman are few and far between. Moreover, as every lawyer knows, judges have enormous influence with jurors and large areas of discretion in their rulings. They are human beings in robes, and hard as they may try to avoid it, if they dislike or distrust a lawyer, it is likely to have an effect on their rulings. Good lawyers go out of their way to learn the idiosyncrasies of the judges they appear before and to adjust their conduct to avoid unnecessary conflict.

However, the word "unnecessary" is essential. Even the best judge, being human, has biases that may affect his or her rulings, and sometimes a lawyer has no alternative but to confront a judge to protect a client. Few other judges—none I have encountered—would employ the combination of one-sided rulings, ridicule in the presence of the jury, and constant threats of contempt that Judge Hoffman heaped on the defense lawyers in the Chicago conspiracy case (and other lawyers in less-famous cases), but less-blatant examples of these problems are not uncommon in the life of a trial lawyer, and the lawyer must be prepared to deal with them, sometimes risking a threat of contempt. A judge who falls into a pattern of one-sided rulings and displays of bias often does so without realizing it. A few may act more deliberately to steer the jury in the "right" direction—but in either event, the lawyer's best remedy is to ask the judge for a conference in chambers, and there present him with an earnest and well-supported complaint that "undoubtedly inadvertently" he has been one-sided in his rulings or comments. Assuming that the record supports the assertion, most judges will recognize, if not admit, the validity of the complaint and attempt to mend their conduct. If not, the lawyer has no choice but to continue to object where appropriate, and look for opportunities to alert the jury to the unfairness when it occurs.

It is in the process of alerting the jury that the lawyer is most likely to tread close to or over the line of contempt. When defense counsel in the conspiracy case violated Judge Hoffman's express order not to tell the jury about his exclusion of former United States Attorney General Ramsey Clark as a defense witness or his refusal to grant a short delay so counsel could call the Reverend Ralph Abernathy as their last witness, they were clearly in contempt of court. Judge Gignoux so found when he retried some of the contempt citations after the Court of Appeals reversal. Nevertheless, given the outrageousness of Hoffman's action and all that had gone before, in my judgment, the lawyers were right to violate the court order and make a last-ditch effort to alert the jury to the unfairness of the trial. If Judge Gignoux had no choice but to find them guilty of contempt, he also had the common sense to assess no jail time or other serious punishment for the transgressions.

The new judge to whom the *Elrod* case was assigned was William J. Bauer, a former Republican states attorney and state court judge from one of Chicago's western suburbs. Bauer was a man of impeccable integrity who became a fine judge of the district court and later the Court of Appeals, but his political background in a Republican organization that controlled DuPage County and its patronage in a manner barely distinguishable from the Democrats' control of Chicago was not likely to make him much disposed to preside over the destruction of patronage politics.

While the case law prohibiting the discharge of teachers and other government workers for expressing unpopular political views was solid, the defense had some attractive arguments for applying a different rule to cases involving the traditional patronage system, not the least of which was the fact that my clients had obtained their own jobs through political sponsorship, often in the wake of firing a predecessor of a different party. Several cases had adopted the proposition that the Constitution is not offended when one who has lived by the sword of patronage dies by it. After considering the case for several months, Judge Bauer dismissed the complaint. My appeal from that ruling was consolidated with the earlier appeal from the denial of a preliminary injunction for consideration in the Seventh Circuit Court of Appeals.

It was October 1973 before my appeal in *Burns v. Elrod* was finally called for argument. In the meantime, a panel of the Seventh Circuit had decided *Illinois State Employees Union v. Lewis,* a case involving legal issues substantially identical to those in *Burns.* Judge John Paul Stevens, who would later ascend to the Supreme Court, wrote the majority opinion in *Lewis,* holding that it was indeed a violation of the First Amendment for an elected official to discharge non-policy-making employees solely because of their affiliation with a different political party. It was precisely the argument I was making, and despite Tom Foran's effort to distinguish it, if the *Lewis* decision was followed, I was almost certain to win my appeal. Knowing this, and encouraged by the fact that Judge Roger Kiley had written a strong dissent in *Lewis,* and Judge William Campbell, while concurring in the result, had written a separate opinion saying the holding should be construed narrowly and applied sparingly, Foran also argued that *Lewis* was decided wrongly and should not be followed.

It was not until the morning we argued the case that I learned that both Judge Kiley and Judge Campbell were on the three-judge panel which would hear the *Burns* case, while Judge Stevens was not. Although neither of us could be sure what Judge Campbell would do, his long connection to the Daley organization and reluctant vote in *Lewis* were worrisome. Overall, Tom Foran must have been as pleased with the composition of the panel as I was concerned. The third member of the panel was Senior District Judge Robert Grant from Indiana, who was completely unknown to me.

To some degree, the argument eased my concerns. From his questions, it did not appear that Judge Grant was buying any of Foran's arguments, and although he asked only a few questions, Judge Campbell also seemed unimpressed with the proposition that the case could be distinguished from *Lewis* on its facts. Judge Kiley was the most active questioner, and I was not surprised when he belabored me with hostile questions about why people who obtained their jobs through patronage should be heard to complain about losing them for the same reason. I was surprised, however, at the vehemence of his reaction to the conclusion of my argument. The citizens who elect public officials, I claimed, are entitled to expect their tax dollars to be used for the public purposes of the office and the benefit of all the people, not as a political slush fund to coerce employees to support the incumbent party. Visibly angered, Kiley snorted and leaned over the bench. "Mr. Tucker," he said, "that's ridiculous. They do no such thing." With that he banged his gavel and announced the case was submitted. I was sorry I had closed with such a contentious and perhaps overdramatic assertion. I never expected to get Kiley's vote, but I was afraid I had goaded him into trying even harder to persuade one of the other judges to join him. In any event, there was nothing I could do to retract my words. I could only wait for the decision.

Meanwhile, perhaps as a result of my work on the contempt issues in the conspiracy case, I was hired in another "political" case which had the added attraction of clients who could pay legal fees—not enough to impress my senior partners, but perhaps enough to give them hope that I might someday bring in more revenue than I was taking out in compensation.

My new clients were sometimes referred to collectively as the "Chicago 59" and, like the "Conspiracy 8" they were accused of contempt of court. Their troubles also arose from their conduct at a Democratic national convention—this time the one held in Miami in 1972. Unlike the Conspiracy defendants, however, my clients lived in Chicago and included some of the city's most prominent citizens.

Following the debacle of the 1968 convention, the Democratic Party was largely taken over by its more liberal wing, especially people who supported one or more of the great liberal issues of the time—promoting civil rights for blacks and other minorities, fostering women's rights, protecting the environment, and ending the war in Vietnam. In the period between presidential election years the party had formed a commission, headed by South Dakota Senator George McGovern, which adopted rules requiring proportional representation of women and minorities in the makeup of convention delegations. Mayor Daley, however, had no intention of changing the way the Illinois delegation was selected. He would lead the delegation, he would decide who was in it, and the machine would see to it that his decision was carried out. It would certainly not include any of the people who opposed him during the disastrous 1968 Democratic convention and its aftermath.

Bill Singer was the best known and most successful of Mayor Daley's "independent" Democratic opponents, having defeated the machine candidate for alderman in his ward a few years earlier. Singer's followers and other independent Democrats were clustered in the wealthy residential areas along Lake Michigan and in the Hyde Park neighborhood near the University of Chicago. When it became clear that Daley intended to ignore the McGovern rules, Singer and his allies decided to select their own slate of delegates, holding "elections" in people's homes around the city and following the McGovern proportionality rules. In the black wards on the south and west sides a group led by Reverend Jesse Jackson was also organizing to resist the plantation politics of the Daley organization, and the Singer and Jackson groups joined forces. Fifty-nine men and women "ran" and were "elected" to the Singer-Jackson slate, and declared they would present their credentials to the Democratic Party at the convention and seek recognition in place of the "regular" slate led by Daley.

As the convention approached and it became clear that the forces supporting George McGovern controlled it and intended to seat the Singer-Jackson delegates, Daley, who had already called in every chit he had with national party leaders, moved at the last minute to a safer venue—the Circuit Court of Cook County. Led by alderman Paul Wigoda, the delegates chosen in the regular, machine-dominated election filed suit asking the court to enjoin the Singer-Jackson delegates from seeking to participate in the convention. The day before the Chicago 59 were to leave Chicago for Miami, Judge Daniel Covelli issued the requested injunction. Process servers (many of whom had been hired by Sheriff Elrod to replace my clients in the patronage case) scurried across the city attempting to serve notice of the injunction on the Chicago 59.

Declaring the injunction invalid and unconstitutional, the Singer-Jackson delegates went to Miami anyway. In a dramatic vote, the convention rejected a last-ditch effort to seat the Wigoda delegation and went on to nominate McGovern for president. It was the most humiliating political defeat of Daley's career.

Meanwhile, the Singer-Jackson group had appealed the issuance of the injunction, but in 1973, the Illinois Appellate Court affirmed Judge Covelli's order and the Illlinois Supreme Court declined to review that decision. The presidential elections were long over, Judge Covelli, much criticized at the time he granted the injunction, had been affirmed by the appellate courts, and most people thought the case would simply fade away. However, Covelli was not about to forget that his order had been violated—at least unless Daley told him to. Apparently Daley didn't, because the judge soon issued a rule to show cause why the delegates should not be held in contempt of court. The delegates had petitioned the United States Supreme Court to review the injunction case, but the pendency of their petition was no bar to Covelli's effort to punish the defendants for violating the injunction. When the delegates realized that they faced fines and possible imprisonment for contempt, they hired me to defend them.

In the end, the Supreme Court reversed the injunction, holding that political parties have a right to make their own rules and decide for themselves whom to seat as delegates to their convention, and that Judge Covelli therefore had no authority to issue his injunction. While the ruling arguably would not prevent the judge from punishing my clients for contempt (some courts have held it is contempt to violate an injunction even though the injunction is later held invalid), Judge Covelli apparently concluded he would look foolish (and might well be reversed) if he did so. By mutual agreement, the rule to show cause was quietly dropped.

In the meantime, while the case was pending in the Supreme Court, I filed and argued a motion challenging Judge Covellli's right to proceed on the contempt charges. When the motion came up for argument, a lawyer who happened to be in the courtroom on another matter observed the hearing and was apparently impressed with my persistence in presenting my legal arguments despite the judge's repeated efforts to cut me off and prevent me from doing so. As a result, he soon became my client and close friend.

The lawyer was Abner Mikva, an independent Democrat who had served two terms in Congress representing the Hyde Park area until Daley gerrymandered him out of the seat in the reapportionment following the 1970 census. Mikva then moved to Evanston, where I lived, and in 1972 ran for the north suburban seat which was vacated by Donald Rumsfeld when he joined the Nixon administration. The seat had been held by a Republican since the Civil War, but the district had gradually become a little more liberal, and Mikva was an extraordinarily attractive and vigorous candidate. He lost—but by a surprisingly close margin given the 1972 Nixon landslide.

I had met Mikva through friends and neighbors and had done some precinct work and served as an "election day lawyer" during the 1972 campaign. Some time after my appearance before Judge Covelli, Mikva called and said he had decided to run for Congress again in 1974 and wanted me to be his lawyer during the campaign and run the election-day lawyers' effort, which involved recruiting and directing the work of several dozen lawyers who would "troubleshoot" on election day. My contacts with Mikva had persuaded me he was an exceptional public servant and one of the smartest people I ever met, so I readily agreed. I'm sure he had no more idea than I did of how much time I would be spending on the "Mikva file" that fall, and for several years thereafter.

The 1974 election in the Tenth Illinois Congressional District was one of the most expensive congressional elections held up to that time. In addition to the large amount of money raised by both candidates, Sam Young, the Republican who had won in 1972, had the advantages of incumbency and the long-dominant Republican precinct organizations in the north lakefront suburbs. Mikva, on the other hand, had the endorsement of several important environmental and "good government" groups, was a far better campaigner than Young, and countered the Republican organizational strength with a sophisticated and dedicated precinct organization of his own that outstripped the Republicans in identifying favorable voters and "running the pluses"—getting those voters to the polls on election day.

For all that, the campaign proceeded in a normal fashion until the week before election day, when Young, who was losing normally Republican voters to Mikva's government-reform proposals in the wake of the Watergate scandal, sought to muddy the water by filing a claim with the Fair Campaign Practices Commission, a voluntary organization promoting clean elections. Young alleged that Mikva had falsely claimed endorsement by certain organizations that did not formally endorse, but had issued statements supporting Mikva's election. The complaint also alleged that Mikva had misrepresented Young's positions and voting record. In our opinion, Young's claims were either false or frivolous, and one possibility was to refute the charges in public and refuse to participate in any commission proceedings so close to the election. The commission had no real power, but refusing to participate would allow Young to claim Mikva was afraid to have the issues examined by an impartial arbiter, and the commission itself might issue a statement about Mikva's refusal to participate which could have an impact on an election everyone believed was extremely close.

Weighing the options, we decided to fight back with a counterclaim: Young—not Mikva—had lied to the public and violated the Fair Campaign Practices Act. The result was a hearing before a panel of arbitrators which began midmorning on Saturday November 2, three days before the election, and continued nonstop through the day and night until after 9:00 A.M. Sunday morning, when both sides realized there was a bitter political fight on the el that would result in nasty charges against both candidates. By agreement, the arbitration was ended without a decision. Both Young and Mikva had spent significant parts of the night at the hearing and had to resume last-minute campaigning all day and into the evening on Sunday. I went home and went to bed.

When it was over, Abner swore he would never again agree to submit an election dispute to arbitration. Quite apart from having to stay up all night, he was right, and both of us should have realized it before agreeing to participate. When it comes to a question of which political candidate is going to prevail in a dispute that could affect an election, it is difficult to find anyone qualified to sit on an arbitration panel who doesn't have a political bias, and since there is no binding precedent to determine what is or isn't a violation of the Fair Campaign Practices Act, the arbitrators have free rein to make any decision they want. Arbitration is often a quicker, less expensive, and perfectly satisfactory substitute for litigation in resolving disputes, but only where most people are unlikely to have a preconceived position on the subject and both sides have adequate time and resources to investigate the prospective arbitrators for undisclosed bias.

On election day, Abner Mikva became the first Democrat elected from Chicago's northern suburbs. His margin of victory was 2,860 out of 164,054 votes cast—less than 2 percent. Although the victory was a little larger than we expected, Sam Young refused to concede and vowed to contest the election (and turn what had started out for me as political volunteer work into some fairly major litigation). Under Illinois law, our victory was within the margin entitling Young to demand a discovery recount of 25 percent of the precincts in the district. The election, except for those who voted absentee, was conducted on voting machines—the kind where the voter enters a metal booth, pulls a large lever to close a curtain, and then votes by pulling down small levers next to the names of the candidates. The number of votes for each candidate are registered mechanically on a counter which is read by the judges after the polls close by opening the back of the machine. The numbers are read aloud and recorded on a poll sheet. In the absence of fraud (moving the counters to record extra votes before or after the polls are open, with the necessary consent of the judges from both parties), the system is essentially foolproof. An error may be made in recording the numbers on the poll sheets, but since the machines are secured and all the numbers checked again in a postelection "canvass" before the winner is certified, any such error is almost certain to be caught. The absentee votes, however, were recorded on paper ballots which were counted by hand—a process considerably more likely to result in mistakes.

Mikva had conducted a vigorous campaign for votes from the large number of young people in the district who were away at college, and had won the absentee votes by a margin of nearly 2-to-1, so Young selected those precincts with the largest number of absentee votes as the ones to be examined in his discovery recount. Only a handful of counting errors were found, but in several precincts the judges had failed to initial absentee ballots when they were counted, as provided by statute. An earlier Illinois Supreme Court decision held that the failure to initial absentee ballots did not invalidate the votes, and the uninitialed ballots—even if thrown out—would have reduced Mikva's margin by only 350 votes. Nevertheless, Young hailed his discovery as evidence a full recount would turn the election in his favor. On that basis he filed an election contest in the U.S. House of Representatives.

Under the Federal Contested Election Act, Young's contest would be heard and determined by the House Administration Committee. Young's complaint seemed frivolous on its face, and with the House firmly in Democratic hands, it appeared unlikely that the election contest posed any real threat to Mikva's keeping his seat. On the other hand, Young's pre-election unfair-campaign claims had also seemed frivolous, and he had almost won them. In addition, there was the question of how Democrats who were loyal to the Daley machine would act in respect to an "independent Democrat" some viewed as worse than a Republican. That aspect of the situation was exacerbated by the fact that Mikva had obtained a seat on the House Ways and Means Committee, the most sought-after assignment in Congress, over the objection of the powerful committee chairman and Daley ally Dan Rostenkowski. Under all the circumstances Abner and I agreed the contest had to be taken seriously, a decision eased by the fact that under the statute my fees and expenses for defending him would be paid by Congress.

In the end, the contest was no contest. After researching the few cases decided since the statute was enacted in 1969 as well as those under prior law, I filed a motion to dismiss the contest for failure to state facts that would change the result of the election. The issues were briefed, a hearing was held before the House Administration Committee's subcommittee on elections in April of 1975, and in December the committee issued a report dismissing the contest by a vote of 18-to-0.

No one had any illusions that Mikva's re-election in 1976 would be easy, but we did think it would be easier than the race two years before. Abner now had the fund-raising and name-recognition advantages of incumbency, the sophisticated electorate of Chicago's North Shore understood and appreciated the power of his position on Ways and Means, and he had put in place constituent service offices surpassing anything his district had seen before. True, the Watergate backlash had faded, and a presidential year was likely to bring out more voters in what was still a Republican district; but Jimmy Carter was running better than Democrats in recent presidential elections, and Mikva's precinct organization was even stronger than it was in 1974. Election day went smoothly, and after waiting at headquarters for an hour or so after the polls closed to make sure no problems arose from the use of a new punch-card voting system, I headed for the victory party expecting that Abner would be re-elected and that this year Sam Young might even concede before the night was over.

I had just arrived at the banquet hall where the victory party was in progress when Ab's campaign manager, Jack Marco, came to a microphone on the stage where he had been announcing and posting vote totals as they came in from the precincts and said, "John Tucker, if you've arrived yet, please come see me." When I got to an office near the stage where the campaign staff was receiving and analyzing vote totals, Jack explained there appeared to be a huge problem with absentee ballots. The law required mailed ballots to be received in the county clerk's office in time to be delivered to the voter's home precinct before the polls closed on election day. The procedure followed by the clerk was for ballots received by the day before the election to be included in the materials delivered to the judges in each precinct on election morning. Ballots received on election day were sorted and delivered to the precincts by contract messengers before the polls closed. Since a significant part of Abner's victory margin had come from absentee ballots in 1974, the campaign had redoubled its effort to enlist absentee voters in 1976. Reports were now coming in from the precincts that instead of record numbers of absentee ballots, very few had been received in the election-morning packets, and no delivery had been received during the day. Some precinct workers were reporting that ballots they knew had been mailed by family members weeks earlier, or even delivered directly to the clerk's office by the voter, were not in the packets delivered to the precinct. The worst news was it looked like the absentee-ballot problem could affect the outcome. A quick analysis of vote totals from key precincts suggested that the election was too close to call.

The first thing I did was to call Stanley Kusper, the County Clerk of Cook County, whose office was responsible for the conduct of elections. Kusper was a "regular" Daley Democrat, but since his office was elected countywide, he needed to keep on the good side of suburban independents as well. He had been cooperative whenever I dealt with him on election matters. Kusper had already left for the regular organization's election-night party in Chicago, but his deputy in charge of elections was still in the office. When I explained the problem, he said everything had been delivered as usual—the voters we were counting on probably just didn't vote. When I said I already had affidavits from dozens of people who swore they had voted and mailed in their ballots over a week ago (I didn't, but I knew I could get them), he said the post office must have screwed up. When I said I also had affidavits from people who voted in person at the clerk's office several days before the election, he said he would check into it and call me in the morning. That meant he would ask Kusper what to do.

There wasn't much more I could do that night other than make sure our precinct workers kept their election-day records, especially the lists of expected "plus" voters, which should show the names of people who had said they planned to file absentee ballots. Later we could check those lists against the list of persons whose absentee ballots were counted in the precincts.

As the night wore on, the vote totals announced to the crowd and posted on a giant chart on the stage continued to show Abner with a slim but steady margin, but those of us in the back room knew we had kept back some Young precincts which, when added to the totals, suggested the race was dead even. Abner arrived at the party and made the traditional "thank you—things look good but it's too early to claim victory—I'll be back" speech and joined us in the back room. Problems with new voting-machine procedures slowed the returns in a few precincts, and there were a few discrepancies between the numbers we received from precinct workers and those being reported by the media, but by a little past midnight, with the crowd beginning to thin out, television stations were reporting Young ahead by a couple of hundred votes with all precincts counted, and our reports showed the same result.

Abner went back out on the stage and said it was so close there wouldn't be a winner declared that night, and everyone should go home. He also mentioned that a large number of absentee ballots had not yet been counted for some reason, and urged everyone who voted absentee or who knew someone who had done so to call their precinct workers in the morning and give them that information. Most of the people left in the room were pretty sophisticated about elections and knew the speech meant Abner thought he was behind.

In fact, when Kusper's office announced their unofficial totals the next morning (unofficial until the canvass was held the following week), Sam Young had a lead of 250 votes out of some 200,000 cast. About midmorning, I finally reached Stanley Kusper. He wasn't sure what happened, but he did know some five thousand or more absentee ballots for precincts in the Tenth Congressional District had arrived on or before election day, but for some reason had not been delivered to the precincts. He thought it was the fault of a contract carrier who was supposed to make the deliveries. I said he should immediately set up a process to have them counted in the presence of representatives of both parties and any individual candidates who wanted to attend, and that I would attend for Mikva. Kusper said what I already knew: There was no provision in the election code for counting absentee ballots except in the precincts on election day. He would like to count the ballots, but was still trying to decide if he could do so legally. Meanwhile, he would preserve the ballots and maintain their integrity.

There was no doubt that if 5,000 absentee ballots were counted, Mikva would win. Even a 60-40 split would give Abner a victory, and in 1974 the absentees had split nearly 70-30 in our favor. The problem was to get them counted—and have the count sustained against Young's inevitable challenge.

The next day Kusper reported that on advice of counsel, he had decided he could not count the ballots unless a court authorized it. Anticipating that result, I had already begun drafting a petition for a writ of mandamus, asking a court to order the county clerk to count the ballots and include the results in his certification of the election results following the official canvass. Mikva agreed with my suggestion that we should hire another attorney to join in the case. Jerry Torshen was a good lawyer who had supported Mikva in the election, but he was also active with the regular Democratic organization. His representation of Mikva should signal to any judge that the Daley machine was supportive—or at least neutral—on the question of counting the absentee ballots.

Jerry also knew Stanley Kusper personally. We agreed he should talk to Kusper and urge him to go ahead and count the ballots, but also tell him if he felt he needed a court order, we would file the mandamus case and hope he would not resist it, although Young would undoubtedly intervene and object. When Jerry came back from the meeting, he said Kusper had told him the mayor himself had asked Kusper not to count the ballots and Kusper had promised he wouldn't unless ordered by a court. It wasn't a matter of wanting to defeat Mikva; the mayor didn't care about that one way or the other. The problem was Joe Power, one of Daley's former law partners who was Chief Judge of the Criminal Court.

Power's term was ending and he was up for "retention"—a process whereby sitting judges submitted to a yes or no vote of the electorate to obtain another term in office. There was no opponent, and if a simple majority of those voting said yes, the judge received another term. If not, he was out of office. The retention system had been adopted as a compromise between those who wanted to retain the system of contested elections at the end of each term and those who wanted state judges to be appointed for life like federal judges, thus freeing them from political influence and public pressure. At first it was unheard of for a judge backed by the Daley organization to fail retention, but by 1976 the Chicago Council of Lawyers had achieved a reputation for careful and impartial investigation of the qualifications of judicial candidates and sitting judges. Largely because of his reputation for slavish devotion to the interests of the regular Democratic organization, the press had joined the council in an intensive campaign to persuade voters to vote no on retention of Judge Joe Power. Now, it turned out, Power's fate placed him in the same boat as Sam Young. The vote on his retention was close, but he was losing badly in the Tenth Congressional District. There was a chance Daley could pull out a slim victory for his friend if no more ballots were counted in the Tenth, but if the absentee ballots were counted, Power was doomed. According to what Torshen reported, that was why Daley had intervened.

According to Torshen, Kusper wanted to count the ballots, but he did not want to defy Daley. On the other hand, he wasn't happy about the idea of our filing a mandamus action that would allege Kusper had a legal duty to count the ballots which he had failed to satisfy. The only alternative Jerry and I could think of was to persuade Kusper he should file an "interpleader" case—a procedure usually employed by someone holding money or property that is claimed by more than one person. Rather than take the risk of resolving the rival claims, the holder files a lawsuit naming the claimants as defendants, explaining the facts, and asking the court to decide who is entitled to the disputed property. Here, we reasoned, Kusper could name Mikva and Young as defendants, recite the facts of his possession of the absentee ballots and the competing demands that he count or not count them, and ask a court to tell him what to do.

Somewhat to our surprise Kusper liked the idea: It got him off the hook with the press and suburban Democrats while passing the buck to the judiciary. Let some judge take the heat, from whatever source. He would run it by his lawyer and do it unless there was a strong reason not to. If Daley complained, he could explain we were going to file a mandamus with the same result, and this way at least it would look like he was trying to do the right thing.

A few hours later, Kusper reported back. He would do it, but his lawyer, whose full-time practice was election law, had never prepared an interpleader complaint. Would Jerry do it? The answer was yes, of course, and Torshen headed to Kusper's office where he could obtain details about the receipt and preservation of the ballots to insert in the complaint.

Working in an office next to Kusper's, Jerry began preparing a complaint, stopping from time to time to get factual information from Kusper or his deputy. Kusper had informed the press he was planning to go to court the next day to resolve the controversy, and a news-radio station had been reporting the announcement for an hour or so when Sam Young's lawyer showed up uninvited to try to dissuade Kusper from filing the case. The lawyer spotted

Kusper in his office so Kusper had no choice but to greet him and invite him in, loudly proclaiming: "So Sam Young's lawyer wants to talk to me. Well, come on in, Sam Young's lawyer, and I'll listen, but I doubt I'll change my mind."

The lawyer was going to walk right past the office where Torshen was preparing the complaint. The office door was open. Hearing Kusper and realizing what was happening, Jerry slid out of his chair and under the desk. There he finished writing the complaint on a yellow pad while in the next room Young's lawyer spent nearly an hour trying to persuade Kusper not to file it.

Stanley Kusper, County Clerk of Cook County v. Abner J. Mikva and Samuel H. Young was filed Friday, November 5. We were delighted when it was assigned to Judge Joseph Schneider, who had a reputation of independence from the mayor.

Because it is much harder to change the results of an election once the vote totals have been certified—as observers of the 2000 presidential vote count in Florida know—time was of the essence. By Monday morning we had already prepared our answer, a counterpetition asking that all the votes be counted, and a memorandum in support of our petition. We asked the judge to hold arguments and decide the matter as quickly as possible. Over Young's objection, he set a hearing only two days later to hear oral argument and decide the case in time for either side to take an emergency appeal before the official canvass and certification. We thought it was an easy call: The ballots had been cast properly, their integrity had been maintained, and all the precedents stressed the importance of not disenfranchising legitimate voters. I argued the case Wednesday morning, and the judge said he would announce a decision that afternoon. When he did, he said he personally thought the ballots should be counted, but he had to dismiss the case because he lacked jurisdiction to decide it. It was a decision that made no logical sense, and was a terrible blow—worse, in a way, than if he had decided against us on the merits. If we were very lucky, we could get the appellate court to consider it and reverse before the canvass and certification, but all they were likely to do was send it back to the county court for consideration on the merits, and the chance of getting that done in time was remote.

Rather than trying to appeal, I decided our best chance was to go back to the idea of a mandamus action against Kusper. We prepared a complaint and gathered evidence to prove that specific legitimate voters had been disenfranchised. By late Thursday afternoon, we were nearly done with everything we needed when I received a phone call from Jack Marco. In preparing materials for the official canvass someone in Kusper's office had discovered a mistake. In transposing vote totals from tapes produced by the voting machines to the tally sheets used to determine the unofficial returns, the judges in one precinct had recorded Young's votes for Mikva and vice versa. Correcting the mistake created a swing of nearly 500 votes—in Mikva's favor. It now appeared that Mikva was ahead, though only by about 200 votes.

Abner wanted to think about whether to go ahead with the mandamus case. We held off filing on Friday and met on Saturday. By then some of Ab's staff and I were leaning against filing. A victory was a victory, pursuing the case would be expensive, and besides, who could say for sure that counting the ballots would increase our margin? What if we fought to get them counted and they produced a victory for Young! Abner was adamant. The people had voted, their votes should be counted, however they came out. Besides, it was impossible to believe they would go the wrong way—the absentee votes that had already been counted favored us by a large margin.

We filed on Monday. The case was assigned to Judge Arthur "Moose" Dunne, who set the case for evidentiary hearing the next day. The final canvass was going on at the same time, and certification of the election was scheduled for a week later. There were two issues to be decided. One was the factual question of whether the integrity of the ballots had been preserved adequately. The other was the legal question of whether, assuming they had been, they could now be counted legally, despite the statutory provision for counting them in the precincts on election day. The judge took the legal question under advisement while we presented evidence on the factual issues. As the evidence came in, it was clear that the absentee ballots had been assembled in the clerk's office on the day after the election and sent to the same secure warehouse where the other election materials were preserved awaiting the canvass. There was no real basis for doubting their integrity, but arguably a few ballots that were received too late could have gotten mixed in with those received on time, and there were enough questions about the chain of custody that a judge determined to reject the ballots could have articulated a reason for doing so. As Judge Dunne listened to the testimony, a few of his comments and questions caused me some concern that he might be leaning in that direction.

Late in the afternoon on the second day of testimony, the judge's secretary appeared through the door from his chambers and handed him a note. The judge read it and then looked up. "Gentlemen," he said, "I have some information that will be of interest. The canvass of votes in the Tenth Congressional District had been completed. Congressman Mikva has been declared the winner by 201 votes."

As I was packing up my materials in the witness room at the end of the day, Judge Dunne stuck his head into the room to say good night. As he left, he made some further comments suggesting a question about the integrity of the ballots, and the fact that with the election this close it would undoubtedly end up in the Congress again, where they might have to decide whether they should be counted.

Whatever the judge said or intended, as I considered the situation, I had no doubt what I should do. It was still possible we would need those votes, and the House was much more likely to order them counted if there was no court ruling that their integrity had been compromised. There was no reason to risk it.

When I got back to the office, I called Abner. I told him about the judge's comments and that I was going to call Young's lawyer and see if he would agree to an order dismissing the case voluntarily. When he resisted, I said, "Abner, we're like Napoleon invading Russia. I think winter may be coming, and it's time to get our asses out of here." Abner finally agreed. Young's lawyer also agreed, and the next day it was done.

As expected, Sam Young filed another election contest in the House of Representatives, but this time he also filed one in the Circuit Court of Cook County and asked the court to order a recount. When the court dismissed his petition on the ground that exclusive jurisdiction to determine election contests for Congress rests with Congress itself, Young appealed to the Illinois Supreme Court. I argued the case in March, and the Court unanimously affirmed the trial court's decision. Shortly thereafter, the House of Representatives dismissed Young's election contest, leaving Abner with an official victory margin of 201 votes. From then on his friends on both sides of the aisle referred to him as "Landslide Ab."

Abner took the "landside" joke in good humor, but the message of such a narrow victory against a weak opponent in a presidential year when the shadow of Watergate was still hurting the Republicans was not funny. At best, it meant he would have to spend much of his time raising money and campaigning for each new election. When the 1978 elections came around, the Republicans nominated a popular state representative from Evanston to challenge Mikva. John Porter was nowhere near the experienced, superintelligent legislator Mikva was, but he was a pleasant, hardworking man who was difficult to dislike, and his moderate Republicanism fit the district's political profile better than Abner's active liberalism. This time all the votes were counted, and with the help of his incumbency, his tremendous constituent services, and campaign appearances by key Democratic leaders including Ted Kennedy and President Carter himself, Mikva squeezed out another narrow victory. That he could barely win with all those advantages, however, made the precariousness of his situation undeniable, and when the president offered to nominate him to a seat on the United States Court of Appeals for the

District of Columbia Circuit, Abner said yes. In a special election to fill his unexpired term, John Porter recaptured the Tenth Congressional District seat for the Republicans and retained it until he retired in 2000.

My representation of Abner Mikva resulted in both a treasured friendship and the satisfaction of playing a small part in the career of a great public servant. And Mikva's entrusting me with his representation clearly played a role in bringing me additional clients who knew Mikva and respected his judgment. That it all started because Mikva happened to be in the same courtroom when I was arguing the "Chicago 59" case is a reminder that you never know who is watching—so you had better always do your best, even when you know the judge is going to rule against you.

While Abner Mikva was making political history in the Tenth Congressional District, the Seventh Circuit Court of Appeals was taking an unusually long time deciding the patronage case, *Burns v. Elrod.* Following the argument in October 1973, months went by with no word from the Court. It was obvious there was a split on the panel and a continuing argument over the crucial second vote. Then, in September 1974, Judge Kiley died. My hope had been the delay was because he was writing a dissent, but when several more months passed without a decision, I began to wonder if the remaining two judges were in disagreement. If so, it was likely the case would have to be reargued with a new third judge. Finally, on January 30, 1975, the opinion was released. Written by Judge Campbell, it was a complete victory. Adopting the reasoning of the earlier decision in the *Lewis* case, the Court reversed the dismissal of my complaint and ordered the district court to issue the preliminary injunction I had requested to stop further patronage discharges. (Since Elrod had now been in office for five years, there were no Republicans left to fire, but the injunction did give protection to employees who had been coerced into changing party affiliation and might want to switch back.)

With the Court of Appeals decision in my favor, I anticipated Elrod and the Democratic organization would negotiate to settle the case. The basis for a settlement was obvious and not terribly expensive. The people who were fired would have to be offered their jobs back, but by this time most had gone on to other careers and would have no interest in returning to the sheriff's office. They would also be entitled to back pay, but on a settlement basis, the case was likely to cost less than $1 million, including my fees. Moreover, to almost everyone's surprise, the Democratic organization had been negotiating for a consent degree in the *Shakman* case that would end traditional patronage practices in the future. The Shakman negotiations suggested that Daley was reconciled to the end of patronage in public employment—at least, in its most extreme form.

But I was wrong. Shortly after the Seventh Circuit decision was rendered, Elrod petitioned the Court of Appeals to rehear the case en banc (that is, to have all of the active Seventh Circuit judges reconsider the case). When the court turned down that request in April, Tom Foran applied for certiorari to the Supreme Court, and in October 1975, "cert." was granted. Now the question of whether the age-old tradition of patronage politics violated the First Amendment would be decided for the entire country, not just the three states of the Seventh Circuit—and I would have an opportunity to argue again in the Supreme Court. As was the case when the Supreme Court granted cert. in *Pate v. Robinson*, my effort to persuade the Court not to take the case had failed, but it was hard to feel too bad about it.

I had briefed the case thoroughly when it was heard in the Court of Appeals, and to the extent pertinent cases had been decided in the months since then, they had been found for the briefs supporting and opposing certiorari, so the bulk of the research was done and the basic arguments had long since been framed. Nevertheless there was much work to be done; a brief in the Supreme Court is different from anything else a lawyer ever does. No matter the time and expense, and despite the fact the lawyers have already combed the books and searched their minds for the relevant cases and arguments, you must consider the case all over again, as if starting from scratch. If possible, it is wise to bring in new lawyers whose minds are not clouded by having developed the arguments presented in earlier briefs. In the end, the cases cited and arguments presented are not likely to change dramatically; but if there is some new line of authority or reasoning to make an argument stronger, it is more likely to emerge from a fresh mind than one who starts out believing he has already found everything there is to find and said everything there is to say.

In addition to the advantages of a fresh mind, I had another reason to enlist new blood for the case. I was engaged in intensive final preparation for an important trial scheduled to begin in mid-November and last for several months, well into the time when my Supreme Court brief would be due. I would need the best possible help to do the new research and write a good draft of our brief so it could be filed in December or January.

A recently hired associate who had graduated with an outstanding record from a top law school was assigned to do the new research and write a first draft, and an older associate who had already proved himself an excellent brief writer would supervise and revise her work. I would have to be content to watch over the project while on trial, reading the drafts on weekends when possible. In this way an excellent brief was produced, primarily due to exceptional work by the older associate, Doug MacDonald. However, the case I was trying was taking much longer then expected. Christmas and New Year's came and went with the end nowhere in sight. Sometime early in the year, I was informed of an argument date in the Supreme Court that was sure to arrive before my trial was over. I succeeded in getting the argument postponed until April 19, close to the end of the time when the Court traditionally hears arguments. Still my trial dragged on, and I began to fear it would last beyond April 19. The trial judge agreed he would, if necessary, adjourn the trial for two days so I could go to

Washington and argue. When I could prepare for the argument was my problem.

My trial finally went to the jury on Tuesday April 13. While the jury deliberated, I spend every waking moment preparing for the *Burns* argument. The jury returned a verdict on Friday, April 16, and on Saturday I flew to Washington to meet with Joe Rauh, a famous civil-rights and civil-liberties lawyer who had written an amicus brief in support of my position in the case. Rauh had argued innumerable cases in the Supreme Court, and I hoped he would be able to suggest some new, especially persuasive idea to add to my argument—or at least give me his sense of where the individual Justices were likely to stand and which arguments were most likely to be interesting to each of them.

Rauh's amicus brief had been prepared on behalf of a coalition of public employees' unions, but at the last minute Mayor Daley had killed it. The NEA was the largest union in the coalition, and its Illinois chapter had persuaded the union to threaten to withdraw from the coalition if the brief was filed. I was surprised to learn Daley had bothered to use his clout with the teachers' union to prevent the filing of an amicus brief, which added little to what the parties had already said and was unlikely to alter the Court's resolution of the case. That he would bother to intervene demonstrated the mayor's power over nearly everything that happened in Chicago, and his attention to every political detail, however inconsequential. At first I had wondered why he fought the *Elrod* case at all in light of his agreement to the consent decree in *Shakman,* but I later realized he must have believed that if the Supreme Court ruled for him in *Elrod,* he could just ignore *Shakman.* Rauh was furious at Daley's intervention, and between us we persuaded Ralph Nader, my friend and classmate at Princeton, to have the brief filed by Public Citizen, the public-interest group he had founded several years earlier.

When I met Joe Rauh in his Washington office, the first several minutes of conversation were devoted to mutual self-congratulation for having outflanked Daley. When we turned to the subject of the

Supreme Court argument and our chances of success, Rauh was less sanguine then I had hoped. The two remaining true liberals on the Court, Thurgood Marshall and William Brennan, were easy to count as votes in our favor, as was John Paul Stevens in light of his opinion in *Lewis*. Beyond that, it was difficult to find the two additional votes needed for victory. Chief Justice Warren Burger and Justice William Rehnquist were unlikely to find a constitutional right outlawing a political practice that went back almost to the founding of the Republic. Although less doctrinaire, Justice Lewis Powell also seemed unlikely to upset such a long-standing political tradition. Harry Blackmun had begun to shed his reputation of simply following Burger's lead, but more often than not the "Minnesota Twins" still voted together. Potter Stewart also seemed more like a no than a yes, according to Rauh, and if Byron White was a possibility, he was far from a sure thing. All in all, Rauh thought the case could be won, but the more likely result was a 5-4 or 6-3 loss. Based on prior votes and opinions, we spent the next hour trying to determine which arguments were most likely to appeal to the four Justices we thought were "in play." They were White, Stewart, Blackmun, and Powell, and we thought we needed two of them to make up a five-vote majority. As it turned out, we actually needed three.

Doug MacDonald, who had done the most work on our briefs, came to Washington on Sunday, as did my wife. The three of us had lunch together, and then Doug and I spent the rest of the day and early evening rehashing the argument and the questions we thought might be asked by the Justices.

Early Monday morning I walked up the steps of the Supreme Court Building to argue a case for the second time. This time I had the comfort of having been there before—but the added concern of believing the case I would argue was one of a handful decided by the Court each year which have the potential to change a significant element of American life.

Tom Foran and I arrived at the Court at about the same time, signed in, and chatted nervously for a few minutes before entering the courtroom. *Elrod, Sheriff v. John Burns*[4] would be the second case argued that morning, so we took our seats at the tables behind those reserved for the lawyers arguing the first case, a boundary dispute between two states. When the Justices appeared from behind the black curtain, John Paul Stevens took the seat reserved for the Court's junior justice on the far left end of the bench. Stevens was the only one of the Justices I knew personally; I had worked with him on a matter when he was a practicing lawyer in Chicago. He looked down at me after he took his seat and seemed to smile and nod in recognition. Then, when arguments in the first case ended and Chief Justice Burger announced, "We will hear arguments next in No. 74–1520, Elrod against Burns," Justice Stevens rose from his chair and disappeared behind the black curtain. For some reason the Justice who was my surest vote because of his opinion in the *Lewis* case had disqualified himself! I was horrified, but Tom Foran was starting his argument and I had to listen. (Years later, Justice Stevens explained to me that he was disqualified because he had voted on the case when the defendant sought rehearing en banc in the Seventh Circuit.)

For the first few minutes, Foran was allowed to give his planned argument interrupted by only a few questions. Suddenly Justices Rehnquist and White began conducting a debate among themselves using questions directed to Foran to frame the issue. (It is common for Justices to use questions to counsel to bring out facts and arguments they think best support the side of the case they favor. The purpose is to try to influence any Justices who may be undecided. Often that effort stimulates another Justice to respond in kind, jumping in with questions that illustrate the other side of the issue.) In essence, Rehnquist's questions were designed to bring out the historical acceptance of patronage and the fact the plaintiffs themselves had once benefited from it, while White

[4] The names of the parties are reversed from the caption in the Court of Appeals because now it was Elrod who was appealing from a lower court decision.

forced Foran to concede that the Court's jurisprudence permitted the kind of infringement on First Amendment rights imposed by the patronage system only if there is a substantial governmental interest in doing so, and that it is hard to articulate a substantial government interest in requiring janitors and process servers to be political supporters of the party in power.

Once Rehnquist and White began their questioning, several other Justices jumped in with questions of their own, and from then until the end of his argument Tom Foran could never return to his planned argument. Even so, the few minutes' grace the Court allowed him in the beginning was more than I received. The transcript shows that when it was my turn to argue, I began with the traditional words, "Mr. Chief Justice, may it please the Court," whereupon, before I could say another word, Justice Rehnquist asked a question. From that moment until Chief Justice Burger declared "Your time is up, Mr. Tucker," every word I spoke except my last sentence was in response to a question. It was the most difficult and exhilarating experience of my career.

Tom Foran and I shook hands and congratulated each other on the arguments as we left the Supreme Court building, pausing for a moment at the top of the stairs. Tom's wife was angry because the Chief Justice had forgotten (or decided to ignore, as it was lunchtime) that Tom had reserved a minute for rebuttal, but Tom was less upset. We agreed this was the most fun we had ever had as lawyers, and that we only wished we could go back after lunch and answer questions for another hour—or all afternoon, for that matter. But as I sat at lunch a short while later, I was glad it wasn't going to happen. The adrenaline had stopped flowing (I doubt there was any left in my system) and I was exhausted.

That afternoon Doug MacDonald and I conducted a postmortem. When we finished we were no more certain about the likely outcome than we had been the day before. From their questions, Justices Rehnquist and Burger had pretty conclusively confirmed our belief that they would vote against us, and although they had not participated much in the questioning, Justices

Brennan and Marshall were still counted as favorable. When Tom Foran's argument was over, I had mentally counted Justice White as favorable because of his persistent and skeptical questions about "governmental interest," but during my argument he had sounded almost equally skeptical about my contention that a viable distinction could be drawn between "policy makers," who could be replaced for political reasons, and non-policy-makers, who should not. On balance, I thought White and Stewart were on our side, but I was by no means sure. Powell, on the other hand, had seemed taken with the defendants' historical argument, concerned that if we prevailed, there would be a flood of new litigation every time an office changed parties. Blackmun was a complete mystery.

For several hours, Doug and I worried over the chance of getting five votes before one of us suddenly realized that because of Steven's recusal, we needed only four to win the case. If the Court split 4-4, the decision of the Seventh Circuit would be "affirmed by an equally divided vote." It wouldn't be nearly as good a victory—such a result would not create a precedent or settle the issue outside the Seventh Circuit—but it would still be a victory, and the largest remaining big-city political machine in America would have to abide by it. We still weren't sure about White and Stewart, but now we felt better.

One of the good things about arguing a case in the Supreme Court in the spring is that you won't have to wait too long for a decision. In modern times, with exceptions that could be counted on one hand, the Court decides every case it hears during the term beginning the first Monday of October before it adjourns for the summer in late June. The harder and more important cases often pile up and are the last to be decided, and this could well be one of those cases, but I returned to Chicago knowing that I would soon learn if I had won or lost.

The answer came on June 28. I was driving cross-country and heard the news on the car radio. Three justices—Brennan, Marshall, and White—had joined in a sweeping opinion written by Brennan declaring that the practice of conditioning public employment in non-policy-making positions on political support of the office-holder violates the First Amendment. Three other justices—Burger, Rehnquist, and Powell—had joined in an equally sweeping opinion holding that historical precedent and the role of patronage in strengthening the political-party system justify conditioning public employment on political support. And two judges—Stewart and Blackmun—while unwilling to join in all of its language, concurred in Justice Brennan's conclusion that a non-policy-making, nonconfidential public employee cannot be discharged solely because of his political beliefs or affiliations. We had won, 5-3.

Several years later, after lengthy negotiations, *Burns v. Elrod* finally ended with recovery of over $1 million in back pay, reinstatement of all who desired it, and a nice six-figure fee for my law firm.

In the meantime there were a trickle of additional patronage firing cases in the Chicago area, mostly from communities outside Cook County. Some of the plaintiffs asked me to represent them, but the amounts involved were too small to justify my hourly billing rates, so I referred them to younger lawyers. Then, in 1980 a new client approached me with a patronage case I could not resist. The case involved multiple dismissals, so the financial stakes were high enough to make it worthwhile, but the reason the case was irresistible was not the stakes but the identity of my prospective client.

Shortly before Christmas 1976, Mayor Daley died unexpectedly from a cerebral hemorrhage. Despite all predictions, the Windy City did not immediately sink into Lake Michigan and cease to exist. Nevertheless, there had to be a new mayor, and the machine quickly settled on Michael Bilandic to hold the seat while more powerful and ambitious figures in the party sorted out who would be the next real boss. Bilandic was a pleasant, mild-mannered man who had been anointed several years earlier to hold the aldermanic seat in the Eleventh Ward, the Mayor's seat of power in Bridgeport, a heavily Irish-American neighborhood on the Near Southwest Side. Bilandic easily won a special election for

Daley's unexpired term in the spring of 1977 and was expected to run and win again for a regular term in 1979, holding the seat for four more years until one of the late mayor's sons was ready to take over. However, in the runup to the 1979 Democratic primary another regular-organization member announced that she would challenge Bilandic for the nomination.

Jane Byrne had been Mayor Daley's Commissioner of Consumer Affairs and Cochairman of the Democratic Organization of Cook County. The first post was a minor bureaucratic sinecure and the other an entirely symbolic gesture to "the girls." Byrne, though, apparently thought her cochairmanship of the party meant she was in line for a major position when Daley died, and felt deeply slighted when Bilandic treated her as largely irrelevant. Despite her claim to be Daley's true heir and some lukewarm support from disaffected blacks and the independent bloc, which could not muster a credible candidate of their own, no one believed Byrne had the slightest chance of defeating the machine, which was solidly behind Bilandic.

Then, in late January, it snowed. And snowed, and snowed and snowed. When it finally stopped, there were thirty inches of snow, and Chicago was at a standstill. The problem wasn't that Chicago had never seen that much snow—the problem was that it had, and expected the city to get it cleared and everything moving again within a reasonable time. For some reason, this snow had gotten way ahead of the removal efforts, and the major streets had become blocked with thousands of stranded cars, which made it terribly difficult and time-consuming to clear them, which meant that the plows couldn't even start on the side streets until many days later. By then the temperature had plunged below zero, cars were frozen in place, much of the public-transportation system was also crippled, and the "city that works" wasn't working at all. The citizens were mad as hell, and quite willing to blame it on this not-the-real-mayor mayor, and even to believe Jane Byrne's claim that if she had been mayor, as the real mayor had intended when he made her his cochair, the snow would have been cleared.

One month to the day after the snowstorm, with some of the side streets still not totally open, Jane Byrne won the Democratic primary. As always, the general election was a walk.

Byrne's victory over the machine had been won with the support of Republicans, independents, antimachine Democrats, and ordinary disgruntled citizens, especially African-Americans, who were angered by the special neglect their neighborhoods suffered in the snow-removal efforts. Byrne understood, however, that machine aldermen and Democratic ward committeemen controlled the city council and a political organization that would have buried her in an ordinary year as deeply as the snow had buried Mike Bilandic. She wanted their support and, thanks to her association with Daley over the years, she knew how to get it. With the help of her husband, a longtime City Hall reporter for the *Chicago Sun-Times* who knew everything about how the city worked and where the bodies were buried, Byrne made it clear that she understood her power as mayor. She determined who would be the commissioner of each of the city's operating departments, and through them had the power to grant or block just about everything an alderman or committeeman could want to happen in his ward. The new mayor also let it be known that if they now pledged their support to her, they would be granted the same mayoral favors and feudal control of their domains as had previously been the case, but if they did not, she would use every power at her command to punish and destroy them—regardless of the *Elrod* decision and the *Shakman* consent decree. And she made sure they knew she meant it with a few sharp preemptive strikes against anyone who appeared reluctant or slow to understand.

There is a dispute about who started the feud between Jane Byrne and the Daley family. Byrne claims the Daleys came to her after she was elected and made a series of demands regarding control of certain matters that she was unwilling to grant. As she put it, "They acted like they were the mayor instead of me." The Daley sons and their allies deny any such thing happened, claiming they offered full support and cooperation. They say Byrne apparently feared they would use the magic Daley name to defeat her re-election, and treated them like enemies from the day she took office. The feud soon broke into the open. In October 1979, Republican Governor Jim Thompson vetoed a bill reducing the sales tax on food and medicine. Byrne supported the veto, but Richard J. Daley's oldest son, State Senator Richard M. Daley, led a push to override the veto. The day before the override vote Byrne fired several well-known city employees who were members of Daley's Eleventh Ward political organization. The next day the override failed narrowly, with several votes from Chicago-area legislators switching at the last minute to uphold the governor's veto.

Next, in early November, Byrne announced she would be supporting Senator Edward M. Kennedy's run for the Democratic presidential nomination against President Jimmy Carter. Richard M. Daley unsuccessfully opposed her effort to have the organization endorse Kennedy. Shortly thereafter, Daley declared he intended to seek the Democratic nomination for States Attorney of Cook County, the only important countywide office then held by a Republican. Most observers assumed he would be endorsed by the party, but Jane Byrne quickly corrected them, announcing that she would support Alderman Ed Burke. Shortly thereafter, Byrne fired several more Daley supporters, and Burke received the endorsement of the regular Democratic organization.

The Democratic primary was scheduled, as always, for mid-March. In January, Byrne announced she had ordered cuts in the city workforce for budgetary reasons. As department heads dutifully began to carry out her order, for the first time in memory, dozens of patronage workers with long years of political service to the Democratic organization began losing their jobs. Some of the good-government organizations and tax complainers hailed the mayor's initiative, but Richard M. Daley and his closest political ally, 19th Ward Democratic Committeeman and Cook County Assessor Tom Hynes, quickly perceived the truth about Byrne's order. When the workers received their pink slips, virtually every one of them had been sponsored for their job by the 11th or 19th

Ward organizations and were political workers in those organizations. The message was loud and clear—and every Democratic politician in Chicago heard it. If you support Richard M. Daley for States Attorney (or, for that matter, cross Jane Byrne in any other way), your workers can kiss their city jobs good-bye, and you will be opposed the next time you're up for re-election.

For Hynes and Daley, it was a double blow to Daley's chances in the primary. Not only were some of their best workers losing their jobs, but far worse, patronage workers all over the city were being warned that if they supported Daley in the wards and precincts where they did their political work, they would very likely lose their jobs too. Daley knew that most of the ward committeemen had to support Burke publicly, but he thought many of them would make it known to their workers with a wink and a nod that they could support Daley if they wanted to. Even more so, he was counting on the belief that whatever their bosses said, thousands of Democratic patronage workers would covertly support Daley's candidacy out of loyalty to his father, who had supported them so well for so many years. Jane Byrne had put a gun to their heads and said no.

Then, on February 4, Ed Walsh, the ward superintendent in Tom Hynes's 19th Ward, received a call from the Deputy Commissioner of Streets and Sanitation. He had been transferred, effective the next day, from his home ward on the Far Southwest Side of the city, to the 50th Ward, on the Far Northeast Side.

Of all the departments of government in Chicago, the largest and most politically important is Streets and Sanitation. As its name implies, "Streets and San" picks up the garbage, fixes potholes and broken pavement, cleans the streets and parkways, and performs other urban-housekeeping duties. It employs by far the most patronage workers of any city agency and is responsible for doing the things that are most visible and important to the city's residents. It was the failure of the Department of Streets and Sanitation to clear the snow that got Jane Byrne elected. The department has an office in each ward in the city, and each ward office has its own workforce.

That workforce is under the command of the ward superintendent, who is traditionally approved by the ward's Democratic committeeman and alderman, lives in the ward, and holds an important position in the ward Democratic political organization. From his position as ward superintendent, he is expected to keep the residents happy by keeping the ward clean and its streets in good repair, and to make sure his workers are also performing their political obligations as contributors and precinct workers for the party. He is the most important patronage worker in each ward.

By 1980, Eddie Walsh had been ward superintendent of the 19th Ward for many years. He was also the secretary of the 19th Ward regular Democratic organization. The 19th was a white enclave on the city's Far Southwest Side and one of the city's wealthiest neighborhoods. Its houses and apartment buildings were neat and in good repair, its lawns were green and trimmed, and its residents expected the streets and public spaces to be equally well maintained. Eddie Walsh made sure that they were. He kept a notebook and pen in his car, and whether driving around the ward during work hours or on his way to church or a ward political meeting, if he saw an unfilled pothole or trash in the street, he made a note of it. Then, as soon as he was back in the ward office, the task would go on someone's work schedule. He was equally diligent in his political duties. He was as much of a public figure in the 19th Ward as the alderman, or even Tom Hynes.

Jane Byrne wanted to send another message to the city's patronage workers and Democratic officials before the primary election, and nothing would send that message quite so dramatically as using her power to humble Ed Walsh. Although, as a practical matter, Walsh worked for Tom Hynes, technically he worked for Streets and Sanitation and its commissioner, who held his position at the discretion of the mayor. Jane Byrne couldn't have Walsh fired because he had civil-service protection, but someone came up with an even better idea: a transfer so obviously irrational and punitive that no one could fail to understand. Support Daley, and one way or another, Jane Byrne will get you.

Soon after getting word of his transfer, Ed Walsh talked to two friends in Streets and Sanitation who confirmed what he already knew: His transfer had been ordered by the mayor's office. In fact, he was told, the call had come directly from the mayor's principal political adviser, her husband Jay McMullen. Walsh called Tom Hynes. For Hynes, this was the last straw.

Tom Hynes had been an associate in my law firm before he left to pursue a political career. As Assessor of Cook County— deciding how much property owners would owe in real estate taxes—he held the best job in the city for raising political funds. Unlike some of his predecessors, Hynes had run the office with scrupulous fairness and honesty, but even an honest assessor was a formidable fund-raiser. When he called me at my office the day after Ed Walsh was transferred, however, it was not to raise money or talk about assessments. He wanted to know if I thought the patronage cases would apply to the firing of supporters of opposing factions within the same political party. I told him I didn't know any case deciding that question specifically, but I thought they would. Could I come to his office the next afternoon to discuss the matter further? I could.

When I arrived at the assessor's office the next day and was shown into Tom Hynes's private office, he introduced me to several people who were already there. One of them was Richard M. Daley.

Hynes proceeded to explain the story of the feud between Daley and Byrne: Byrne's recent tactic of systematically firing patronage workers loyal to Hynes and Daley, and now the transfer of Eddie Walsh. Would I file an action on behalf of the fired workers, charging that their dismissal was the result of their political support for Richard Daley in the approaching Democratic primary? Tom Hynes asked the question, but when I responded, I turned to Rich Daley.

"Yes," I said. "I really didn't expect to do any more of these cases, but I can't resist filing a case complaining about patronage abuses on behalf of someone named Richard Daley."

If Daley was offended, he didn't show it. He laughed and nodded his head. And that is how I got back into the patronage business.

For the next several weeks leading up to the Democratic primary, I devoted significant time to the Daley-Hynes patronage case, although neither of their names appeared as parties to the litigation. I decided to file the case as an enforcement petition in the *Shakman* case, charging Mayor Byrne and the regular Democratic organization she now controlled with violating the consent decree in which they had agreed to end political persecution of public employees. Filing a *Shakman* petition rather than a separate action under the *Burns* case had two advantages: It was simpler, and it meant the case would be assigned to the federal judge who had already heard a number of similar petitions. It was not that Judge Nicholas Bua was especially favorable to *Shakman* plaintiffs, but he was throughly familiar with the applicable law, knew how to move cases quickly and make up his mind without endless briefing and procrastination and, perhaps most important, had grown up in the local political world, having come to the federal bench from the state court. He knew how the system worked and was unlikely to be fooled by some contrived nonpolitical reason for Byrne's conduct. While on the surface his ties to the system might have seemed a negative, as a federal judge, Nick Bua had long since proved he would call cases as he saw them, regardless of the politics.

Within a few days of the meeting in Tom Hynes's office I had interviewed many of the fired workers and identified several who would be named plaintiffs. After checking to be sure Judge Bua would be available to hear an emergency motion, on February 26 I filed two petitions. The first was filed in the name of several of the fired city workers. It described the political background and the pattern of firing supporters of Daley and Hynes. That pattern, I asserted, proved the discharges were politically motivated. The petition was supported by affidavits of the plaintiffs and included an emergency motion for an order requiring the city to post a notice in every city office informing employees that it was illegal for anyone to alter or threaten their employment status because of their support or nonsupport of any candidate in the March primary. I also asked that the city include a copy of the notice in every employee's next pay envelope. Employees who believed their rights were violated were urged to call their own attorney or me. A separate second petition was filed for Eddie Walsh alone, seeking his immediate retransfer to the 19th Ward.

In addition to filing the pleadings in the clerk's office, that morning I hand-delivered a copy to Judge Bua's chambers. Since it was important that Daley supporters learn of the effort to protect them as quickly as possible, I also dropped off a copy of the petitions in the office of the City News Bureau, which supplied court news to the print and broadcast media. I wanted them to have it in time to cover the hearing on my emergency motion and get word to city workers in the late editions and on the televised evening news.

When my emergency motion was called in Judge Bua's court that morning, an assistant corporation counsel reported that the mayor was consulting private counsel about representing her in the case and asked to continue it to the next day. Recognizing the time constraints of my request that notices be included in the end-of-February pay envelopes, three days later, Judge Bua agreed only to continue it until that afternoon, when he granted the notice I had requested. By agreement the case was then continued until February 28.

When the case was called that day, the lawyer who approached the podium and announced he now represented Mayor Byrne and the Democratic organization was Don H. Reuben, one of the most prominent lawyers in Chicago. For many years, Reuben had been the most powerful partner in the city's largest law firm. Among his many clients were the *Chicago Tribune* and the Catholic Archdiocese of Chicago. Reuben used his influence with clients freely to attack his enemies, and his clout with elected state-court judges was legendary. He was a smart, hardworking lawyer, but his overbearing personality led him to treat opponents with disdain and intimidate them whenever possible—characteristics that engendered both jealousy and intense dislike among many in the legal community. Apparently he treated some of his partners at Kirkland & Ellis the same way, because despite the enormous business he controlled, one day he returned to Chicago from a trip to discover that he had been voted out of the firm. He promptly formed a new firm, Reuben & Proctor, taking with him many of his largest clients and quite a few good lawyers. Reuben had also reputedly been influential in Judge Bua's nomination to the federal bench.

Recognizing the political practicalities, Bua's first order of business was to craft an agreement between the parties to continue the hearing on the multi-plaintiff petition for reinstatement until after the election, with the city promising not to fire any employee in the interim except for cause. I anticipated a similar agreement would be reached to continue the *Walsh* petition, but I was wrong. The *Walsh* petition, Reuben said, was a blatant political ploy aimed at affecting the upcoming election. Moreover, if granted it would deprive the Commissioner of Streets and Sanitation of the power to run his department, and even its pendency was an impediment to his authority. Reuben said he had been instructed by the mayor not to agree to anything regarding Walsh—we had alleged it was an emergency matter, and that was fine—he was ready to go to trial immediately.

I understood at once what had happened. Reuben believed that even though it was obvious to everyone, it would be difficult for me to prove that Walsh's transfer was politically motivated. Our claim that Walsh's transfer was ordered by Jay McMullen was based on statements to Walsh by men who would be reluctant to testify, even assuming they had direct knowledge of McMullen's action. And, quite apart from his relationship with Bua (which he doubtless thought would help), Reuben knew the judge would require me to present real evidence of political motive, not just an argument that "everybody knows it."

It was a clever tactic and vintage Don Reuben. If we tried the merits of the *Walsh* petition before the election and lost, it could adversely affect the election, not to mention Eddie Walsh. In the face of his intimidating confidence, Reuben figured I would try to stall, or perhaps even agree to dismiss the petition. Either way, it would appear that I was afraid I would lose, which would be just as bad. Fifteen years earlier, it might have worked, but I had long since learned not to be intimidated by the Don Reubens of the world. We would go to trial the next week.

I began my opening statement by reciting the history of the political rift between Byrne and Daley. When I moved on to Byrne's "reduction of force" order and asserted the evidence would show it was a subterfuge for firing public employees who supported Daley, Reuben objected, claiming that only the Walsh transfer was at issue and the earlier discharges were irrelevant. I responded by citing analogous cases holding that evidence of a pattern of racial discrimination is admissible to show discriminatory intent. Judge Bua said he would consider the evidence "for what it's worth," adding that if I succeeded in showing a pattern of political firing, he would decide later what weight he should give it in deciding whether Walsh's transfer was also politically motivated. (In bench trials, judges frequently listen to evidence before making a final decision about its relevancy. In jury trials, they don't have this luxury—they know that if the jury hears the evidence, it will be impossible to erase it from their minds—although they often pretend jurors can ignore it when something prejudicial happens before the judge can stop it. "The jury will disregard it," the judge announces, and everyone solemnly nods.)

Although generally opening statements in bench trials are shorter than the detailed recitation of favorable evidence that should be presented to a jury, I decided to describe my evidence in full. I wanted the judge to understand from the start that the petition was more than a political response to the Walsh transfer as Reuben had claimed. I had a theory of the case and facts sufficient to prove that the transfer was ordered for political reasons.

When I finished, Don Reuben gave a short opening statement of his own, essentially repeating his assertion that it was
our petition—not the transfer of Eddie Walsh—that was politically
motivated. He especially attacked our claim that the transfer had
been ordered by Jay McMullen, which, he said, was a malicious
effort to smear the mayor through her husband.

The next morning, Reuben was accompanied by a younger
partner from his firm and one or two associates. When we recon-
vened after lunch, Don was not there, and Carole Bellows, another
partner in his firm, appeared and told the judge that Mr. Reuben
had a commitment to another matter that afternoon and she
would be sitting in for him. When the evidence began, however,
the partner who had been there in the morning handled all of the
trial work, and continued to do so for the balance of the case
except when Reuben reappeared to cross-examine Tom Hynes and
a couple of other newsworthy witnesses. Carole showed up that
one afternoon, watched wordlessly, and never appeared again. I
could only laugh. Carole was a good lawyer, but I did not believe
Reuben had sent her there to try the case—I thought he sent her
there because she had played an important public role in supporting Nick Bua for his federal judgeship. Again, it was classic
Don Reuben, and I suspect Judge Bua was equally amused.

Over the next couple of days, we put in evidence that the recent
public-employee firings were aimed almost exclusively at supporters
of Richard Daley. Additional testimony from Walsh, Hynes, and the
19th Ward alderman described the nature of the job of ward superintendent and the universal practice of appointing superintendents
who were residents of the ward and supported by local elected officials. As we neared the close of our case, I was confident the evidence proved Walsh's transfer was political punishment for his and
the 19th Ward organization's support of Daley. Our proof that
the transfer order had come from Jay McMullen, however, was
weak, and although I thought it was unnecessary to prove who
ordered the transfer, we had alleged it was McMullen and I knew
Reuben would try to make it an essential issue. I had persuaded

the judge to let Walsh testify to the reports he received that McMullen gave the order to show he had made the allegation in good faith, but that was not proof it had actually happened. At the end of the day on Friday, I rested my case.

On Sunday I received a phone call from Tom Hynes. Ed Walsh and a friend had gone into the ward office while it was closed and located the logbook that recorded the name of everyone who called the ward office by date and time. There was a rumor that a suspected Byrne spy in the office had received a call about the transfer even before Walsh was notified of it. Walsh wanted to see if the logbook reflected a call from someone in the mayor's office on the day he was transferred. It did, and the identity of the caller was recorded as Mr. J. McMullen.

Walsh made a copy of the page reflecting the call and returned the logbook to its place. I told Hynes to bring Walsh and the photocopy to my office early Monday morning. After satisfying myself that the entry was legitimate, I prepared a subpoena for the logbook itself and a motion to reopen my case and recall Ed Walsh as a witness.

When I presented the documents to Judge Bua the next morning and described the circumstances, I was met with a flurry of objections and outraged assertions that my story showed my client was a burglar and a thief. It was almost exactly twenty years since I had heard the same accusations shouted at Jim Sprowl in a courtroom in central Illinois. Recalling the incident, I repeated the substance of Mr. Sprowl's words with a sense of pleasure well beyond the circumstances of the moment. "I don't believe Mr. Walsh did anything wrong," I said, "but whether he did or didn't isn't the issue. The issue is whether the photocopy I have handed up is a genuine copy of an authentic entry in the 19th Ward Streets and Sanitation office telephone log. If it is, it is strong circumstantial evidence of our claim that Mr. McMullen was involved in Mr. Walsh's transfer. So let's get the logbook and see."

Judge Bua agreed, and a delegation was dispatched to the Southwest Side to collect the evidence while the defense began its case.

Near the end of the morning the logbook arrived, and confirmed the authenticity of the copy Walsh had obtained. The judge said we would take up the matter after the noon recess. When I arrived back in the courtroom after lunch, I saw Don Reuben coming out of the door that led to the corridor containing the judges' chambers. He had not been in court during the morning session. Now, he said, Judge Bua wanted to see the lawyers in chambers. Reuben said he had told the judge's secretary he wanted such a meeting to discuss a possible settlement, and the judge had agreed.

The negotiation did not take long. Reuben proposed we continue the case until after the election at which time the city would agree to transfer Walsh back to a ward in the city's South District, which encompassed several wards including the 19th. I said it had to be the 19th, and a consent decree reflecting the agreement had to be signed now. After some backing and forthing and persuasive comments by the judge, an agreement was reached. A consent degree and settlement agreement would be prepared and signed that afternoon. It would provide for Walsh to be transferred back to the 19th Ward or promoted to deputy commissioner for the South District. The parties would agree, however, to continue the trial until the day after the election, and the fact of the consent decree and settlement would not be disclosed until then. This latter provision had been insisted on by Reuben and supported by Judge Bua, and while it would have been nice to have a public pre-election victory, with Daley ahead in the polls, he and Hynes felt it wasn't worth the chance the judge might rule against us if we refused a solution for what could only be political motives. Continuing the case would not hurt anything; losing it might. I thought the case was won and didn't think Bua would rule against us for refusing to go along with the continuance, but I agreed we should do so. The agreement was in the best interest of my real client, Ed Walsh, and I would have recommended he agree to it even if Hynes and Daley objected.

On Tuesday, March 18, Richard M. Daley soundly defeated Ed Burke for the Democratic nomination for State's Attorney. In

November, with little support and, in some instances, active opposition from the Democratic officials who supported Byrne and Burke in the primary, Daley went on to win the office by a razor-thin margin.

After the election, I settled the first petition, obtaining reinstatement of all the plaintiffs with back pay, and successfully handled another case for a former appellate court judge whom Byrne had ordered fired from his position as counsel to the supposedly independent Chicago Transit Authority. (Byrne and the CTA settled as soon as Judge Bua denied their motions to dismiss, clearing the way for me to take Byrne's deposition and question her under oath about her role in the matter.)

In each of the cases arising from the Byrne-Daley feud, the defendants were ordered to pay my legal fees and expenses, bringing the total fees for my excursion into the world of politics to some $500,000. Chicago politics was a hobby I would have indulged for the fun of it, but my experiences proved you can sometimes turn a hobby into a paying enterprise.

CHAPTER 7

LOSING—AND WINNING

The case I tried for five months from November 1975 until the Friday before the Supreme Court argument in *Elrod v. Burns* was titled *Wells v. F & F Investment Co.* To everyone involved, however, it was called the "Contract Buyers League case," one of two connected cases that challenged racial profiteering in Chicago's notoriously segregated real estate market.

The CBL cases were filed in early 1969, but the issues they explored went back to the early 1940s and the great African-American migration from the South to Chicago and other northern industrial cities. The movement that led to filing the cases began in the summer of 1967.

On the Fourth of July that summer, a young college student named Peter Welch left his home in Massachusetts and began hitchhiking to Chicago, arriving several days later. Following directions received in a telephone call, he made his way to Presentation Church in the Lawndale neighborhood of Chicago's West Side. Entering the church, he found the man who had phoned him and several other young men and women in an excited mood. They and a group of black residents of the neighborhood had just returned from downtown, where they had dumped several large containers of ripe garbage onto the steps of Chicago's City Hall. The next week, for the first time in recent memory, the Department of Streets and Sanitation picked up the garbage in Lawndale on the day it was supposed to be picked up.

The next Saturday, Welch accompanied the same young men and women, together with fifty or sixty neighborhood men, women, and children, on a bus trip from the church to Bridgeport, the all-white neighborhood where Mayor Daley lived. There they entered a city-maintained playground not far from the mayor's house and played with the swings, teeter-totters, and sandboxes for several hours while a growing crowd of local residents looked on in amazement and anger. There were some curses and racial epithets from the crowd, and when the Lawndale invaders left the playground, a bottle and a few rocks were thrown as the bus pulled away. But the next week a city crew arrived in Lawndale and created a children's playground on vacant land across from Presentation Church.

As Welch explained at a Contract Buyers League reunion thirty years later, "I thought to myself, this is fun. I think I'll stick around for a while." He did, and so did many of the other young men and women who had received similar telephone calls from the man who had called Welch—a young Jesuit seminarian named Jack Mcnamara.

But it wasn't Jack Mcnamara who started it. It was Monsignor Jack Egan, the pastor of Presentation Church. For some years, Jack Egan, as director of the Office of Urban Affairs of the Catholic Archdiocese of Chicago, had struggled mightily to maintain the presence of the Church in the inner city and to direct as many of its assets and services as he could to the mission of assisting the urban poor. He was one of Chicago's best-known and most-beloved priests. Then, when John Cody became archbishop and then cardinal of Chicago, he named Egan pastor of Presentation Parish in the heart of Chicago's new West Side ghetto. As Egan diplomatically put it, "I was Cardinal Cody's second appointment to a parish. It was the biggest favor anyone ever did for me. I don't think he meant it that way, but it was the biggest favor he could have done. I had been in the civil-rights movement for many years, but now for the first time I began living with black people. I was an arrogant priest. I thought I would bring God to the West Side, but I found out that God was already there in the courage and spirituality of the people."

What Jack Egan didn't say, but everyone knew, was that Cody had put Egan into Presentation (while theoretically retaining his title of Director of Urban Affairs) because Cody had no intention of maintaining the Church's service to the black, largely non-Catholic population of the inner city. Cody considered Jack Egan a troublemaker and the Office of Urban Affairs an impediment to his plans. By making the assignment, he hoped to place the troublemaker where he couldn't make trouble and let Urban Affairs die a slow death. To a shameful extent, Cody's plan worked insofar as the Church's commitment to the inner city was concerned, but it was a miserable failure if he thought it would keep Jack Egan from making trouble.

Not long after he came to Presentation Church, Egan persuaded sixteen Catholic seminaries in the Chicago area each to give him a seminarian to help him in Presentation Parish every Saturday for two months in the summer of 1966. Each seminarian was assigned to one square block and told that block was his parish. Egan told them: "Get to know every single person who lives on your block, regardless of religion, and talk to them and find out what their problems are, and offer them our help." Then, every Saturday afternoon, the seminarians would return to Presentation Church for a meeting where they told what they had learned from the people and discussed how they could help with the problems they had unearthed. One of the sixteen seminarians was Jack Mcnamara.

It is not clear that any one person involved in Jack Egan's project suddenly seized on the issue that caused the formation of the Contract Buyers League. Jack Egan kwen about it, but had been unable to find a solution. The seminarians began to learn about it, but had no idea anything could be done. The people certainly knew its results, but did not understand its causes or imagine there could be any relief from it. One of them, Ruth Wells, "the Rosa Parks of Lawndale," may have been the first person to get angry enough to try to do something; but by herself, there was really nothing she could do. And nearly everyone in Chicago was aware of the fundamental events that precipitated the problem, even if they could not identify the problem itself.

For many years prior to World War II, Chicago enjoyed a substantial and relatively stable African-American population. They were postal workers, steelworkers, manual laborers, teachers, shop owners, doctors, lawyers, and businessmen. And they all lived in a fairly small and compact area on the city's South Side. With the war, however, the migration of rural southern blacks to Chicago and other northern cities accelerated in response to thousands of newly created factory jobs. When the war ended, the migration turned into a flood. Chicago was one of the most residentially segregated cities in America. Newly arriving blacks could not buy or rent a place to live outside the existing black neighborhood on the South Side—property owners, realtors, and mortgage lenders would not deal with them.

As a result, the black South Side bulged with people, a condition that caused serious deterioration in every aspect of black life—crowded schools, increased crime, inadequate police protection, deteriorating buildings. Most of the people had steady jobs with incomes sufficient to rent or purchase homes in better neighborhoods, but they could not do so.

Into this breach moved the blockbusters. They started on the Near Southwest Side and spread their message block by block, with astonishing speed. "Did you know a colored man just bought the house across the street?" they would ask, from door to door. "You better sell now, while you can—I'll give you $15,000 cash—sign here." A week before, the house was worth $20,000, so the owner might resist for a few days or weeks; but as the "for sale signs" multiplied and neighbors were consulted, it wasn't long before they caved in. Especially when a couple of threatening-looking black men appeared on the front porch of the house next door, drinking whiskey out of a bottle wrapped in a paper bag. Oddly, those same men kept showing up over and over, block by block.

If the blockbusters had turned around and sold their newly acquired property to a black family for the $20,000 it had previously been worth, thus making a healthy 33 percent profit, things might have turned out differently. But they knew they didn't have to settle for such small pickings. The demand for housing available to blacks was so great, they could charge much more. Moreover, since lenders would not provide mortgage financing, there was only one way an African-American could buy: on a contract financed by the new owner. No appraisal, no fuss—and no title until the contract was paid in full. Miss one payment, and the blockbuster could take back the house without any return of equity. And the contract price could be double what the blockbuster had paid.

By the mid-1960s, Lawndale, which was one of the first areas "busted," had changed from a neighborhood of neatly maintained bungalows and small apartment buildings to a violent, over-crowded crime-ridden slum—just what its white former residents had feared and predicted when they sold out and fled. But the African-Americans who purchased those houses were mostly solid middle-class people with good jobs, trying to find a better place to live for the sake of their children. How could they be responsible for this dramatic decline?

From their work in Presentation Parish, Jack Egan and Jack Mcnamara began to reach some conclusions. First, with the help of Ruth Wells and others, they began to realize how much housing prices had been inflated, how the onerous terms of the contracts had put the buyers at the mercy of the sellers, and how willing many of the sellers were to use that imbalance of power to extract even more from the buyers, through high interest rates and exorbitantly priced insurance. The excessive prices charged the black contract buyers and the high interest tacked on to their monthly payments were beyond the buyers' ability to pay from their existing incomes. So they took second and third jobs—and the women went to work—and the financial strains broke up marriages—and the children, no longer supervised, began to skip school, hang out on street corners, and join gangs. Needing more income, the buyers might rent out a room—or break up a large flat into two or three apartments. The people who rented those rooms often had no jobs—or only marginal ones—and some were on drugs and had to sell drugs or rob stores to feed their habits. Almost before you knew it, Lawndale was a slum.

Jack Mcnamara decided after that first summer of talking to the people of Lawndale that he wanted to stay and try to do more about the problems he saw. He wanted to organize the people and find ways to help them relieve themselves of their problems, including the crushing financial burdens he believed were most responsible for the mess. Jack told Father Egan what he wanted to do. Egan approved, and helped Mcnamara get permission to postpone his studies at the seminary for two years to work in Lawndale. Joe Putnick, another of the seminarians, made the same decision. The two of them solicited help from other young people they knew.

Mcnamara had taught in a Catholic high school in Cincinnati the year before he came to Chicago. He was a charismatic teacher, as he would become a charismatic organizer and leader. Before he was done, he had lured a large contingent of his former students to Lawndale. Jack Egan was a good friend of Saul Alinsky, the legendary organizer and author. Egan introduced Mcnamara to one of Alinsky's disciples who provided a short course in community organizing, which is why the garbage at City Hall and the Lawndale folks in a Bridgeport playground sound so familiar to anyone who has ever done Alinsky-style organizing. It is also why the enterprise was based on asking the people what their problems were, instead of telling them, and helping them lead their own way out, instead of dragging them behind on a path determined by outside leadership.

Thus began the Contract Buyers League. Its story soon spread across Chicago, and the nation. It was chronicled in books and magazine articles and dissertations and newspaper stories and law journals in far greater detail than can be told here,[5] but not even the fullest telling can ever capture the richness of its impact on the lives and spirits of those who were involved in its struggles.

Most of the properties the blockbusters purchased and resold to African-Americans in Lawndale were first placed in land trusts, which both hid the name of the true owners and made it difficult to determine how much the blockbuster had paid for the property and how much he resold it for. Jack Egan introduced Jack Mcnamara to someone who knew about real estate and taught Mcnamara how to research property at the Chicago Title and Trust Company. Once he assembled his army of college students, Mcnamara sent them off to the title company to begin tracking down the names and address of the real owners of the houses, how much they had paid the panic-stricken white sellers, and what they had charged, on contract, to their black purchasers. The pattern that emerged was even more startling than Mcnamara had originally thought. Many of the homes were sold to blacks within one or two days of their purchase at double the purchase price. Contrary to common belief, many of the purchasers put up substantial down payments—some as much as 30 to 50 percent of the purchase price—yet they still had to purchase on contract, at interest rates nearly twice the prevailing mortgage rates.

On Wednesday nights the people of Lawndale were invited to a meeting at Presentation Church to discuss their problems, and every Wednesday Jack Mcnamara raised the issue of contract buying and the prices the people had paid for their houses as a possible subject of discussion. But for some reason, no one would talk

[5] The struggle over contract selling and the exorbitant prices charged black home buyers in Chicago, including the Contract Buyers League story, is the subject of a forthcoming book by Rutgers University historian Beryl Satter, expected in 2004. The story of CBL was also told in a long cover story in the April 1972 *Atlantic Monthly* titled "In My Father's House There Are Many Mansions—And I'm Going to Get Me Some of Them Too" and is the subject of a chapter in Margery Frisbie's *An Alley in Chicago: The Ministry of a City Priest* (Sheed & Ward, 2002).

about it. Every movement has a hero and a legend surrounding its birth, and the Contract Buyers League's hero is Ruth Wells. The movement's time and place of birth was one of these Wednesday-night meetings in the basement of Presentation Church. Some time earlier, Wells, with Egan and Mcnamara in the background, had confronted her seller face to face and backed him down when he arbitrarily added another $1,500 to the amount she owed. Faced with the reluctance of others to discuss their own problems with the sellers, Mcnamara tried to persuade Wells to tell her story, but she had never spoken to a group in public and was afraid to do so. Then one Wednesday night, she screwed up her courage and stood up, clutched the back of the chair in front of her for support, and told her story—what she had paid; how much less the seller had paid; how the property was worth much less than her purchase price according to an FHA appraisal; the seller's effort to add even more to her payments; the way these events had impacted on her life and that of her family in struggling to make their payments. When she finished, she looked around the room at her neighbors and asked, "Is anybody else in the same boat?" Nearly every hand in the room was raised, and everyone started talking at once. The Contract Buyers League had been born.

"They didn't want to tell their story to Jack because he was white and they didn't want to admit they were taken advantage of," Ruth Wells says. "But once I told my story, it just kind of made it all right for them to tell theirs." The floodgates opened.

Soon attendance at the Wednesday meetings was standing room only. A foundation was created. Money was raised. An office was opened, and several of the founding members were hired to staff it. The number of volunteers quickly grew—college students and recent graduates, nuns, seminarians, and just plain people. The objective was to get the sellers to renegotiate their contracts to a fair price, which CBL decided was 15 percent more than the seller had paid, and to convert the contracts to conventional mortgages. (Embarrassed by the redlining of black neighborhoods that had made it impossible for blacks to get mortgages, several large lending institutions set up programs to provide mortgages to buyers who succeeded in getting their balances down to a reasonable level.)

When the sellers refused to renegotiate, pickets marched in front of the sellers' real estate offices. When that didn't work, the pickets moved to the suburban neighborhoods where the sellers lived, and when picketing with signs failed to move a seller, leaflets were passed out to his neighbors, giving the purchase and sale numbers which starkly condemned him as a racial profiteer. All of this found its way into the press, and then into the calculations of the politicians, who began showing up at meetings and offering support.

A group of blacks who purchased newly constructed houses on contract on the South Side read the stories and showed up at Presentation one Wednesday night to see what was going on. Soon a substantial number of South Siders were showing up as well. Research suggested they too had been overcharged for their houses, and a South Side branch of CBL was formed.

Slowly, some of the sellers agreed to renegotiate. A major breakthrough appeared imminent when one seller called Jack Mcnamara and told him he had discussed the situation with his wife a few days earlier, and she had said she agreed with the Contract Buyers League—he had overcharged the buyers, and it was immoral. He had spent several sleepless nights and finally concluded she was right. He had eighty contracts, and he renegotiated all of them on the basis of the CBL formula despite objections and threats from his fellow sellers. That and a few other successes led one Chicago newspaper in March 1968 to call CBL's successes "very close to an economic miracle."

After a while, the successes slowed, and then stopped. The West Side sellers formed their own organization and hired a lawyer. They vowed not to renegotiate, or tried to pick off CBL's leaders with terms they would not offer to anyone else. No one agreed, but something had to be done to put more pressure on the sellers. In November 1968, the people decided to begin a payment strike even though they knew the sellers could throw them out of their homes. Some time earlier, a sympathetic judge named Harold Sullivan had organized a group of volunteer lawyers to advise CBL and help with renegotiations and conversions to mortgage financing. Most of them were real estate lawyers. Jack Mcnamara asked them if they could do anything in the courts to challenge what the sellers had done, but they said no. Contract sales are legal, and so long as there is no misrepresentation, there is no such thing as an excessive price for real estate—it's worth whatever people will pay for it. When the people started talking about a payment strike, these lawyers said there was nothing that could be done to avoid evictions.

Although Judge Sullivan's court was in the north suburbs and would not be involved in the eviction cases, he was worried—partly because of his concern about what would happen to the people, but also because of the civil disorder he feared would result from massive evictions. Judge Sullivan thought maybe a good, imaginative trial lawyer would have a better idea of what to do. He called Bert Jenner, who had earlier expressed some support for CBL. Jenner referred him to Tom Sullivan. When Judge Sullivan called Tom Sullivan (no relation), Tom set up a meeting at his office the following Saturday. Jack Mcnamara, CBL president and contract buyer Charlie Baker, and some other buyers and supporters came downtown for the meeting and described the predicament in full. They told Tom the committee of lawyers had said there was nothing to be done from a legal standpoint. Tom said, "I'd be very surprised if that's true. I don't believe there's nothing we can do." And that, for better or worse, is how CBL became a "case" as well as a community organization. It is also why I got involved with the CBL cases several years later, and spent more time on them than any others in my career.

Asked about his own role in the cases thirty-four years after that meeting, Tom Sullivan insists, "I was no hero, and I never looked at the case as some kind of crusade. Judge Sullivan called me up and asked me to take on the matter, so I did. It was just another case, although of course I didn't realize at the time I would be working on it off and on for the next decade or that the firm would end up donating millions of dollars of legal time and tens of thousands of dollars in out-of-pocket expenses." The last statement is undoubtedly true, but the rest is nonsense. In fact, if anyone but the people themselves were heroes, Tom was perhaps the biggest. It was Tom Sullivan who first perceived there could be a legal remedy for the contract buyers, and it was Tom who put together the team that pursued the cases, without compensation. Many lawyers made substantial contributions to CBL, but by any measure the CBL cases were, from the beginning, his cases. And he was as dedicated to them and to CBL as anyone.

Another lawyer, Tom Boodell, had become interested in CBL and started attending the Wednesday night meetings in 1968. That fall he obtained a fellowship from the Adlai Stevenson Institute to spend full time working on the contract-sales issue. He says he just kind of doodled around with some ideas. He and Tom Sullivan were both aware of *Jones v. Mayer,* a case decided that summer by the United States Supreme Court. Interpreting the provisions of a civil-rights act passed by Congress during Reconstruction, the Court had held that a section of the act, which prohibited discrimination against blacks in the sale of real estate, applied to individuals as well as governments and governmental entities. In arriving at its decision, the Court had announced that the law, Section 1982 of the 1866 Civil Rights Act, was meant "to assure that a dollar in the hands of a Negro will purchase the same thing as a dollar in the hands of a white man." Seizing on the *Jones* case and that language in particular, Boodell, Sullivan, and John Stifler—the associate who had helped me in the *Robinson* case when he was still in law school—prepared a complaint charging the defendants with taking advantage of the separate real estate market for blacks that had been created by racial discrimination, in order to charge black homebuyers more than whites had to pay for equivalent housing. This difference, or "race tax," was made possible by the excess demand for housing in those few areas where housing for blacks was available.

When the complaint was finished, Sullivan, Boodell and Stifler met with Jack Mcnamara to go over it one last time. When they finished, Sullivan said, "There's something wrong with it. It covers all the bases, but it needs something more. I'd like to ask my friend Bob Ming to look at it." Bob Ming, a partner in the best African-American law firm in the city, had worked with Thurgood Marshall on *Brown v. Board of Education* and many other important civil-rights cases, while maintaining a distinguished and profitable private law practice with clients ranging from individuals to the City of Chicago. He agreed to look at the complaint over the weekend. On Monday he sent it back, revised, and offered to join in the case. When Tom Sullivan read the revisions he called Tom Boodell and Jack Mcnamara. He was excited. "Now it sings," he told them. "You can't read it without wanting to do something for the plaintiffs."

Most cases involve trying to prove facts that fit into a settled legal framework. As long as you touch the required bases, the language of the complaint doesn't much matter. The *CBL* case was different. It sought to establish a claim most lawyers and judges would have said did not exist. In traditional civil-rights cases, the complaint alleges the defendant himself performed some act of racial discrimination, which caused injury to the plaintiff. Here the claim was not that the sellers themselves had engaged in racial discrimination, but that they had taken advantage of the societal discrimination against blacks which created a separate, racially defined real estate market.

It was one thing to say that *Jones v. Mayer* had established a cause of action against private parties for racial discrimination in real estate sales; it was quite another to assert that the *Jones* decision meant that taking advantage of the discrimination of others to charge higher prices and reap higher profits from blacks was a violation of the 1866 civil-rights law. First impressions are important, and it was important that the judge to whom the CBL case was assigned feel the injustice the people had suffered and understand the consequences of the sellers' greed when he first read the complaint. If Bob Ming had done nothing else, his work in turning the CBL complaint into a compelling cry for racial justice was a giant service to the cause of the Contract Buyers League. In fact, however, he did much more, participating actively in the case for many years and serving as the master of its theoretical underpinning.

The West Side CBL case was filed the first week of January 1969 and assigned by lot to Judge Hubert Will, one of the smartest judges on the U.S. District Court. Two weeks later, the South Side case was filed and also sent to Judge Will as a related case. Other than the names of the parties and the fact that the homes involved on the South Side were new construction, the complaints were substantially identical. As expected, the defendants moved to dismiss, claiming the complaints failed to state a cause of action because they did not allege the defendants themselves had sold comparable homes to whites for any less than the prices at which they sold to the plaintiffs. In fact, if you defined "comparable" homes as only those located in the same area, they hadn't sold homes to whites at all—white families were not buying houses in Lawndale or on the South Side. Judge Will set a consolidated briefing schedule on the motions to dismiss in both cases.

The payment strike had started in December. Each month a participant bought a money order for the amount of her monthly payment payable to herself and deposited it with CBL to hold. Some people just stopped paying and kept the money, but they were not considered part of the payment strike. Each Wednesday night, Charlie Baker would announce the number of people who had joined and the amount being held. According to the *Atlantic Monthly* article, by March 1968, nearly six hundred families had joined the strike and withheld over $250,000. But by mid-January, when the South Side case was filed, eviction actions had been started against nearly one hundred of them.

The defendants were using the payment strike to claim their own status as victims in proceedings before Judge Will, who expressed some sympathy for their position and urged the lawyers to control their clients. Both because they feared it would injure their chances in the lawsuits and because they were afraid many of the people would be evicted from their homes and lose everything, the lawyers opposed the strike, even though some of the sellers had begun expressing more interest in renegotiation when they stopped receiving their payments.

Finally, in March, the South Side CBL members agreed to resume payments, pending the outcome of the case, in return for some minor concessions by the sellers, and in April a similar agreement was reached on the West Side. Then, in May, in a decision hailed across the country as one of the most important developments in civil-rights law since *Brown v. Board of Education*, Judge Will denied the motions to dismiss. As a result of *Jones v. Mayer*, he said, it is now understood " . . . there cannot in this country be markets or profits based on the color of a man's skin." The judge ridiculed the logic of the defendants' claim there was no cause of action because the defendants had not sold properties to whites at a lower price, responding that such an interpretation "would mean that the 1866 Civil Rights Act, which was created to be an instrument for the abolition of discrimination, allows an injustice so long as it is visited entirely on Negroes."

It was a decision with implications far beyond home sales to blacks in Chicago. Not only were there dual real estate markets in other large cities in America, there was a "race tax" on many products besides real estate. Commodities like groceries, medicine, furniture, and gasoline cost substantially more in many black inner cities than in white areas of the same cities, and while the merchants claimed higher costs due to higher rates of theft, vandalism, and the like, many observers doubted any serious analysis would justify the prices being charged. If the Civil Rights Act prohibited taking advantage of segregated markets to obtain a higher profit from the sale of real estate to blacks, the same logic should apply to groceries.

Judge Will's decision was cause for celebration among everyone associated with CBL, but as the cases settled in to the long process of pretrial discovery, the initial enthusiasm of the people began to wane. Meetings continued to be held on Wednesday nights, but once you announced that so-and-so's deposition had been taken, or was about to be taken, or that some politician would speak at the next meeting, there wasn't much to say or do. The leaders sensed that an organization that had thrived on the people's acting together in their own interest was slowly fading away, and the lawyers could only tell them that it could be a year, maybe two or three years, before the case went to trial. Moreover, the judge's favorable decision had not resulted in any wave of renegotiation— if anything, the sellers seemed more intransigent than ever. In July the people took matters into their own hands and declared another payment strike.

This time, the South Side sellers decided to go after the buyers with a vengeance. By September, eviction proceedings had been brought against nearly half the strikers. Under the Illinois eviction statute, there was no defense based on a claim you had been over-charged or cheated in some way. Unless you could prove you had paid the money you owed, the seller was entitled to throw you out and take his property back.

By December, the legal process had reached the point where the sheriff was ready to begin evicting people physically. They started with one home on the South Side. Deputies came to the house, ordered the family to leave, and threw their possessions out on the sidewalk. As soon as the deputies left, a crowd of CBL members and supporters moved the people and their possessions back into the house. At the next house, it happened again. The next day's papers were filled with pictures of the families and fur-niture on the street and descriptions of how much each had already paid the seller and the profit he had made. Then the sheriff announced he would do no more evictions until after Christmas.

When evictions began again in January, twenty-five deputies arrived at the first house, only to find several hundred CBL mem-bers and supporters crowded inside, preventing them from entering. The same thing happened at the next house. For the next month, a well-rehearsed stylized dance was played out between the sheriff and CBL. Evictions would be scheduled, the information would be leaked to CBL the night before, word would go out, and when deputy sheriffs arrived at the first house on their list, they would find it surrounded by the people and their supporters. A deputy would go to the door and tell the buyer he had been ordered to leave and was guilty of criminal trespass if he stayed. The buyer would refuse to leave, and the deputies would go on to the next house. The dispute between buyers and sellers had moved from the courtroom to the media.

Then, at the end of the month, under extreme pressure from the sellers, the sheriff sent a posse of several hundred deputies and Chicago policemen to a house where they knew the family wasn't home. They arrived before the CBL forces could get there, broke into the house, threw out the furniture, and installed armed security guards hired by the sellers. Soon the house was surrounded by an angry crowd, shouting at the guards to leave. A scared guard fired his gun in the air, causing the crowd to grow larger and angrier. Finally, a CBL leader was able to calm the crowd and persuade the guards they would be safe if they left, which they did. The family and their possessions moved back in. It was the lead story on television news broadcasts that evening.

The sheriff said he would never again send two hundred men to evict a family. If the people were convicted of criminal trespass, the police could arrest them. He was promptly sued by the sellers and threatened with contempt of court by the judges in housing court. The evictions began again, this time with several hundred police and deputies closing off an entire city block, clearing out every house on the block where there was an eviction order, posting guards with shotguns, and arresting anyone who tried to interfere.

Still the people would not give up. Marshall Patner, a wonderful public-interest lawyer, had been asserting that the failure of the Illinois eviction statute to recognize defenses based on the condition of the property and CBL's civil-rights claims was a violation of due process. Representing a CBL member who had been evicted during the first payment strike, Patner managed to persuade the Illinois Supreme Court to consider his arguments. Struggling to find a way to help the CBL members (while continuing to urge them to end the payment strike), Tom Sullivan and Bob Ming raised similar claims in a separate action in federal court. When the federal court declined to rule due to the pendency of the issue before the Illinois Supreme Court, Sullivan and Ming somehow persuaded the state courts to consolidate their clients' cases with Patner's case, enabling them to avoid eviction while awaiting that decision.

While the eviction battles produced angry confrontations on the streets of the South and West sides almost every week, another element of the conflict produced equally intense—if less public—emotions. Because Lawndale was a Jewish neighborhood before it changed to a black one, most of the real estate dealers who "busted" it and became the contract sellers were also Jewish. Perhaps by coincidence, the companies that built and sold the new homes on the South Side were also owned by two Jewish families. The sellers asserted the charges against them were motivated by anti-Semitism and sought to rally the Chicago-area Jewish community behind them. It was an unfounded charge—but not entirely unsuccessful. Rabbi Robert Marx, a prominent Jewish leader and president of the Chicago Jewish Council on Urban Affairs, had worked closely with Monsignor Egan for years. He was a strong supporter of the Contract Buyers League from the start, and tried to rally other Jewish leaders to their side while using his influence to try to persuade the sellers to reach an accommodation with the buyers. But the sellers labeled him a traitor, and he was ultimately forced to resign as president of the Council on Urban Affairs and leave Chicago. Gordon Sherman, president of Midas Muffler, was the single largest contributor to CBL, and he too was attacked as a traitor by his coreligionists. While these disputes, unlike the evictions, seldom reached the press, they cast an unfortunate pall over the struggle.

Finally, Mayor Daley himself was persuaded to try to negotiate a settlement of the second payment strike lest the street battle over evictions burst into a full-fledged riot. After two days of intensive negotiations, a settlement was announced in April 1970. From the buyers' standpoint, it was not much better than the settlement of the first strike. Some of the South Side buyers rejected it while others signed on and resumed their payments. Most of the South Siders who continued their holdouts were evicted and lost their houses, but the money they had saved allowed some of them to purchase other homes and end up better off for their intransigence. On the West Side, quite a few buyers also refused to end the strike at first, but most resumed payments when Judge Will announced that those who continued to strike would be dismissed from the case.

Thus ended the payment strikes, which, if they did not fully achieve their intended purpose of forcing the sellers to renegotiate their contracts, precipitated more settlements than any previous tactic. The strikes brought the people together with a courage and resolve that, for many CBL members and supporters, was the highlight of their experience and an inspiration for the rest of their lives. At the CBL reunion thirty years later, it was the courage of the buyers in standing together in the face of losing the roofs over their heads that was mentioned most frequently by the seminarians, students, and lawyers in attendance. Mark Splane, now a hard-bitten AFL-CIO organizer for thirteen western states, wept when he spoke of it. Peter Welch spoke of the fundamental difference between men and women like himself, supporters who always knew where they would eat and sleep the next night, and the strikers, who had the unfathomable courage to risk their homes, even when their children asked, "Where will we be tonight?" and there was no answer.

As Tom Sullivan put it, "By acting on principle in ways we could not support in the law, the people forced us to become better lawyers, to expand our thinking and find new ways and new theories to support what they showed us was morally right."

I became involved in the CBL case in 1971. From the beginning, the lawyers had planned to join the Federal Housing Authority and Veterans Administration as defendants in the case because of their refusal to provide mortgage financing in racially changing neighborhoods. Initially, the two agencies were left out of the case to avoid a conflict that would prevent the Justice Department from filing an amicus brief in opposition to the defendants' motions to dismiss, but in 1970 they were added as defendants, along with the Federal Savings and Loan Insurance Corporation (FSLIC). Questions arose about how to prove a case against the FSLIC, whose role was as successor to savings and loan associations that had become insolvent. I had litigated against the FSLIC, knew their lawyers, and knew something about the real estate appraisal issues involved in the CBL case. So I volunteered and overnight became the newest member of CBL's legal team.

I use the word "team" deliberately. Anyone who has participated in team sports knows the communal effort of a team creates a closeness, a sense of purpose, and feelings of hope, joy, and despair which are never forgotten and rarely experienced in any other endeavor. But preparing and trying a major lawsuit with a team of lawyers, assistants, clients, and witnesses evokes a similar response, and where the case involves people and principles deeply important to the members of the team, the emotions are that much greater. For many of us, the Contract Buyers League became the most important team we had ever played on.

Since I obtained my place on the team by claiming expertise with the FSLIC, I thought the first thing I should do was try to make good on that claim. My friend Don Moore, who had represented FSLIC in litigation, set up a meeting with John McCarthy, a Chicago lawyer whose small firm did most of the day-to-day legal work for the agency in Chicago. Fortunately, McCarthy was sympathetic to the buyers. Before long, instead of trying to figure out how to defeat the FSLIC's legal defenses, I was negotiating with them for a settlement. The amount we ultimately agreed on was not many dollars per home, but in total it was a significant sum, a portion of which provided a much-needed contribution to CBL's expenses.

In 1971, Judge Will recused himself from the cases as a result of complaints of bias by the sellers. We had been concentrating on preparation of the West Side case, which was supposed to be the first to go to trial, but in the fall of 1971, the new judge assigned to the South Side case declared that case, formally known as *Clark v. Universal Builders,* would be tried first, in the spring of 1972. Everyone scrambled to prepare for a case that had received little attention except for the eviction battles. As a result of illness or other commitments on the part of some of the other lawyers, the trial team, when the case began, consisted of Tom Sullivan, Tom Boodell, Dick Franch, a Jenner & Block associate, and myself. We were assisted by a veteran team of dedicated paralegals who had organized the evidence.

Due to the high public interest in the case and the large number of buyers expected to attend, the trial was moved from a regular courtroom to the ceremonial court, a larger chamber normally used for swearing-in groups of new citizens, swearing-in ceremonies for new judges, and similar occasions. The judge, J. Sam Perry, was a senior member of the court. Perry had grown up in Alabama, but spent most of his adult life in the same western suburb where Tom Sullivan grew up. Perry was no legal heavyweight, but he had a reputation as something of a populist, with sympathy for the underdog. On balance, we thought he was not too bad a draw. We didn't realize until the trial started that an Alabama populist—at least one of Judge Perry's age—is still from Alabama.

Even before the trial started, Judge Perry had made some troublesome rulings. When the trial date finally arrived, the defendants' lawyers used their peremptory challenges to eliminate every black potential juror. We objected and tried to persuade the judge to assure the presence of at least one black on the jury, but we failed.

The plaintiffs' case in *Clark v. Universal Builders* was lengthy, but straightforward. Much of it was presented through the testimony of experts who, like the lawyers, worked without compensation. An expert in the interpretation of census data traced the influx of blacks into Chicago, their concentration in the South Side ghetto, and the slow block-by-block expansion against white resistance.

The data demonstrated the pervasive racial segregation of Chicago's residential neighborhoods. That data and the testimony of additional experts demonstrated that the influx of African-Americans greatly exceeded the slow expansion of areas where housing was available, creating a severe imbalance of demand over supply in the black housing market. Other experts demonstrated that the dual housing market was the result of racial discrimination against African-Americans by real estate boards and agents, lenders, lending agencies, neighborhood associations, and individual white homeowners, all of whom refused and encouraged others to refuse to sell property or lend money to blacks to purchase property in white neighborhoods.

Individual plaintiffs were called as witnesses to testify to their experience with the sellers. They testified that the sellers refused to sell except on contract, even to buyers with substantial down payments and incomes that easily qualified for mortgage financing. They described the shoddy construction of the houses. Representatives of the defendants were called as hostile witnesses and required to verify books and records demonstrating their construction costs and profits and to admit certain facts and details of the transactions and events testified to by the buyers.

Appraisers experienced in evaluating residential real estate in both black and white areas of Chicago testified that prices in comparable white neighborhoods were 20 to 35 percent lower than those paid by the buyers. The sellers had themselves obtained mortgages on the houses they sold to the buyers on contract, and records subpoenaed from the savings and loans produced fair-market values consistent with the testimony of plaintiffs' appraisers.

One significant difference between the South and West Side cases was that the South Side homes were in a stable African-American neighborhood where some mortgage financing was available to qualified black purchasers. The former commissioner of the Illinois Savings and Loan Associations shed light on the defendants' insistence on contract sales: In addition to the advantages the contract method provided the defendants in high interest payments and the right to retain the plaintiff's entire equity in the property in case of default, by selling on contract the defendants were also able to hide the fact that their prices were substantially above fair-market value. If the buyers were allowed to seek mortgage financing, the lenders would have obtained appraisals, and the low appraised values would have become known to the buyers.

John Royer, an accountant serving without compensation, spent hundreds of hours analyzing the defendants' books and records. From them he prepared extensive data showing the defendants' costs and profits. Experts in residential-housing development compared the markup over cost obtained by the defendants in sales to the buyers with markups obtained by sellers in the white market, demonstrating that the profits on defendants' sales to the buyers were substantially higher. But the most startling evidence was the fact that the same men who controlled the South Side sellers also controlled companies that built nearly identical houses in two white suburbs of Chicago. They sold the suburban houses to white buyers at much lower prices than they charged the contract buyers in Chicago. Moreover, the defendants' claim that the differences were justified by differences in building and land costs was refuted by John Royer's analysis of the defendants' own records, which proved that, in fact, their total costs on the South Side were lower than in the suburbs, so that a comparison of profits produced a disparity even larger than the disparity in price. This evidence proved the defendants had not only taken advantage of the dual housing market to charge purchasers in the black market a higher price than would be paid in the white market, but also that they themselves had charged blacks more than they charged whites for comparable homes. In the face of all law and logic, Judge Perry refused to allow this powerful evidence to go to the jury, claiming that because the suburban houses were "miles away" from, Chicago's south side, they were irrelevant to the case.

Despite Judge Perry's rulings, when we finally rested our case after six weeks of trial, we felt comfortable with the case we had presented. The defendants had experts of their own, but their testimony seemed either irrelevant or designed to dispute facts that most citizens of Chicago knew to be true. The individual defendants would doubtless deny any personal racial animus and claim that by going into a black neighborhood and building badly needed new housing, they had alleviated the very shortage we were complaining about. But if the judge instructed the jury in accordance with Judge Will's interpretation of *Jones v. Mayer*, as he was legally required to do, and if the jury understood and followed those instructions, they would see that none of those pleas were a defense against the charge the defendants had taken advantage of the dual market to charge excessive prices and enjoy excessive profits in their sales to black purchasers.

In civil trials, when the plaintiffs complete their proof, the defendants often file a "motion to dismiss at the close of plaintiffs' case." It is a routine motion which can be granted only if the plaintiffs have failed to produce any relevant evidence in support of some essential element of their case. We rested on a Friday, defendants' motion was argued briefly by both sides, and the case was adjourned until Monday morning, when we expected the defendants would begin their case. The judge's taking the motion under advisement rather than denying it outright was a little unusual, but not worrisome—there was simply no basis for dismissal under Judge Will's opinion, which was the applicable law of the case until and unless reversed by a higher court.

When we arrived on Monday morning, I thought something was odd, but it took me a while to figure out what it was. Scattered around the front row of the spectator benches were eight or ten men I recognized as members of the United States marshal's service. Usually there was only one marshal in each courtroom.

There were several of our paralegals and perhaps two dozen contract buyers sitting in the spectator section. All but one or two of the contract buyers were women, none of them less than fifty years old. When Judge Perry entered, everyone rose, but when the judge was seated and everyone else sat down, the marshals remained standing in the front of the courtroom, facing the audience.

And then, suddenly and overwhelmingly, I realized what was happening. Judge J. Sam Perry was going to dismiss the case—take it away from the jury—and he was afraid the middle-aged postal workers, domestics, and housewives who had come to his courtroom for the past six weeks wearing their best clothes and standing quietly and respectfully whenever he entered the room, were going to start a riot.

They should have.

Speaking rapidly, the judge, without mentioning Judge Will's opinion, flatly rejected it and announced we had failed to prove our case. As he read from a document he must have prepared over the weekend, his eyes were glued to the paper as though he was afraid to look up:

"Counsel for the plaintiffs have not painted a pretty picture of the defendants, but that picture is a picture of exploitation for profit, and not racial discrimination. . . . Nowhere in the six weeks trial is there one scintilla of evidence that the defendants . . . ever refused to sell to a white person or a black person . . . any house, or refused to sell one or the other at a higher or lower price, absolutely no positive evidence of discrimination in this record."

Accordingly, the judge said, the defendants' motions for directed verdict are granted. If the plaintiffs do not appeal, he went on, he would dismiss the defendants' counterclaims and not assess costs against the plaintiffs; but if they did appeal, he would reinstate the counterclaim and reconsider assessment of costs. With that the judge rose and fled out the door to his chambers just as Tom Sullivan began objecting to the shameless effort to coerce the plaintiffs into waiving their right to appeal. Tom continued making his record to the court reporter after Perry had left, and when the judge realized it, he came back and angrily ordered the reporter to stop taking down Tom's objections.

It was over. Utterly dejected, we gathered up our papers. One of the paralegals was crying, and several buyers tried to comfort her. As we left, we told the buyers who were still there how sorry we were, and they said they knew we had done everything we could, and they hadn't trusted the judge from the start. Most of the members of the Contract Buyers League were deeply religious—far more so than their lawyers or even most of the young Catholics Jack Mcnamara had attracted to the cause—and several of them spoke of God's will, and how they had endured so far and knew God would give them the strength to endure this as well and keep fighting. We said we would keep fighting too and were confident we could prevail on appeal. And then there wasn't anything more to say, so people just stood around looking at each other and murmuring awkward reassurances until someone took the initiative of saying they had to leave and the people headed back to the South Side while the lawyers and paralegals dragged our suitcase-sized briefcases and bankers' boxes full of documents back to our offices. I felt more tired than I had ever felt in my life.

We had said we would appeal, but it wasn't quite that simple. The judge had threatened to assess legal costs against the plaintiffs and reinstate the defendants' counterclaim, charging them with a variety of alleged misconduct in connection with the eviction wars. The one thing we were confident about was that the Court of Appeals would not approve Judge Perry's effort to coerce the plaintiffs into forgoing their right to appeal, but we had also had some confidence in Judge Perry. The people had to understand that nothing was certain. If we were wrong, they could be facing a whole new problem.

The most active participants in the case were unanimous in wanting to appeal. We let everyone who remained in the plaintiff class know they could exercise an individual election to withdraw and not be included in the appeal. Only a handful did. We also explored the possibility of a settlement, but the defendants offered nothing of interest. We filed our notice of appeal within the short time allowed by the rules and began putting together the record and preparing a brief. Because of the length of the trial, putting the appeal together was a slow process, with many extensions of time. Even after all the briefs were filed, there was a substantial delay before the court set the case for argument; but finally we were notified the argument would be held on October 24, 1973, some sixteen months after Judge Perry dismissed the case.

For reasons neither of us can now remember, Tom Sullivan and I had decided some time earlier that I would present the argument on appeal. Neither do I recall whether I received notice of the CBL argument date before or after I learned that the Seventh Circuit argument in *Burns v. Elrod* would be held on October 23. Either way, I was going to be awfully busy in mid-October preparing for two of the most important cases I would ever argue.

The panel assigned to hear the argument in *Clark v. Universal Builders* consisted of Luther Swygert, the chief judge of the Seventh Circuit, Robert Sprecher, and Robert Grant, the same senior district court judge who sat on the *Burns v. Elrod* panel the day before. I knew nothing about Grant except that he had seemed sympathetic to my argument in the *Burns* case. Sprecher was neither especially liberal or conservative and was one of the smartest judges on the court. Luther Swygert was a big man with white hair and a white beard whose friendly, welcoming demeanor with the lawyers who appeared before him never failed to remind me of Chief Justice Earl Warren. And, like Warren, Swygert was an unapologetic liberal. I was delighted to see his name on the panel.

Clark v. Universal Builders was the first case on the docket on October 24. When I walked into the courtroom a few minutes before the argument was to begin, quite a few contract buyers were sitting in the spectator section. There was no time to talk, but we smiled at each other, and several of them gave me a little wave of recognition and encouragement. As appellant, I argued first, and while the judges asked quite a few questions, most of them involved clarification of Judge Perry's rulings. Wasn't his statement of the reasons for directing a verdict in direct contradiction of Judge Will's ruling upholding the complaint? It was. What reasons did he give for excluding the comparison between the prices and profits obtained by the defendants and those obtained by companies owned by the same individuals in selling substantially identical homes to whites in the suburbs? There was no mistaking the tone of the questions—they were expressions of puzzlement and disbelief at Judge Perry's ruling.

When I finally sat down, feeling dangerously confident, the judges began immediately to ask many of the same questions of the defendants' lawyer, but in a very different tone. Isn't Mr. Tucker right that the judge's decision effectively overruled the exploitation theory of the case which Judge Will sustained? Assuming that Judge Perry had any right to revisit that issue, did he ever do so—was there ever any briefing or argument or ruling on the subject before the trial started? And didn't the very evidence Judge Perry excluded also provide a basis for finding the more traditional kind of discrimination that he then said was missing when he dismissed the case? With each question and look of skepticism, my confidence increased. Then, when I rose to say a few words in rebuttal, Chief Judge Swygert asked me the most astonishing question I had ever heard in an oral argument:

"Mr. Tucker, in your brief you ask us to reverse Judge Perry's order and remand the case for a new trial. But if we uphold Judge Will's exploitation theory, can't we reverse outright and enter judgment for the plaintiffs?"

For all the years that have passed since that moment, I have tried to figure out some way I could have said yes. In his disgust and irritation with Judge Perry's clearly erroneous ruling, Judge Swygert had momentarily forgotten that the sellers had a right to put on a defense. I had to say I didn't think so.

As I have said before, experienced lawyers know better than to assume they know how an appeal is going to come out from the questions asked by the court—but when the argument in *Clark v. Universal Builders* was over, I knew we had won.

I was right, but for some reason it took the court another nine months to say so. When it did, on July 26, 1974, it was as complete a victory as we could have asked for, short of Judge Swygert's finding a way to give us judgment without letting the defendants put on a defense. The court adopted the exploitation theory in full, adding its own rhetoric to Judge Will's rebuff of the claim that the defendants could be liable only if they sold houses to whites in the black market at a lower price than they charged blacks, and that there could be no liability for exploiting someone else's discrimination:

"It is no answer that defendants would have exploited whites as well as blacks. To accept defendants' contention would be tantamount to perpetuating a subterfuge behind which every slumlord and exploiter of those banished to the ghetto could hide by a simple rubric: The same property would have been sold to whites on the same terms. . . . We find repugnant to the clear language and spirit of the Civil Rights Act the claim that he who exploits and preys on the discriminatory hardship of a black man occupies a more protected status than he who created the hardship in the first instance."

The judge who now was in charge of the West Side case had decided without objection that he would not set that case for trial until the South Side appeal was decided. Once the Supreme Court denied the defendants' petition for certiorari in *Clark v. Universal*, he proposed a trial date in the spring of 1975. Despite the delays that had already occurred and drained much of the energy from the Contract Buyers League, I had no choice but to ask for a later date. Almost the entire staff of CBL had dispersed to other lives after the South Side case was dismissed. Reconstituting a support team and bringing the West Side preparation back to where it had been when attention shifted to the South Side was going to be a big job which would be followed by a substantial final push to be ready for trial. At my request, the judge continued the case until November. Patti Randolph came back to work as a paralegal. Ellen Duggan, a former nun who had stayed on in a paralegal job at Jenner & Block, was reassigned to CBL. Linda Mullenbach, whose parents had been CBL supporters when Linda was starting high school, had now graduated from college and signed on as a paralegal. Slowly but surely the case came back together, and on

November 19, 1975, we began selecting a jury for the second CBL trial. I would serve as lead counsel, assisted by Dick Franch and Tom Boodell.

Judge Frank McGarr was an experienced lawyer who had served many years in the Illinois attorney general's office before becoming a judge. He was a Republican and quite conservative, but by today's standards he would be called moderate; on the bench he had earned a reputation as a good trial judge. When jury selection began and it was apparent there were hardly any blacks among the fifty or so citizens who had been sent up to the courtroom as the panel from which the trial jury would be selected, we were encouraged to learn he had ordered up additional jurors and made it clear he wanted some of them to be black. However, even with the additional panel the best we could do was have an African-American as the first alternate, and for that we had to accept as a regular juror an elderly man whose background suggested a likely bias against the plaintiffs but who was in such frail health we thought he would probably have to be replaced sometime during a long trial. That would get us to the black first alternate. Among other problems, the juror we were hoping to lose had been the victim of a poison-gas attack that had injured his lungs in the First World War. Some days he seemed barely able to walk, but he came every day and was still there five months later when the trial ended. So were the other five regular jurors we started with—all white.

Ruth Wells had replaced Charlie Baker as the first named plaintiff in the West Side case. The plaintiff's evidence in *Wells v. F & F Investment Co.* closely followed the evidence we had presented in the South Side case, with some important differences in degree. For one thing, unlike the South Side defendants, who presented the appearance of respectable businessmen, it was difficult for the West Side sellers to disguise the truth: Most were sleazy men who made huge profits by methodically promoting panic among white homeowners and purchasing their homes for prices well below their true value, and then turned around and sold those homes to black contract purchasers at prices well above their true value. One of them, the Reverend Wallace Reid, was the white pastor of an evangelical church with a largely black membership. He had sold houses to members of his congregation. Solemnly assuring the buyers he was doing the Lord's work in trying to help them, his markups were the highest of all the defendants.

On the South Side, the evidence suggested a markup of about 20 percent above the white market for similar houses. On the West Side, the markup was often 50 percent or more, and because of the below-market prices they paid panicked whites, their profit margins sometimes reached 100 percent. In addition, our questioning of the defendants resulted in several examples of outright dishonesty and false testimony to go with their exploitation of the buyers. As for the plaintiffs themselves, those who we called as witnesses presented a picture of honest, hardworking men and women who had tried to make a better life for themselves and their children. They had moved out of the overcrowded South Side ghetto into homes of their own in a better neighborhood, only to find that the price they paid had led to disintegration of family life, loss of control over their children, inability to maintain their property, and ultimately to a neighborhood with worse problems than the ones they had sought to escape. In early February, when I announced, "The plaintiffs rest," I was confident we had made an even stronger case than we made on the South Side.

The plaintiffs' case had taken two months and two days from the first witness to the day we rested, and the defendants' case took exactly two months more. In part, the length of the trial was due to an extremely relaxed schedule and several longer-than-ususal recesses for holidays and for Judge McGarr to attend to other duties. George Feiwell, who represented the largest defendant in number of homes sold, organized a joint defense based primarily on the theory that the high prices charged to plaintiffs were due to the fact they were buying on "credit"—i.e., on contract—rather than for "cash," with a mortgage. Several appraisers called as witnesses claimed it was this difference—not race—that created a dual market. One problem with that theory was that many of the buyers had down payments and incomes that qualified them for mortgages—if they "had" to buy on contract, it was simply another manifestation of the racial discrimination that created the dual market in the first place. Moreover, there was no evidence that sales on credit justified the higher prices—the delay in receiving full payment and increased risk, if any, was more than made up for by the high interest rates the sellers imposed.

The "credit" argument was supplemented by the testimony of several defendants that they would have charged whites the same prices they charged blacks for the houses they sold—and in a handful of instances, they claimed to have done so. That claim had been expressly rejected by the Court of Appeals as a defense to the exploitation theory of liability, but it had a certain superficial appeal. We asked the judge to reject the testimony, but throughout the trial it had become increasingly obvious that Judge McGarr was himself no fan of the Court of Appeals decision. Over our objection, he allowed the defendants to identify certain sales they claimed had been made to whites at similar prices and conditions. However, whenever those buyers could now be located, we discovered that the defendants' claim was false, or the sales were to mixed-race couples. The truth was that white home buyers were not moving into Lawndale and paying excessive prices during the 1950s and 1960s, but even if a few had done so, it didn't change the basic fact that the defendants had exploited a racially segregated dual market.

As the case drew to a close, the jury was excused for several days as we fought over instructions. At first the judge rejected the instructions we proposed that he give to reflect the exploitation theory, even though they were taken almost verbatim from the Court of Appeals decision. Ultimately, he agreed to include a general instruction that recognized the basic elements of our case, while continuing to resist instructions which incorporated language from the Court of Appeals decision rejecting the defense that the sellers would have treated white buyers as badly as they treated the blacks—if only they could have found some willing white victims.

At my suggestion, Tom Boodell gave the initial closing argument for the plaintiffs. Tom's regular law practice was as a transactional lawyer, not a trial lawyer, but he had represented CBL longer than anyone and was completely familiar with the facts of the case, and the law too. He provided the jury with a logical, low-key, complete, and compelling road map through the evidence and instructions which would require the jury to return a verdict for the plaintiffs. When he was finished and the lawyers for the defendants had made their responses, I spoke in rebuttal for a final seventy-five minutes. It was the most intense, deeply felt argument I ever made in a courtroom.

The next day, Tuesday, April 13, Judge McGarr instructed the jury and sent them off to deliberate. There had been lumps and bumps—some rulings I thought were dead wrong, some important instructions refused, some cross-examinations I would have liked to try over—but all things considered, I thought the case had gone well enough.

With my Supreme Court argument in the patronage case scheduled for the following Monday, I had to turn my attention to that preparation, but it was difficult to concentrate, and more so each day as the jury deliberations continued. Finally, late on Thursday afternoon, a call came from the court. Judge McGarr had received a question from the jury. They had reached a verdict on all but one defendant, but could not find or recall any evidence about that one and wanted to know what to do. The defendant involved had made only one or two sales, the buyers could no longer be located, and we had simply forgotten to dismiss him from the case before the trial started. We agreed that the jury could be told the next morning to return the verdicts they had and the defendant in question would be dismissed. All of us felt certain the question meant the jury had decided in our favor with regard to the other defendants—why would they be concerned about what to do with a defendant who had never even been mentioned in the case if they weren't finding the others guilty? We spread the word to all concerned that a verdict would be returned the next morning, telling those who asked that we were cautiously optimistic.

It was Good Friday. Every seat in the courtroom was occupied by CBL members, staff, well-wishers, and press. When everyone was settled and the judge called for the jury, the first juror through the door would be person who was selected to be foreman so he or she could take the seat closest to the bench and deliver the verdict sheets to the clerk. It was the same person who had sat in that chair throughout the trial, a middle-aged accountant named Francis McLennand. He was one of our less-favorite jurors, and hadn't seemed like a leader, so I was a little surprised to see that he had been elected foreman.

It is widely believed you can tell what a jury has done by watching them when they enter to return a verdict, especially in criminal cases. (They supposedly avoid looking at the defendant if they have convicted him.) But I have never thought I could tell any such thing, and I couldn't this time. The judge complimented the jury for noticing there was no evidence about the one defendant, said he would be dismissed from the case, and said he understood they had a verdict. Mr. McLennand said they did, and was instructed to hand the verdict forms to the clerk. The clerk handed them to the judge, who read them to himself and handed them back to the clerk. I was sitting with my elbows on the table in front of me, clasping my hands tightly together to try to keep from shaking with tension. The minute or less that elapsed from the time the clerk took the verdicts from the foreman until the judge handed them back so the clerk could read them aloud dragged on and on. Before returning them to the clerk, the judge had folded the verdict forms in half the way the foreman had presented them to the clerk and the clerk had presented them to the judge. The clerk took another hour or two to unfold them. My shoulders ached.

When the clerk finished unfolding the forms, he picked up the first one on the pile, held it up in front of him and, looking out into the audience, read it. "We the jury find the defendant Joseph Berke not guilty." My shoulders stopped aching. They were numb. Paralyzed. But my mind raced. Joseph Berke had the fewest sales of the defendants who remained. He had come to court poorly dressed and had represented himself. The jury may have believed that whatever he had done, he was now impoverished and felt sorry for him. The clerk picked up another verdict form and began reading. "We the jury find the defendant Jay Goran not guilty." My mind stopped racing. It stopped doing anything. My head felt full of little bubbles, fizzing and popping like carbonated water. My neck would no longer hold my head up, so I unclasped my hands and rested my forehead between them with my elbows still planted on the table while the clerk read another not guilty verdict and then another and another until all six defendants were acquitted. Even the execrable Reverend Reid.

Somehow I croaked out a request that the jury be polled—that each juror be asked individually if the verdicts that were read were in fact his or her verdicts. Two of them looked unhappy, but they all said it was their verdict. And that was all.

The analogy between lawsuits and sports extends beyond the camaraderie of working as a team. Courtroom lawyers and people who play sports are engaged in an endeavor where there is a winner and loser of every contest, and no matter how good they are, sometimes they lose. In fact, in both endeavors it is often true that the better they are the harder their contests and the more often they will lose. Lots of basketball players go through a high-school season or two without a loss, but no NBA player does. You don't have to like it—in fact, you had better not—but you won't last long if you don't learn to get over it, or at least put it far enough behind you to go on to the next case or the next game. Twenty-six years later, I still haven't gotten over the verdict in the Contract Buyers League case, but in a way I was lucky. I had no choice but to put it behind me in a hurry. I had to argue in the Supreme Court on Monday.

Of course, when a case means as much to you as the Contract Buyers cases had meant to me, you can't help wondering what went wrong. We knew we had make some mistakes, you always do, but had we made some horrible mistake we didn't know about? No way to answer that. I had a couple of other theories, and I believe they are probably at least partially true. For one thing, public attitudes had changed between the late 1960s and 1976. From strong support for civil rights, at least in the North, many had come to believe blacks were asking for, and getting, too much "special treatment." And there was no denying the CBL case was seeking relief for blacks that would not have been available to whites if they had entered into the same contracts. Of course, whites didn't *have* to enter into such contracts, they had housing available on better terms—but plenty of them felt they had been cheated at some point in their lives, and nobody had claimed their civil rights had been violated.

Another factor was that by 1976 the prices the plaintiffs paid for their houses in the 1950s and early 1960s seemed extraordinarily low, despite the comparisons we provided for similar houses in white markets. The plaintiffs had bought two- and three-flat brick or stone buildings for $25,000 or $30,000. Anywhere the jurors looked, such buildings were now worth at least twice that much. Even if the plaintiffs were overcharged at the time, some of the jurors may have felt, they probably came out all right.

Then, a year and a half later, some information emerged that provided additional insight into what happened. The foreman of the jury had kept a diary throughout the trial and jury deliberations. He had sent a copy to one of the defense lawyers, who shared it with me. Reading it, it was apparent that from the first day of the trial he had been against the plaintiffs and determined to rule against them. Although generally couched in polite, non-racial terms, his overall attitude toward the plaintiffs themselves was revealed early on by comments like "I don't think she understands what interest is" or " I think this witness wasn't 'aware' of things until the Contract Buyers League projected thoughts to her." As his description of the trial progressed he would find some negative explanation for every point made by the plaintiffs' witnesses, ridiculing one of the experts as an arrogant Harvard intellectual and commenting that the "Harvard liberals in government" are responsible for many of the country's problems. At some point during the trial, he noted that the higher prices paid by blacks were "not a matter of civil rights, but supply-and-demand economics," as though supply and demand was a defense rather than a central part of the exploitation theory of the case. Finally, during his description of the jury deliberations, it becomes clear that despite the jury instructions, he slowly but surely persuaded the three jurors who started out voting for the plaintiffs to accept his view.

McLennand's diary proved we had indeed made a terrible mistake by not using one of our challenges to eliminate him from the jury. But none of us could recall a thing about the voir dire (preliminary examination of a juror) to warn us he would be against us from the start. Then it got even worse. Jeff Fitzgerald, who had written his Ph.D. thesis at Northwestern University on the Contract Buyers League in the early 1970s, had come back to Chicago to observe the trial and perhaps write a book about the case. After the case was over, he managed to locate and interview several of the jurors, including McLennand—who told him, in so many words, that he hoped the verdict would help to reverse "the mess Earl Warren made with *Brown v. Board of Education* and all that nonsense."

In his diary, McLennand also said that after the case was over, Judge McGarr had called the jury into his chambers and told them they had reached the right verdict: The case was about economics, not civil rights. I thought it was just McLennand justifying his own conclusion. I didn't think the judge would make such a comment— he would praise the jury for their service, but not comment on their verdict—especially by saying something that showed he didn't accept the Court of Appeals decision—even if it was true. But it turned out he did; the juror who held out the longest for a plaintiffs' verdict confirmed it to me as I was preparing this book.

What would have happened without McLennand on the jury we will never know, nor can we be sure what would have happened if the judge had given stronger instructions. I remain a strong believer in the jury system, but nothing is perfect. It does argue against the perfunctory voir dire that has been the practice in most federal trials for many years, although the voir dire in the CBL case was broader than in most cases and there is no guarantee even the most searching questions would have uncovered the biases of the determined Mr. McLennand.

So what can I say about a case I worked on for seven years and more hours than any other case in thirty years of practice; a case that produced no revenue and thousands of dollars of out-of-pocket expenses; a case I tried twice, once for six weeks and once for nearly five months, and lost both times?

I can say that while we lost the legal battle, there were also some victories. Over four hundred buyers renegotiated their contracts on CBL terms and saved some $6 million—$29 million in today's dollars. Probably twice that many buyers renegotiated on their own for less per contract, but even more in total dollars. The case ended contract selling as a vehicle for discrimination in Chicago and most of the country, nudged the government into forcing lenders and its own agencies to provide mortgage financing for African-American home buyers, and scared the crap out of a bunch of really bad people. Jack Egan and Jack Mcnamara and all the people who supported them helped the people of CBL create an organization that empowered them to work together and stand up for themselves in ways they had never known before, and never forgot.

In one sense, Tom Sullivan was right. We were not the heroes, the heroes were the Ruth Wellses and Charlie Bakers and all the other home buyers who went to meetings, withheld payments despite the threat of losing their houses, and defied authority by resisting eviction. They suffered the indignity of harassment and ridicule by the defendants' lawyers, and the strange, fearsome experience of testifying in a federal courtroom. The lawyers, the expert witnesses, the students and staffers, the priests and seminarians, the rabbis, the fund-raisers, were not heroes—but we were given a rare opportunity to work with heroic people, for which I am deeply grateful, and which is my proudest experience as a lawyer. Everyone who has the privilege of becoming a courtroom lawyer should hope for such an extraordinary opportunity.

Incidentally, several years after the case was over, one of his buyers—not a CBL member—shot the Reverend Wallace Reid dead in his living room. Sometimes justice does come only from the barrel of a gun. *I AM PISSED!!!*

❧ CHAPTER 8 ❧
SOME GOOD GUYS AND SOME BAD GUYS

In 1976 one of Chicago's best criminal-defense lawyers referred two clients to the firm to handle a case that was too complicated for his one-man office. And that is how I met Dominic Cortina and his best friend and partner, Donald "The Wizard of Odds" Angelini.

For many years, Cortina and Angelini operated the largest sports-gambling business in the Midwest. On a day-to-day basis Cortina managed the sports book that had the wealthiest customers and highest volume in Chicago. His book also took layoff bets from other bookmakers seeking to reduce their exposure to risk. Angelini was the oddsmaker, providing a betting line for the books managed by Cortina and other midwestern bookmakers. Three bookmaking offices allegedly supervised by Cortina were wiretapped by the FBI during 1974 and 1975. Thereafter, the two men and five of their associates were indicted by a federal grand jury on charges of running an illegal gambling business.

Tom Sullivan and I agreed to represent Angelini and Cortina, respectively. We soon discovered that Donald and Dominic were delightful company and men of impeccable honesty and candor in their dealings with us. That was also their reputation with their betting clients, their employees, and even the FBI agents who had spent many years trying to catch and convict them.

From our first meeting in 1976 until his death in December

1999, I represented Dominic Cortina whenever he was in trouble, which was often. In the course of those cases I learned a great deal about sports gambling and the "Outfit," Chicago-speak for the local branch of Italian organized crime. Federal criminal cases against alleged members of the outfit were investigated and prosecuted by the "strike force," a special unit of the Justice Department with its own detachment of lawyers and FBI agents. Rather than finding a crime and trying to solve it, they targeted suspected organized crime figures and tried to find a reason to prosecute them. From representing Cortina and other targets of the strike force, I also learned about some of the problems of target prosecution which led to the disbanding of the strike force in the 1980s and termination of the "independent counsel" statute following the Kenneth Starr/President Clinton debacle in the 1990s.

Dominic Cortina was born in Chicago in 1925 to parents who emigrated from Italy the year before. In a conversation not long before his death, he described the life that led to our meeting fifty-one years later. Dom's father, Joe, was a laborer—a pick-and-shovel man who spoke no English and "worked like a dog from dawn to dark." His mother, Anna, stayed home with the six children.

Dom went to the local grammar school and high school in the predominantly Irish and Italian neighborhood where the family settled, but he had no interest in school. "I was an idiot—I didn't know any better, and nobody could tell me anything." He wasn't a troublemaker, but he skipped school almost every day. When he was fifteen, he quit altogether.

There were pool halls every couple of blocks in those days, and Dom began working in one of them, cleaning the tables and taking fifty-cent and dollar bets on horse races for the owner. Hanging around the neighborhood, he met many of the people who would become his best friends for life, including Angelini, Joe Spadeveccio (always known as "Joe Spa"), George Collucci, and Joe Ferriola, who years later would become the boss of the Chicago outfit.

When he turned eighteen, Dom volunteered for the army. He had flat feet and failed the physical, but was finally accepted for "limited service." Eight months later, they changed the rules to eliminate "limited service," and he received a medical discharge.

When he got out of the army, Dom did factory work for about a year and a half, and hated it. In 1945 he went to work as a doorman for a real "book joint" at 19th and Blue Island. If Chicago's neighborhoods in those days boasted a tavern on every corner and a pool hall every few blocks, there were also a couple of book joints in every ward. All the bars, pool halls, and cigar stores took horse bets, but a real book joint was a walk-in business devoted exclusively to gambling. Dom's employer was "Big John" Cimitelli, a large man who always wore a vest and a straw hat. Dom was a big guy too and served as a "lookout" for potential troublemakers or unexpected visits from law enforcement. "But they really didn't need me, everybody was OK in those days."

The book joint had open phone lines covering all the tracks, all day. Phones were not allowed at the track, but someone with high-powered binoculars would be stationed in a building where he could see the races. He would call each race over the telephone. In the book joint, loudspeakers broadcast the call to the assembled bettors: "They're off in the second at Arlington." There would be fifty or sixty people in the joint every afternoon and evening. Between races, they would rush to the counters to make their bets—a dollar or two—ten dollars was a big bet. When the call started, everybody went crazy, yelling for the horse they had bet on while the progress of the race was described over the loudspeakers. "It was great," Dom said wistfully. "Everybody should see what a real book joint was like."

On the same day I interviewed Dom in early 1999, I interviewed Donald Angelini. He was a year younger than Dom. After his junior year in high school, he quit, and in 1944 was drafted into the army, where he became an MP. When he got out he connected up with Dom, who got him a job in Big John's book joint as a "sheet writer"—writing down the customers' bets. At night he went to DePaul University Law School on the GI Bill, but after a year, he quit.

In the two years Dom and Donald worked for Big John, his book joint was never raided by the police. Gambling enforcement was all local; the federal government wasn't involved. The primary level of "enforcement" were the gambling squads within the Chicago Detective Bureau. They were run from downtown and could roam all over the city to make arrests. The first of every month, the "bureau cars" would come by Big John's for their cut. All day long they would come, dozens of squads, each car getting maybe fifteen, twenty bucks. Then they would move on to the next joint. "They had a regular route." At the local level, only the district police captain or "his man" got paid. No local cop was allowed to bother them. If one did, the captain would have him transferred out the next day. If for some reason there was going to be "heat," the captain would let them know and tell them to close down for a day or two. Big John didn't like to close down, so he had an alternate location several blocks away. When the captain said to close down, everyone would grab the counters and betting sheets and other paraphernalia and carry it to the alternate location. One day, after coming by and telling Big John to close for a couple of days, the captain left and then for some reason doubled back, just as everyone was carrying stuff down the street. "The captain starts yelling at Big John. He's out of his car, in the middle of the street in broad daylight, yelling, 'I told you to close down, damn it, I told you to close down.' He was screaming, in the middle of the street. Everyone in the neighborhood could see and hear him. That's how open it was."

The pay with Big John wasn't much, so sometime in 1947 Donald and Dom, joined by their street buddy Joe Spa, opened a telephone office booking the "wire." The "wire" referred to horses who were for some reason expected to win, either because of a fix or because they were.part of a consortium of racing stables that commonly held back horses in several races until the odds were good and then ran them for the gambling winnings. Word about which horses were "on the wire" would spread quickly among bookmakers, who would then refuse to take bets on them. Of course, the wire horses didn't always win, and sometimes the word that a horse was "wired" would result in it getting bet down so far at the track that even if it won the bookie didn't have to pay off much, and if it lost, he made a bundle. Those situations looked to Dom "like ice cream." With the arrogance of youth, Dom, Donald, and Joe thought they could beat the wire, and they knew they could get lots of customers—bookies wanted to get rid of bets they had inadvertently taken on wire horses, and savvy bettors wanted to find a place to bet on them. They let a few bookies know they would book the wire, and the bookies would send them bets they had taken and give the phone number to their good customers. For a while the wire was cold, and the new entrepreneurs built up a nice bankroll. But soon the tide turned. "We were young and stupid. In the long run, you couldn't beat 'em. We lost the bankroll we'd built up, and then we lost our asses."

A friend of theirs owned a pool hall and hired Dom and Donald to run it, together with a regular all-night poker game on Fridays. After about a year, the pool hall was sold and Dom and Donald went back to working for a bookmaker. His name was Joe Amato, and his book joint was in the back room of a pricey restaurant and lounge—a roadhouse—called the Bigfoot Inn. It was located just 200 yards south of the Wisconsin border on U.S. 14, the main route from Chicago to the west end of Lake Geneva, a recreational haven for some of Chicago's richest families.

Like Big John's, the book joint in the Bigfoot Inn was wide open. A sport service provided a call of the races from tracks across the country, and the call was broadcast over speakers at the Bigfoot. The speakers, however, were in the restaurant and lounge as well as the back room, and travelers who stopped in for lunch or a beer during the day would hear the call and ask if there was a book joint on the premises. Told yes, plenty of them would linger for a while to bet, or come back again for that purpose. Slot machines supplemented the horse betting for those so inclined.

Donald and Dominic pretty much ran the place; Joe Amato was seldom around. They got $15 each per day plus bonuses. Business was great. The two men, both bachelors, moved up to Harvard, Illinois, ten miles south of the joint, and took a room in the town plumber's family home, sleeping together in a large double bed with a quilt. Dom had a defensive tackle's body and a broad face that remained youthful into his seventies. Donald was also tall, but otherwise Dom's physical opposite: slim, with sharp features, large blue eyes and a deeply tanned complexion. Some time before I met him, his hair had turned pure white. They shared a car, and they had a great time. Most of the people who lived in the area and many of their most loyal customers were dairy farmers. There's no telling how many farmers' daughters learned the ways of the big city from Dom and Donald at the Bigfoot Inn.

Then, on November 1, 1951, a new federal gambling law went into effect, and every book joint in the Chicago area closed overnight, including the Bigfoot Inn. There was no way to hide your operation in a joint where anybody could walk in, and the word was the feds were serious about it and were going to send treasury agents in plainclothes into book joints all over the country. No one wanted to find out if that was true—there were prison sentences at risk.

Dom and Donald returned to Chicago and opened a real estate office on the Near West Side. Donald did tax returns to pay the rent while Dom tried to sell real estate. It wasn't long before they had another idea. "If you were around when Prohibition came in, and all you really knew how to do was run a bar, but the bars had to close, what did you do? You opened a speakeasy." Because of the new federal law, all the old book joints were closed. Still, people wanted to bet, and the bars, pool halls, hotel doormen, and all the other small fry still wanted to take bets. But big bettors had nowhere to go. There was a vacuum, and Dom and Donald thought they could fill it by taking bets the way they had when they were booking the wire—on the telephone. "The feds couldn't find us on the telephones." Dom paused. "Supposedly." He laughs. "They found *us.*"

Though they had no bankroll, Dom had a friend who agreed to back them if they needed money. They started winning from the beginning and never had to call on him. They were the only game in town, and business built up to a tremendous level almost from the start.

Before long they had several wire rooms and hired others to work the phones and take the calls. They took horse bets and, as it became popular, sports bets. For the most part, they had few problems with law enforcement. On the rare occasion when local law enforcement arrested someone for gambling, the punishment was a small fine or a few days in jail. When the federal law came in, the city gambling squad had been disbanded. With the bureau gone and the wire room hidden, it was no longer necessary to pay anybody off. Only the feds had the desire and resources to try to track down the wire rooms and until Bobby Kennedy became attorney general, the FBI didn't pay any attention—only treasury agents went after the bookies.

One time treasury agents located a wire room, put it under surveillance, and got a search warrant to raid it and arrest the employees who were running it for Dom and Donald. By chance, Dom was there checking to see how things were going when the raid started. The wire room was in the attic of a garage. The garage door itself was locked and reinforced, and if someone got it open, a light went on in the attic, signaling an intruder. Once you were inside the garage, the only way to get into the attic was through a trapdoor in the ceiling. When the treasury agents got into the garage and the light went on, the men in the attic jammed precut two-by-fours between the top of the trapdoor and the roof of the garage. It was impossible for the agents to get any leverage into their efforts to ram the trapdoor open from below. The wire room had four phone lines that came into the attic inside a fat cable behind a desk. Dom had a sharp ax next to the desk so anyone inside could cut the phone cable with one blow. That way, if the agents got in, they couldn't continue to take phone calls from bettors who could then be traced and coerced into testifying against the bookies. Dom cut the cable and the three men started burning all the gambling paraphernalia in a big metal wastebasket—betting slips, line information, racing forms, and the like. When they were sure everything was burned beyond reconstruction, they pulled out the two-by-fours and let the agents in. One of them hurried up a ladder into the attic with a fire extinguisher and directed it into the still-smoking wastebasket, but it was too late.

There were six or seven treasury agents in the operation. They had arrest warrants for Dom's two employees, but not for Dom. When everyone got down into the garage, one of the agents asked Dom his name. He gave an obviously phony name. The man asked him again. Dom said, "You already asked me that. I'll tell you again, just one more time," and he repeated the phony name. When the agent kept asking, Dom just stared at him and refused to answer any more questions. "Then the prick called me un-American for not answering his questions. Can you imagine that? I was furious. I'm as good an American as he is. I volunteered for the army, had to go back and beg 'em to let me in after they first turned me down because of my feet. The prick!" Except for two FBI agents who later lied in a case against him, I never heard Dom say a bad word about any other law-enforcement agent he encountered over the years. He figured they were just doing their jobs, like he was. And when he told me this story, near the end of his life, he still sounded a lot angrier at the guy who called him un-American than he ever did about the agents who tried to send him to jail by lying.

If Dominic Cortina thought he was just doing his job and was as good an American as anyone, and he absolutely did, it was because to the day he died he never thought there was anything wrong with being a bookmaker. Illegal, yes, but immoral, sinful, un-American? Absolutely not. When he started out, the local book-maker was as welcome and respected in the community as any other businessman. He raised a family, went to church, and didn't hurt anyone. Illegal, yes, but that was simply the hypocrisy of the state, which for its own purposes provided legal gambling of all sorts.

Later, with the full force of the Justice Department's Strike Force on Organized Crime after him, Dom would say, with a look of genuine amazement on his face, "The government takes millions of dollars from poor people in the lottery and pays back only 50 percent of the gross, while I take bets from rich people and pay back all but 5 percent, and I'm Public Enemy Number One? Ridiculous!"

Betting on sporting events came to Chicago gradually in the 1950s. The betting was primarily on baseball. Betting on football, now by far the most popular gambling sport, didn't heat up until the games were shown on television and everybody had a TV set. Dom and Donald's book took only horse bets until their old friend Joe Spa went broke in 1954. Joe had been booking baseball out of his house. He ran into a bad streak, got hit hard, and lost his bankroll. He needed money and asked Dom and Donald to go in with him. They agreed to partner with him—they'd supply the money and split the profits 50-50.

That fall the World Series was between the Cleveland Indians and the New York Giants. The Indians had three of the best pitchers in baseball, Bob Lemon, Early Wynn, and Mike Garcia. They were big favorites and the bettors were heavily on their side. When the Giants won the first game, the Indians' bettors doubled their bets for the next game to get even, but the Giants won again. The bettors doubled up again. The Giants swept the series four straight. When it was over, the book had won $64,000. In today's dollars, it was the equivalent of nearly $500,000. Dom and Donald's cut was $16,000 apiece.

With his 50 percent share, Joe Spa went back on his own and Dom and Donald also decided to start up a sports book. Booking sports is a whole different business than booking horses. With horses, you just pay the track odds. With sports, you work on a much smaller margin, but you don't have to worry about somebody's hitting big on a long shot and breaking you, and to some degree you can control betting so you don't get too many bets on just one side.

The profit margin was provided by a built-in advantage for the bookmaker called, variously, the "juice," the "vigorish," or, for short, the "vig." If you bet $100 with a bookmaker and lose, you have to pay $110; but if you win, you collect only $100.

Obtaining bets on both sides of a game is accomplished by using a "line" which "gives" a certain number of points to the underdog. If the New York Giants are six-point favorites over the Chicago Bears, the line is "Giants minus six." If someone bets on the Bears and they lose the game by less than six points (or win it), she wins the bet, but if the Bears lose by more than six points she loses. If the Giants win by exactly six, it's a tie and no one collects.

Donald Angelini's job was to set the line for every game at a number that would encourage some bettors to pick the favorite and others to pick the underdog. That way the vig allows the bookmaker to make money no matter which team wins. Making a line for bookmaking has more to do with knowing the psychology of bettors than knowing the teams; someone in Las Vegas will put out a well-publicized line based on the relative strength of the teams. Donald had to adjust that line to fit the habits of his bettors. It was because he was so good at it that he became known as "The Wizard of Odds" throughout the Midwest.

Whether Dominic Cortina thought it was justified or not, the strike force considered sports gambling the lifeblood of organized crime. If not Public Enemy Number One, Dom and Donald were high up on the FBI list, and in 1969 they were indicted for conspiracy to violate a law that made interstate transmission of gambling information a felony carrying a maximum sentence of five years in prison. Included in the same indictment were Jackie Cerone and Joe Ferriola, two men known as important members of the Chicago outfit.

The man who made the government's case was an informant named Louis Bombasino, who claimed to have been part of the gambling business and to have met with all of the defendants on various occasions. To the day they died, Dom and Donald swore they had never met Bombasino or known who he was, and that

Cerone and Ferriola had nothing to do with the sports book. Nevertheless, everyone was convicted together. Because of the involvement of two top-level mobsters, Dom and Donald received maximum sentences.

Cortina and Angelini were released from prison in late 1973. By the opening of the 1974 football season, the word on the street was they were back in business.

There was nothing more than a rumor of any crime, but the strike force set out to try to prove Dom and Donald had committed one. When a small-time bookie named Tony Galano was arrested taking bets, he was threatened with prosecution and agreed to become an informant. One of the phone numbers he obtained for placing bets turned out to be that of a man named Frank Aurelli, who was working for Cortina and Angelini. When a wiretap was obtained, FBI agents familiar with their voices soon determined that the man who gave Aurelli the line was Donald Angelini and the man who "cleared the bets" was Dominic Cortina. Further investigation identified two more wire rooms, the men who took bets in them, and the fact that Joe Spa cleared the bets in one of them.

In the summer of 1976, the strike force obtained the indictment against Donald and Dominic that brought them to my office. Spadeveccio and four men who worked in the wire rooms were also indicted.

The indictment charged violation of a 1970 statute making it a federal crime to own, operate, or manage an illegal gambling business involving five or more participants and either thirty days of continuous operation or $2,000 in bets taken in a single day. The theory is that a gambling business with those characteristics necessarily has an impact on interstate commerce, thus giving the government jurisdiction to make it a federal crime. But the indictment did not stop there. Based on the same facts, it also charged the defendants' bookmaking business violated RICO, the Racketeer Influenced and Corrupt Organizations Act. Thus, by the magic of a presumption that sports gambling affects interstate commerce and that receiving payment from a losing bettor is the collection of an "illegal debt," the strike force elevated conduct that for decades had occurred openly in every city in America, that the state itself was engaged in, and that was still treated as a minor misdemeanor by local law enforcement, into a felony carrying a sentence of twenty years in prison.

Ridiculous, as Dom would say, but with two RICO counts and the five-year gambling count, he and Donald were facing a maximum sentence of forty-five years in prison.

The case was assigned to Judge John Grady, a recently appointed District Court judge who had been in private practice in Waukegan, Illinois, and before that served as an assistant U.S. Attorney in Chicago. Grady had quickly developed a reputation as a tough sentencer—but fair in his rulings and straitlaced in his expectations and management of lawyers who appeared in his courtroom.

It was three years before the case went to trial. In the meantime, we persuaded Judge Grady to suppress the wiretaps due to the FBI's failure to comply with the statute authorizing electronic surveillance, but the Court of Appeals had reversed, holding that the government had an adequate excuse for its mistake. Thereafter, Dom and Donald pled guilty, but then withdrew their pleas when Judge Grady arguably gave them a longer sentence than he had promised.

The judge was furious. He had sentenced the defendants in good faith and doubted any court would say he had broken his promise; but if our clients thought so and wanted a trial, a trial they would have. But they must understand that all bets were off on the sentences. They would now be facing the full range of sentencing, including that provided by the RICO charge. Paging angrily through his docket, he vowed to clear the way for a quick trial and set a date in mid-April 1979.

Tom Sullivan had become the United States Attorney for the Northern District of Illinois when Jimmy Carter was elected president, and I had persuaded my partner Jerry Solovy to take over the representation of Donald Angelini while I continued to represent Dominic Cortina. As Jerry and I worked to complete our trial preparation we had one new advantage: Joe Spa had gone to trial in the case and lost. His lawyer had provided us with a transcript of Joe's trial. It included the testimony of the two most important live witnesses who would be called in our case: the FBI gambling expert and the bookie, Tony Galano, who claimed he had met with Dominic, Donald, and Frank Aurelli in September, October, and November of 1974. That claim was recited in an FBI agent's affidavit and provided the "probable cause" required to obtain approval of the wiretaps. Galano had repeated the claim in his testimony at Joe Spa's trial.

Dom and Donald swore they had never heard of Tony Galano, much less met him and talked to him about bookmaking. In fact, the idea that Dom and Donald would have such meetings with this two-bit horseplayer and barroom bookie was ludicrous to anyone who knew anything about sports gambling in Chicago—but there it was. We knew Galano's testimony was false, but we still had to prove it and, if possible, prove the FBI knew it when they filed the wiretap affidavit and put Galano on the witness stand.

On that score, there was additional help from the Spadeveccio trial in the form of reports of FBI interviews with their witnesses, which had been turned over to Spa's lawyer before each witness testified, as required by law. Two things stood out: First, the records showed that although Galano had been a paid FBI informant starting in early 1974, there were no interview reports about his alleged meetings with Dom and Donald until just before the wiretap application in December. Then a single report summarized all the alleged meetings from September through November. It made no sense that there were no contemporary reports of these crucial meetings—at least, not if the meetings had ever occurred. Second, in the Spadeveccio trial, Galano had been asked to describe Frank Aurelli, whom he said he had met several times with Dom and Donald. His answer was that Aurelli was "skinny, very skinny." In fact, Frank Aurelli was about 5'6" and 230 pounds.

These reports—and lack of reports—would be extremely helpful in impeaching Galano's testimony about meetings that I was convinced had never happened.

Persuading the jury that Galano was lying about the meetings with Dom and Donald was essential, but not necessarily enough to obtain an acquittal. The fact that Dominic managed and Donald supplied the line to a sports book was proved by the wiretaps. Jerry thought about challenging the FBI identification of Donald's voice, but I was doubtful it would work. The government had obtained voice samples from Donald, and they sure sounded the same as the man on the tapes. Of course, I might have been influenced by the fact that I *knew* it was Donald. I was afraid that denying it might injure our credibility with the jury. Jerry agreed not to raise the voice issue in his opening statement and see how things went. When one of the first phone calls the government played had Donald identifying himself as "the man from Glad," a reference to a character in a television commercial who had a snow-white pompadour like Donald's, the jurors looked at Donald and laughed. Jerry abandoned the voice-identification defense.

My theory of defense for Dominic was that although he was a bookmaker, his business did not include the required five owners or managers. In my opening statement, I said Dominic had been a bookmaker all his life, knew the federal law, and made sure he didn't violate it by limiting his operations to fewer than five people. The government claimed all three of the wire rooms they had wiretapped were part of the same business. I said they were not. Although the same person provided the line to all three rooms, I argued that the person who provides the line is an independent contractor. Like a supplier of equipment, he sells his line to many different bookmakers. Cortina's business, I said, was himself and the people who took bets in two of the wire rooms: Aurelli and Sam Molose. The other wire room was Spadeveccio's, and while they were friends, they had separate businesses.

I had two pieces of evidence to support my theory. One was a series of conversations the government had recorded but didn't intend to play for the jury and probably hadn't focused on. The other was our own gambling expert, who had read transcripts of the wiretaps. He would testify that in his opinion, the third wire room was a separate business from the other two.

The conversations I planned to use had been discovered by the paralegal we had hired to listen painstakingly to the hundreds of hours of wiretaps, after receiving a short course in bookmaking from Donald Angelini. They took place on a Saturday afternoon during the basketball season. Indiana was playing Michigan State and was favored by 12 points. The game was on television, and Sam Molose was going to watch it while he took bets on games that started later in the afternoon. During the pregame broadcast, it was revealed that the Michigan State coach had suspended his entire starting team because of a locker-room infraction. Michigan State would start all freshmen. Immediately Molose "took the game off"—that is, stopped taking bets on it. When Dom called in to clear bets, Molose told him about it. Meanwhile, in the wire room managed by Joe Spa, the man taking bets received a flood of last-minute bets on Indiana right up to the scheduled tip-off. He clearly had no clue about the benching of Michigan State's starters. By halftime, when someone finally called Joe Spa's wire room with the story, Indiana was 30 points ahead.

If the two wire rooms were part of the same business, this would never happen. The minute Molose learned about Michigan State's benching, he would have contacted Dominic or called the other room to make sure they knew about it. That he didn't proved they were separate operations—or so I would argue. And my expert would rely in significant part on that evidence, together with his long career and extensive knowledge of sports gambling, to support his opinion that the two wire rooms were separate.

The government's expert was an FBI agent. I had reason to hope the jury would find my expert more persuasive. He was Jimmy "The Greek" Snyder, the most famous sports oddsmaker in the country. Like Dom and Donald, Snyder started in the gambling business at an early age, working as a bookmaker in the wide-open town of Canton, Ohio, before moving to Las Vegas to make a line for legal sports books, then selling his line to newspapers across the country (the papers were shocked, shocked to learn the lines they published were used in illegal gambling), and finally landing a job as an "analyst" for CBS-TV. Jimmy appeared every weekend on the National Football League telecasts to discuss his predictions for the games being played that day. Everyone in the country who watched pro football had seen Jimmy the Greek, and millions more had read his newspaper columns or his best-selling "as told to" autobiography.

It was Donald Angelini who persuaded Jimmy to be our expert. Jerry and I had agreed I would cross-examine the government gambling expert and put Jimmy on in our case, while Jerry would have primary responsibility for cross-examining Galano, the informant. I sent Jimmy transcripts of the conversations the government planned to put into evidence and their expert's report. I also sent him the Indiana–Michigan State transcripts and a few other pieces of evidence that might be helpful. Well before the trial started, we met to go over his testimony.

I thought Jimmy would be a terrific witness—if he actually showed up, which he was clearly reluctant to do. He had been hugely relieved when Donald and Dominic pleaded guilty, and distraught when I told him they had withdrawn their pleas and we now needed him for trial. We were required to reveal his name to the government, and someone from the FBI had gone to CBS and asked if they knew their football analyst was planning to testify for the Mafia. While CBS did not say he would be fired if he testified, Jimmy was desperately afraid he would be, especially if his testimony became a big deal in the press.

When I told Donald I was afraid Jimmy might fail to show up at the last minute, he reassured me: "He'll squeal like a pig, but he'll come." Then, when the judge learned I planned to use him as my expert, he too was unhappy. Jimmy the Greek was a colorful character, and Judge Grady was afraid he would "turn the courtroom into a circus." Grady was uptight about such matters. (He is the only judge I ever tried a case with who insisted the lawyers remain squarely behind the podium when examining witnesses or addressing the jury.) He decided he wasn't sure sports gambling was an appropriate subject for an expert. When I reminded him the government was planning to call one, he tried to persuade them not to, and said if they would agree not to call their expert, he would prohibit me from calling Jimmy. The prosecutors were reluctant—they were afraid they couldn't satisfy their burden of proof without an expert. When they cited several gambling cases in which experts had testified, I pointed out that the logic of those cases supported my right to call an expert whether or not the prosecutor did. The judge finally threw up his hands. Praying that Donald was right, I told the jury in opening statement that Jimmy the Greek would be an expert witness for the defense.

There is nothing quite so boring as listening to tape recordings of people placing bets with a bookmaker. For the first three days of the trial, the prosecutors played such tapes, occasionally interrupted by the testimony of an FBI agent explaining some phrase on the tape. By the third day, some of the jurors were asleep. So was Dominic. I could tell because the judge, the lawyers, the defendants, and the jurors were all wearing earphones to hear the calls more clearly, and when the prosecutor was through playing a particular tape, she would take off her earphones with a kind of flourish that signaled everybody else could take theirs off. When a juror failed to take off his earphones, a neighbor in the jury box would nudge him awake. I would do the same for Dominic.

Additional testimony came from agents who had watched Dominic calling the wire rooms from a pay phone. After court, Dominic would laugh and shake his head over their testimony. "It's December in Chicago and I'm out there freezing my ass off in a phone booth feeding quarters into the telephone and trying to write down the numbers, and that son of a bitch is sitting in his car with the heater on watching me! What a life. I shoulda stayed in school."

Then the prosecutor called Tony Galano. Galano was the quintessential mope. Slow-witted, inarticulate, forgetful, and willing to say anything the government wanted him to say but too dumb to remember what that was with any consistency. Alexandra Kwoka, one of the prosecutors, led him through direct testimony in which he repeated his story about a series of meetings with Angelini and Cortina starting in September 1974. According to Galano, the meetings resulted from his asking a tavern owner named Mario Caputo if he knew someone he could send bets to. His question supposedly resulted in the first face-to-face meeting with Donald Angelini a week later in which he said Angelini had bragged about being the biggest bookmaker in Chicago and gave him phone numbers for calling in his bets.

On cross-examination, Jerry confronted Galano with a series of inconsistencies between his story and details from the FBI reports, demonstrated Galano's confusion about parts of his story, and impeached him with statements he had made in the Spadeveccio trial, including his description of Frank Aurelli as "skinny." I followed up with more questions along the same lines, and played a wiretapped conversation in which Galano made statements that were contrary to his trial testimony. His effort to explain the inconsistencies only made them worse. By the end of his testimony, Galano's credibility had been compromised, if not destroyed.

The most important things Galano said on cross-examination were about his contacts with FBI Agent William Herman, the man he reported to. First, he said he had reported each meeting with Angelini and Cortina shortly after it occurred. He also said he had known about the meetings in advance, and gave Agent Herman advance notice when a meeting was scheduled. It was impossible to believe that Agent Herman would not have prepared contemporaneous reports of these meetings and arranged for surveillance of them if Galano's testimony was true. But there were no reports, no surveillance, not even a record of the wire-room phone numbers Galano had supposedly received from Angelini and Cortina. The only reasonable conclusion was that the whole story was false.

Galano gave two additional answers on cross-examination that turned out to be equally important. We had not been provided with any of the records Galano would have had to make for his bookmaking business, which an informant would routinely turn over to his FBI handler for preservation as evidence. When Galano said he *had* turned such records over to Agent Herman, we asked to see them. Jeff Johnson, one of the prosecutors, said, "They don't exist." It wasn't clear whether he meant Galano never had such records, or that something happened to them after they were turned over. But when I asked Galano if Agent Herman had taken notes when he reported his meetings with Dom and Donald, the plot thickened deliciously. Galano said yes. I asked for the notes, and this time the prosecutors said, "Those notes . . . are no longer in existence. They were destroyed prior to this trial."

We demanded an investigation, and Judge Grady agreed. If the government didn't have a logical, innocent explanation of why these notes and records were destroyed, there was a chance Galano's testimony would be stricken and a mistrial declared. But what actually happened was even better.

The investigation, conducted outside the presence of the jury, began with the government explaining that because the case file had become so large, a portion had been sent to storage. Somehow that portion had been destroyed in the course of a file-reduction program. The betting records and Herman's notes of his meetings with Galano must have been among the destroyed documents. Dave Kelley, the FBI agent in charge of the case, and an FBI file clerk were called to support this explanation.

On cross-examination, however, the accidental-destruction explanation crumbled. Sending material to storage when it could be needed for a trial was contrary to regulation. Moreover, there was no record that any part of the file had been sent to storage, and no record of any part of the file being destroyed. The storage-room supervisor testified she was under strict instructions not to destroy anything unless the file folder was stamped "closed" and the attorney in charge of the case had drawn a line through his name on the file to signify that it could be destroyed. The person in overall charge of files was ordered to appear. She agreed it was unlikely the material had been destroyed in the manner suggested, and promised to trace the file through the record-control system and to make another search for the missing documents. On Friday afternoon, Jeff Johnson said he had been told the file room had now located some records that might be relevant. The judge ordered the prosecutors to examine the new records over the weekend and produce anything we were entitled to see.

Depending on what happened, we might have to begin the defense case on Monday or Tuesday. I had asked Jimmy the Greek to come in on Saturday so we could spend the weekend on final preparation of his testimony. To my relief, he arrived as scheduled, and we worked together Saturday afternoon and part of Sunday. I called the prosecutors on Saturday morning to arrange to pick up the new documents, but they were still going through them. Jeff Johnson would call me when they were ready. I was concerned the FBI would now produce phony reports about meetings I was certain had never occurred. I told Johnson bluntly that if he produced any documents, he'd better be damn sure they were genuine. He was offended, and told me angrily there were no other reports of the meetings, which is what I had hoped. I heard nothing for the rest of the day, and in late afternoon I called again but got no answer at the strike-force office. I was furious, but there wasn't anything to do about it. In the end, we got nothing until Monday morning.

When I opened the thin envelope of documents that arrived by messenger early Monday morning before court, there were a few undated papers with numbers on them that might be some of Galano's betting records. There were no notes of Agent Herman's meetings with Galano, nor any contemporaneous witness reports covering the supposed meetings with Cortina and Angelini. There were, however, a few reports of contacts between Herman and Galano that we had not seen before.

The betting records were no help. The absence of any notes or witness reports reflecting meetings with our clients gave further support to our contention that these meetings had never occurred. And three newly produced reports of Herman's contacts with Galano proved it.

The three new reports covered conversations between Galano and the bar owner, Mario Caputo, on July 6, 1974, December 3 and 4, 1974, and December 17, 1974. The July report said that Mario Caputo had given Galano a phone number through which he could place his bets and that Galano would try to determine the name of the bookmaker at that number. Apparently that bookmaker was not connected to our clients, as no report of his name or the inevitable FBI follow-up of the phone numbers was ever provided to us. After July, there were no further reports from Galano until the one covering December 3 and 4. It said Galano had trouble getting paid by his prior bookmaker and had asked Caputo if he knew anyone else who would take his bets. On December 4, Caputo gave Galano the phone number of another bookmaker. (The number was recorded in Herman's memo.) Galano called the number and spoke to a man with a "heavy voice." Galano told Herman he would try to find out his name.

In fact, the phone number was the wire room where Frank Aurelli answered the phone, and the "heavy voice" was the distinctive foghorn voice of Frank Aurelli. The fact that Galano did not already have Aurelli's number and did not recognize his voice demonstrated beyond question that Galano's claim he had been betting with Dominic and Donald through Aurelli between September and December was false. Obviously, Galano's initial contact with Aurelli and the Cortina-Angelini sports book was on December 4, when he called Aurelli for the first time. Further evidence of that fact was provided by the third new document, which reported that on December 17 Mario Caputo had told Galano he was now "working for Donald Angelini."

Before Agent Herman testified, we were permitted to present our view of the significance of the new documents, and the judge took a few minutes to himself to study the documents and consider our arguments. When Herman finally took the stand, the prosecutor asked only about the betting records that Herman said he had summarized and then destroyed as a matter of routine practice. Alex Kwoka's effort to limit our cross-examination to the subject of the betting records was rejected by the judge, who soon demonstrated that he now understood our arguments. Taking over the cross-examination, Judge Grady began sharply questioning Herman about the newly discovered reports and the alleged meetings between Galano and the defendants. Herman claimed he had not reported the September, October, and November meetings because he didn't want to write down anything that might endanger Galano if a report leaked outside the FBI (a claim belied by the fact that the file contained dozens of post-December reports from which one could clearly identify Galano). His failure to make a record of the phone numbers Galano supposedly received from Angelini and Cortina was because "he wasn't thinking about this investigation that much" (although he was spending most of his time on it). He tried to explain the early December report of what appeared to be Galao's first call to Aurelli by saying he "didn't think Galano was very good at recognizing voices," and therefore didn't realize the man with the "heavy voice" was Aurelli, even though he had supposedly talked to Aurelli almost every day for three months. And what was the reason for Herman reporting on December 17 that Galano had just learned he was working for Angelini, as though this was new information? Herman pretended he didn't really understand that question and never answered it.

If there was any doubt that Judge Grady now understood the situation fully, it ended when Herman left the stand. The government offered to call another agent who would say he handled betting records the same way Herman did, but the judge replied, with obvious disgust in his voice, "I don't think we need him. If his testimony is the same as Agent Herman, I've heard enough."And when the government suggested recalling Galano so we could cross-examine him on the newly discovered records,

Judge Grady was equally uninspired: "My inclination to proceed by that route is so imperceptible it would not warrant the expense of bringing him back from wherever he is."

"Oh," said Jeff Johnson, "we researched the wrong issue over the lunch hour."

"Until we heard from Agent Herman," the judge replied, "nobody could really tell what the issue was, but right now the issue is whether this case is going to die a very unnatural death."

We floated back to the office and prepared a legal memo in support of a motion to dismiss the indictment for prosecutorial misconduct. I told Jimmy the Greek it looked like we might get the case thrown out. He wanted to leave at once, but I told him he had to stay; we wouldn't know until the next day.

In addition to the problem of the now throughly discredited "meetings" with the defendants, the examination of Galano and Herman showed that in his wiretap affidavit, Herman had made false statements about Galano's reliability as an informant. The next morning, Judge Grady examined Herman on that subject in chambers. When he returned to the courtroom, the judge again rejected the prosecutors' request to recall Galano for cross-examination on the new documents, and took the initial step of declaring a mistrial:

> THE COURT . . . Well, I believe that the case cannot be tried from this point on in anything resembling a fair and proper way. . . . This trial has turned into a shambles, and the agents of the Federal Bureau of Investigation are the ones who have turned it into a shambles. I will not lend the auspices of this Court to a continuation of this kind of travesty. . . . I am going to call in the jury, declare a mistrial, . . . and then we will discuss the defendant's motion to dismiss the indictment.

After explaining the situation to the jury in blunt terms and sending them home with thanks and an apology for wasting their time, Judge Grady gave the prosecutors a final chance to persuade him that the FBI misconduct in the case was not so egregious as to require the case to be dismissed rather than retried with a new jury. After a recess to consider his decision, the judge returned to the bench and minced no words in announcing it.

The government, Judge Grady said, called a witness, Galano, whose testimony was powerful evidence against the defendants. However, the government had in its possession reports that strongly suggested Galano's testimony was false. The government was required to produce those documents, but did not do so. The prosecutors did not know of these documents, but were told that some records from the case were destroyed. They should have reported that to the court and defense counsel before trial. Their failure to do so was a mistake of judgment, not bad faith—they were trying to avoid what they assumed was a red herring the defense would raise about the destroyed documents—but "the problem is that you really can't tell which herrings are red and which aren't, as the experience in this case should amply demonstrate as a lesson for the future."

The FBI, Judge Grady said, was a different story. In fact, the records had not been destroyed, and the way they turned up demonstrated the FBI knew it, and deliberately concealed them from the defense. Someone went through the file and carefully removed these records.

> THE COURT: I waited for some [other] explanation. . . . [It] was offered by Agent Herman. It gives me great pain to say that I did not find him a credible witness. I do not believe that Agent Herman told the truth yesterday. I believe that he deliberately lied, and I do not say that lightly because I realize the implications of what I am saying; but the things he said were simply absurd. No person with any sophistication, let alone someone who spent five years in the United States Attorney's office and three years on the Federal District bench, as I have, could believe the story he told.

Herman's story was indeed too absurd to be believed by anyone whose eyes were not closed to the truth. The documents the government was finally forced to produce showed beyond question that far from having a four-month betting relationship with Frank Aurelli and the Angelini-Cortina wire rooms, the first time Tony Galano ever bet with Aurelli was after Caputo gave him Aurelli's phone number on December 3. Moreover, the first time Galano ever heard of Angelini—much less met him—was when Caputo told him on December 17 that he was now working for Donald Angelini. But even without those records, who could rationally believe that for three months Agent Herman had received incriminating information about meetings with top targets of the Chicago strike force but never made a report of that information, never arranged surveillance of the meetings, never even wrote down the phone numbers of their wire rooms? Absurd is an inadequate description.

The FBI had deliberately withheld records that should have been produced and then lied about it. Because of that misconduct a mistrial had to be declared after the defendants were in jeopardy. The judge therefore dismissed the indictment "with prejudice," meaning that it could never be reinstated.

Before leaving the courthouse I called my secretary to tell her what happened. By the time I got back to the office, Jimmy the Greek had left for New York. Years later, I asked Donald Angelini why "The Greek" had agreed to testify when he so obviously didn't want to. "He owed a favor to a friend of mine," Donald explained. "Jimmy loves to play the horses. He's a degenerate gambler, and he thinks he's a great handicapper. He owes my friend over $70,000." I was glad I had not heard that story before the trial—it would have raised a serious question about whether I could use Jimmy as a witness.

Judge Grady was furious at the FBI's conduct. Some time later, he granted our motion to expunge the record of the charges against Dom and Donald, and later still, set aside the verdict against Joe Spadeveccio, allowed the other defendants to withdraw their guilty pleas, and dismissed the charges against everyone. For a year or more, I tried to find out what the FBI had done about Agents Herman and Kelley. As near as I could tell, the answer was nothing. A few years later, I talked to Judge Grady and asked if he knew anything different. No, he said. In fact after a year or so, he had written FBI headquarters to complain that nothing had been done. They never responded.

Dominic was free of the charges involving the sports book, but he was still under indictment in another case, which was set for trial in September. Several years earlier, a Chicago lawyer named Frank Oliver had decided he could make money by creating an offtrack betting service. The state legislature had declined on several occasions to approve legalized offtrack betting, but Oliver concluded he could legally accept bets in an offtrack office and relay them to the race tracks for a fee of 10 percent of the amount bet. He opened several offices and was doing a good business. When police tried to shut him down, a court held that as long as he was taking orders to make legal bets at the track, the business was legal.

That caught the attention of Bill McGuire, a smart, enterprising, happy-go-lucky rascal. McGuire had joined the police force as a young man, but before he could complete his probationary year, he got fired. He had already started taking money from shady businesses in the neighborhood he patrolled. Soon he was involved in gambling and, according to some stories, was bag man for a crooked alderman. Bill was delightful, but he was what the English call "bent." As Donald Angelini put it, "Bill could do anything, but he always had to do it the wrong way. If he'd been president of General Motors he'd have put four bad tires on every car."

Soon Bill McGuire started Mr. Lucky, a rival racetrack messenger service on Chicago's South Side. He installed an African-American as president and hired a black lawyer as the company's attorney. Bill was the day-to-day manager of the business. Soon Mr. Lucky had over a dozen storefront locations. Chicago had four racetracks, ranging from high-end Arlington in the north suburbs to Hawthorne in the gritty blue-collar suburb of Cicero to the south. There was racing somewhere every week of the year, and the "orders" were rolling in. Next, Bill decided to expand the business to the Loop and North Side. He formed another corporation called Finish Line, which expanded even faster than Mr. Lucky. At the height of their success the two companies had fifty storefront offices, including one right across the street from City Hall in the Loop and another within sight of Chicago's police headquarters at 11th and State. The latter was a typical Bill McGuire thumb-on-the-nose to the police, who had been raiding the stores and disrupting his business until restrained from doing so by a court.

The racetrack owners were unhappy. Revenue was down, and they were sure it was because of the messenger services. It was bad enough that the messengers were taking away from attendance, where the tracks could charge admission and sell food and beverages to the patrons—they didn't believe the messengers were sending all the bets to the tracks. But that was difficult to prove. Some tracks set up a special window to serve the messenger services, and the messengers were, in fact, bringing in large sums of money and buying thousands of pari-mutuel tickets every day. It didn't seem like enough, but no one knew or could tell how many bets were being made at the services. Other tracks refused to set up special windows and even harassed the people they identified as messengers to make it hard for them to place bets—a practice that defeated their own interests and provided a handy defense against a charge that the messenger service was booking bets. Customers signed a form specifying whether they wanted the service to cash their pari-mutuel ticket if it was a winner, or bring it back to the customer. In the rare cases a customer checked the "bring it back" box, you could be sure a ticket would be purchased and returned to the customer if he won. If somehow things got screwed up and there was no ticket, it was because the messenger got hassled and couldn't make all his purchases—but the messenger service magnanimously paid off on the wager anyway.

When the courts stymied the effort to close down the messenger services as illegal, the racetracks, supported by Mayor Daley and Illinois Governor Dan Walker, pressed the legislature to pass a new law explicitly making racetrack messenger services illegal. The law was passed and signed by the governor, but the messenger services amended the complaint they had filed to stop police harassment and alleged that the new law was unconstitutional. The case was heard by a respected judge who enjoined the state from shutting down the businesses while he considered the constitutionality of the statute. Ultimately he found it constitutional and set aside his injunction, but the messengers appealed, and the appellate court promptly stayed enforcement until it could decide the case. Over a year went by while the case was under advisement.

Meanwhile, the strike force was conducting its own investigation of the services, convinced they were nothing more than a clever front for a tremendous bookmaking operation. FBI agents questioned a number of employees of the services, who reported that fact to their bosses. A special grand jury was convened in early 1977, and on April 22, 1977, FBI agents raided the office where the records and money collected each day in the Finish Line and Mr. Lucky storefronts were analyzed overnight. The proper amount of money had to be delivered back to each storefront the next morning to pay off winning customers and conduct the new day's business. The agents had a search warrant, and stripped the offices of all of their records and some $50,000 in cash.

When the agents entered a room in the back of the Finish Line office, they found Dominic Cortina trying to hide under a desk. As Donald said later, there was no desk big enough to hide Dom, whose nickname was "Large."

"Dominic!" exclaimed Ray Shyrock, an FBI agent who had been after Dom for years and knew him well. "What are you doing here?"

Dom grinned. "Ray! What are *you* doing *here?*"

"We're conducting a federal gambling investigation."

"Here?" Dom asked, as if Shyrock must be out of his mind.

The next day Dom came to see me.

"Well, what were you doing there?" I asked.

"Counting the money," he replied, and went on to say he was on Finish Line's payroll, paid by check, withholding taxes, and everything. He had to make a living, didn't he?

"Sure," I said, "but not that way. The government now thinks you're the boss of the messenger services and that for sure you're doing something illegal." (I didn't tell him I thought so too.) "Quit." I told him. "Right now. Don't take any more money, don't go in those places, and give Bill McGuire a letter of resignation." I knew that if the government returned an indictment Dom would be the first-named defendant no matter what he did now, but quitting, with a formal letter of resignation to go with the payments by check and the payroll taxes, might help with a jury if shit happened. Which, of course, it did.

The racetrack-messenger investigation dragged on. Meanwhile, the most active investigator in the case, FBI Agent William Brown, contacted as many employees of the two services as he could find, using persuasion or threats of prosecution to try to get them to provide incriminating information about the business. Dominic had hired me to monitor the investigation, and knowing Brown was likely to get some people to say what he wanted, whether it was true or not, I began taking sworn statements from Finish Line's supervisory-level employees to get them saying under oath that to their knowledge the business operated legally.

In 1978, the appellate court struck down the statute outlawing racetrack messenger services as unconstitutional. The state promptly appealed to the Illinois Supreme Court. Meanwhile, a newspaper reporter found evidence suggesting that the assignment of the case to a panel of judges in the appellate court had evaded the random-assignment system. Mysteriously, the case had been directed to a panel whose presiding judge was long suspected of corruption. The Supreme Court expedited the appeal, reversed the appellate court, and issued its mandate immediately, instead of waiting the usual fifteen days. The order was delivered by helicopter from the capital in Springfield to the court in Chicago where a team of process servers delivered it to the storefronts on the same day. One could infer that the Supreme Court thought there was some merit to the newspaper's suggestion of corruption. Finish Line and Mr. Lucky shut down immediately.

Then, on February 1, 1979, the strike force returned an indictment charging Cortina, McGuire, twelve other individuals, and the two corporations with violations of RICO and various anti-gambling statutes. An examination of the indictment and the affidavit in support of the search warrants showed the essence of the charge was that most of the bets taken in by the storefronts were not being sent to the racetracks, but instead were being "booked" by the companies behind the scenes. As I had predicted, Dom was the first-named defendant and was alleged to be the owner and overall boss of the operation. The prosecutors would be Alex Kwoka, again, and Mike Groark from the regular U.S. Attorney's office. The assigned judge was Bernard Decker, a pro-prosecution judge who was also known for moving cases to trial quickly and rushing them to completion.

For a search warrant to be issued validly, the application for the warrant must demonstrate probable cause to believe a crime has been committed and that evidence of the crime will be found in the premises the government wants to search. Like the wiretap application in Dom's case before Judge Grady, the bulk of the "probable cause" information in the search-warrant application came from an unnamed "confidential informant" who supposedly worked as an employee of Mr. Lucky and Finish Line and had incriminating conversations with the managers of those companies, especially Bill McGuire. According to the affidavit, McGuire and others had expressly admitted to the informant that only 25 percent of the bets were going to the tracks and the rest were being booked in-house. The informant also claimed to have observed McGuire in the Finish Line offices "handicapping" the races in order to determine which bets to send to the track and which to book. (At that point it was apparently the government's theory that McGuire was sending the bets he thought might be winners to the track while retaining the rest. In fact, what McGuire was probably doing was trying to make sure that if the return on a long-shot bet exceeded a certain amount and someone had placed such a bet, a ticket would be purchased and returned in case he won.)

The idea that Bill McGuire had sat around telling low-level employees of the messenger services that he was really booking the bets was as silly as the idea that Dominic and Donald had sat down in a meeting with a two-bit bookmaker like Tony Galano and told him all about their bookmaking business—but, again, there it was. Among the pretrial motions we filed was one to suppress the evidence seized under the search warrant on the ground that the affidavit was false. In support of the motion, McGuire and others filed affidavits saying they had never told *anyone* the things the confidential informant supposedly told the FBI. We asked for an evidentiary hearing to determine the truth of our claim, but the motion was denied on the ground that even if the informant did lie or exaggerate, there was no proof the FBI agent who made the affidavit knew that the claims were false.

The government had been investigating the case for over two years and there were tens of thousands of documents to analyze, but over our protest, Judge Decker set a trial date of September 12. I worked on preparation as much as possible during the summer. On August 30, as we were scrambling to get ready, we learned that because of a shortage of judges needed to comply with the recently enacted Speedy Trial Act, the case had been reassigned to Judge Ronald Davies, a senior district judge from North Dakota, who had agreed to come to Chicago for the trial. Our first reaction was relief—now that the Seventh Circuit Judicial Conference had ordered that no more criminal cases be assigned to Judge Julius Hoffman, Judge Decker was the worst judge in the district for criminal defendants. When I made some inquiries with lawyers in North Dakota, however, I learned that Judge Davies was also considered pro-prosecution and, if anything, even more prone to rush through a trial, usually putting the defense at a disadvantage.

Judge Davies was a small man (disturbingly similar in size to Judge Hoffman) who, despite being in his seventies, exuded great energy. He had been specially assigned to a court outside his District on at least one other occasion—to preside over *Aaron v. Cooper*, the famous case involving the desegregation of Central High School in Little Rock, Arkansas. When Arkansas governor Orville Faubus refused to enforce his order that the high school be integrated, and ordered the Arkansas National to prevent integration, Judge Davies enjoined the governor's action and ordered the Federal government to enforce his integration ruling. Ultimately President Eisenhower reluctantly deployed troops from the U.S. Army's 101st Airbourne unit to Little Rock to enforce the order. Judge Davies obviously had the guts to do what he thought was right.

The judge also ran an exceptionally tight ship, as he let us know when we first appeared before him two days before the trial was scheduled to start. Court would start at precisely 9:30 (a half hour earlier than most judges), would resume at 1:00 after a one-hour lunch, and run until 5:30. It was a trial day at least an hour longer than most, and when Judge Davies gave the starting times, he meant it. Any lawyer who was even a few seconds late would be ordered to pay a fine to the court's library fund, and it would increase dramatically if it happened a second time. He meant it, too, as two lawyers in the case soon found out.

The defense of a case with fourteen defendants goes a lot better if one person is designated by agreement as lead counsel, with the authority to resolve disputes of strategy. I was that person. I decided early on that, because I would be very active in the conduct of the trial, it would be best for me to represent one of the corporations rather than Dominic Cortina, whose best strategy was to be as nearly invisible as possible. The government had no real evidence that he was the owner, not just a salaried employee with no role in management of the business. Accordingly, I filed my appearance for Finish Line, along with Barry Sullivan, a terrific young associate who had worked with me on numerous other cases. Tom Mulroy, a young partner in my office who was a former assistant U.S. attorney, would represent Dominic. Pat Tuite, one of Chicago's best defense lawyers, would represent Bill McGuire, whose open management of the enterprise meant his lawyer also needed to participate actively in the defense; if the government could prove the basic elements of its case, there was no place for Bill to hide.

In truth, our theory of defense did not go much beyond trying to poke holes in the government's case and rely on the government's burden of proof beyond a reasonable doubt. Based on its analysis of company records, the government asserted that between them, Finish Line and Mr. Lucky had been taking in gross bets of between $50,000 and $100,000 a day. Nothing I had seen or heard from our clients suggested this was the kind of gross exaggeration the FBI normally put out in gambling cases. If it was true, and you took the average and assumed the government was right that 75 percent of it was being booked, and the book was making the roughly 20 percent the tracks kept plus the 10 percent messenger fee, you came up with gross income of close to $600,000 a month!

So far as I could tell, the government could not prove the exact volume of bets the messengers were taking in, or how much did or didn't go to the tracks. The only live witness who claimed to know Finish Line was "booking" appeared to be the "confidential informant" cited in the search-warrant affidavit. The government did, however, have records of multiple bets FBI agents had made with Finish Line and Mr. Lucky on long-shot combinations, and the pari-mutuel tapes from the tracks showed that not all of those bets had reached the tracks. Our defense against that evidence was a combination of "The pari-mutuel tapes may have been wrong because of machine failure," "The tracks and FBI were out to get us and altered them," and "On the days they were going to do their test-buying, the tracks harassed our messengers and kept them from buying the tickets." That is to say, our defense had some problems. It was in that posture that I spent most of the day on Tuesday, September 11, finalizing my thoughts about jury selection and the opening statement I expected to give late the next day or the following morning.

Then, late in the afternoon, a letter arrived from the prosecutors. It was a copy of a letter they had sent to the judge, and it said that while conducting final preparation for the testimony of their first witness, who was also "Source One" in the search-warrant affidavit, they had reviewed the witness's FBI informant file. Based on that review, they said, they anticipated we would renew our previously denied motion to suppress evidence and for an evidentiary hearing. While they said they didn't believe we would be able to meet the test for a hearing, rather than take a chance of having the issue arise after a jury was impaneled, they were sending the judge and us the reports of interviews with the witness, her grand-jury testimony, and other materials they would be required to produce when she took the witness stand. The letter was accompanied by a batch of FBI reports and other documents.

I did not have to look at the documents to understand what they contained. They obviously must contradict the claims attributed to Source One in the search-warrant affidavit, in which she was said to have had incriminating conversations with McGuire and others. The prosecutors did not want to risk another fiasco like the last trial, in which lies by their witness were uncovered after the trial began, resulting in dismissal of the indictment. If the FBI was going to be caught lying again—and they knew I would be looking for it—better to get it over with before the defendants were legally placed "in jeopardy."

My only question was how gross the misrepresentations were, and I knew they had to be bad or the prosecutors wouldn't have sent the letter. When I began looking through the documents I saw they were very bad indeed—or, from my perspective, very good.

Source One, the confidential informant, was one Pamela Bridges, a low-level employee of first Mr. Lucky, and later Finish Line, although she did not go to work at Finish Line until after she supposedly supplied Agent Brown with the material included in the search-warrant affidavit.

The information attributed to Pamela Bridges in the affidavit was lengthy and detailed, and it took our team of lawyers most of the night to prepare a point-by-point list of the differences between the affidavit and the material supplied by the prosecution. I saw immediately that the claim McGuire had told Source One he was booking most of the bets was false. By 2:00 A.M., when we gathered in my office, bleary-eyed but exhilarated, we were able to conclude that every one of the allegedly incriminating conversations and observations that made up the heart of the affidavit was contradicted by Pamela Bridges's grand-jury testimony or Agent Brown's contemporaneous reports of his contacts and conversations with her, either expressly or by omission of any reference to the incriminating information. It was no more likely that Bridges had reported important incriminating facts and Agent Brown had somehow failed to write them down than it was that Agent Herman had deliberately decided not to report Galano's supposed information about meeting with Angelini and Cortina. For a fleeting moment, all I could think about was how Alex Kwoka's face must have looked when she began to read the contact reports and realized she had another Agent Herman on her hands.

By the next morning, we had to prepare a renewed motion to suppress and for an evidentiary hearing. I needed to be ready to begin cross-examining the government agents and Pamela Bridges in order to demonstrate that the information in the search-warrant affidavit was not only false, but that Agent Brown knew it. I decided to go home and get a few hours' sleep and come in early to begin preparing for a hearing. Barry Sullivan stayed on to prepare the motion and get it typed by the night secretarial staff. The motion itself alleged generally that the Bridges contact reports and grand jury testimony showed that the information attributed to Source One was false—and Agent Brown knew it. That general allegation was supported by our detailed comparison between the affidavit and the Bridges documents. I had decided to file the detailed analysis only with the judge, asking him to consider it ex parte[6] so the details of our claim would not be set out for the prosecutors before we could cross-examine witnesses. We notified the prosecutors that we had made such a submission even though we didn't share it with them.

When we arrived in court the next morning, the prosecutors strenuously objected to the ex parte filing and asked the judge to make us give them a copy, but he refused and took the question of whether he would order an evidentiary hearing under advisement until after the noon recess. Then, after listening to a brief argument from the government, he announced that in the interest of justice, he would conduct a hearing.

It had been agreed that, if a hearing was granted, I would question the witnesses for all defendants. With fourteen defense lawyers and a judge who guarded time jealously, it would have been foolish to have everyone chiming in, especially since everyone's objective was the same. If, after I finished with a witness, someone else had a few questions I hadn't asked that were important to their client, they could, of course, ask them.

In the morning Judge Davies had told the prosecutors to have the witnesses we wanted available in the afternoon so we could begin the hearing immediately if he decided to grant one. As soon as the judge ruled I called our first witness, FBI Agent Linda Stewart. For some reason, instead of having Agent Brown give an affidavit telling what Bridges had said to him, Stewart had written the search-warrant affidavit. In each instance, she had presented the incriminating material by saying, "Source One told Agent Brown, who told me. . . ."

As I expected, Agent Stewart testified that all of the incriminating evidence in her affidavit had come from Agent Brown. She herself had never met or talked to Pamela Bridges. The information she put in the affidavit had come to her both from reading

6 Meaning, in this instance, that he consider our submission without providing it to our opponents.

Brown's reports and talking to him. She had prepared a handwritten draft of the affidavit primarily from the reports and shown it to a strike force attorney, who suggested it was insufficient because the claims that the messenger services were booking bets were conclusory. The draft didn't disclose the specific facts that supported the conclusion or from whom those facts had been obtained. Stewart had gone back to Brown with that problem, and Brown had said he would recontact Pamela Bridges. Brown then came back to Stewart and told her Bridges had learned the incriminating facts in conversations with McGuire and others, as stated in the affidavit. I obtained the draft affidavit. It contained almost none of the alleged conversations and incriminating facts that were in the final affidavit Stewart had taken to the magistrate who approved the search.

Agent Brown was next, and if anything he made Agent Herman look candid and competent. In the period between midmorning of September 13 and the noon recess, covering fifty pages of transcript, Brown answered sixty-three times that he was not sure or did not recall. Virtually the only unequivocal statements he made during that portion of his interrogation were that he had only discussed his testimony with Kwoka and Groark on one occasion, Monday evening, September 10; that he had not seen or talked to Pamela Bridges recently except for a brief greeting in the hall of the courthouse the day before; and that Bridges had, in fact, told him that in March 1977, Bill McGuire told her he was booking bets for Mr. Lucky and Finish Line. All three of those answers were later shown to be false. Finally, just before the noon recess, when Brown said he couldn't recall whether in his meeting with the prosecutors they had asked him about the statement that McGuire had told Source One he was booking bets, Mike Groark could no longer stand it. He rose and stipulated that had been one of the subjects of their discussion. Brown still couldn't remember.

After the noon recess, Groark asked to be heard. He said that over the lunch hour, he and Kwoka had met with Brown and admonished him that he had an obligation to listen to the questions and try to answer them. "We told him that he had an obligation to recall answers to questions that were put to him and if he had a present recollection of the answer, . . . he should state it." Groark went on to say he and Kwoka had in fact met with Brown to discuss his testimony not once, as Brown testified, but three times: Monday evening, Tuesday evening, and Wednesday morning (the previous day).

When I resumed my examination of Agent Brown, he remained forgetful and evasive, but gradually and tortuously began making some concessions. He admitted that when he first talked to Bridges, she was unemployed. She had been let go from Mr. Lucky some months earlier, and had not gone to work at Finish Line until long after the search-warrant affidavit was filed, thus making it obvious that the information about Finish Line attributed to her in the affidavit had to be false. Bit by bit, Brown finally conceded that Bridges had not told him most of the incriminating things attributed to her in Stewart's affidavit, and that the assertion in the affidavit to the contrary was false. He could not recall telling those things to Stewart, although when asked where, then, she had gotten the information, he said it "would possibly have been me." With regard to a few of the incriminating conversations, however, he said Bridges had, in fact, reported them to him, and he had repeated them to Agent Stewart, even though in each instance he was compelled to admit that there was no mention of any such information in his contact reports.

The final witness I planned to call was Pamela Bridges. Brown had been such a terrible witness, and his claim that some of the incriminating material was true even though he hadn't reported it was so obviously false, that for a moment I considered resting my case without her. I didn't really know what she would say—she might even support Brown on the things he still claimed she told him, just as Galano had supported the story Agent Herman made up. I decided, however, that I might as well call her. If she was going to support some of Brown's story, the prosecutors would surely call her anyway. If that was the case, there might be an advantage in getting to her first, before her story was set in stone by questions posed by the government.

My concerns were unwarranted. Bridges testified in detail about her contacts with Agent Brown and the information she supplied him. The bottom line was she had never had any of the incriminating conversations attributed to her in the search-warrant affidavit, nor had she ever told Agent Brown she had any such conversations. Neither had she told Brown she had observed McGuire "handicapping races" or any of the other incriminating observations attributed to her. In fact, prior to June 1977, when she went to work for Finish Line, she had never even been inside the office where the observations supposedly occurred and the search warrant was served. She also testified that Brown was mistaken about having recently seen her only briefly in the hall on Wednesday—in fact, he had questioned her for about an hour on Monday night.

When the hearing was over, Judge Davies cut to the chase:

THE COURT: Gentlemen, I have prepared some brief notes I think will do much to solve this problem. During the course of these proceedings it has become very clear to this Court that the testimony of Agent William I. Brown was just short of incredible; and it follows that the Court is of the opinion that a great share of the information furnished to Agent Linda Stewart by Agent Brown, who knew that the information was to be used by her in an affidavit to establish probable cause for the issuance of a search warrant, was false.

When Mike Groark claimed the only things we had shown to be false were two paragraphs Brown had explicitly conceded were untrue, and that there was no showing of intentional or reckless misconduct, the judge was unpersuaded.

THE COURT: Mr. Groark, you are a very charitable man, but I will say to you . . . I think all materials attributed by Agent Stewart to

Agent Brown by Source One should be deleted from the April affidavit.

MR. GROARK: You are making a finding that they were all intentionally misrepresented?

THE COURT: I think they are intentional misrepresentations. Certainly shows a reckless disregard for the truth. . . .

There was so much of his testimony I found unbelievable, that I have no hesitancy in characterizing it as false. I don't know how I can make it any plainer than that. . . .

But I can tell you one thing: that if he were still living, J. Edgar Hoover would be rolling over in his mausoleum if he heard that man in this courtroom.

Judge Davies's comment may have been a malapropism, but it certainly couldn't have been stated any plainer.

Without the false information attributed to Pamela Bridges, the prosecutors were forced to concede there was no probable cause and the evidence seized under the warrant was suppressed. While the judge also held that information allegedly obtained from Pamela Bridges should be deleted from an affidavit in support of a second search warrant executed in June, he declined to suppress that evidence because the warrant was supported by a second affidavit reporting the purchase of tickets that didn't get to the pari-mutuel machines. While agreeing with our characterization of the government's conduct as outrageous, he denied a motion to dismiss the indictment since jeopardy had not attached and he thought throwing out the indictment altogether was too extreme.

The prosecutors also argued that only the corporations had standing to complain about the illegal search which resulted from Brown's lies. It was a crucial issue, since the material seized in the search could be used against the individual defendants if the government won that point, and they would have simply dismissed the corporations as defendants and proceeded to trial, but Judge Davies disagreed and suppressed the evidence against all the defendants.

The government appealed, but only on the standing issue, apparently hoping that by not challenging Judge Davies's findings about Agent Brown's lies, they could avoid having those embarrassing facts presented in detail to the Court of Appeals. If that was their hope, it was foolish. In their opening brief they said nothing about the facts that led to the suppression, but our responding brief described Brown's lies in full detail.

I argued the case before the Court of Appeals in February 1980, and it was decided in September. The Court of Appeals affirmed Judge Davies in full, pointedly repeating the judge's finding that Agent Brown had "deliberately lied" and his comment that "J. Edgar Hoover would be rolling over in his mausoleum if he heard that man in this courtroom."

It was a rare and devastating public rebuke of FBI misconduct by an appellate tribunal. Several years later, when we were appearing together in a trial program for practicing lawyers, Judge Bauer, who wrote the Court of Appeals opinion, remarked, "I wonder who was the genius in the Justice Department who decided to authorize an appeal in that case."

Not long after the court's decision, I reached an agreement for dismissal of the indictment against all of the individual defendants.

Within less than eight months, two FBI agents attached to the Chicago strike force had been found to have lied under oath by two different federal judges. In both cases, Dominic Cortina had been a target of the strike force investigation and a defendant in the indictment. And, in both cases, the indictment against him was dismissed. Anyone who has defended criminal cases knows that law-enforcement officers sometimes lie to get a conviction. But to catch them doing it requires egregious conduct—and enormous luck.

Alex Kwoka was pregnant when we began trial in the racetrack messenger case, and I saw her a few days after Judge Davies entered his suppression order. As we parted, she looked at me with a wry grin and said, "If I have a boy I'm going to name him Dominic."

"Why?" I asked innocently.

"Because it's a very lucky name."

It was a nice bit of humor that surprised me—in the two cases we had been opponents I had never seen her smile. I laughed, and acknowledged she was right: Dom had been extraordinarily lucky. There was no point in adding that in my opinion, targeted prosecution and the strike force mentality had played a big role in his luck.

The judges in both *Cortina* cases went out of their way to say the prosecutors had not known about the lies of the FBI agents, and I would not suggest otherwise. But they should have known. The oldest cliché in the legal profession is that a lawyer who represents himself has a fool for a client—meaning that a lawyer with such a strong personal stake in the outcome of a case may lack the objective judgement essential to see the weaknesses of his case and make good decisions. The same is true of a lawyer so imbued with the righteousness of his cause that he accepts without question any claim that confirms his belief, no matter how improbable.

In any case where a person is targeted for prosecution, it is nearly inevitable that the investigator will see every fact as pointing to his target, and rationalize away any evidence to the contrary. It is only a short leap from loss of objectivity to manufacturing evidence. After all, when good is in pursuit of evil, doesn't the end justify the means? Agent Brown was certain the racetrack messenger services were booking their bets and the mob was involved, and the whole purpose of his assignment to the strike force was to prove it—so why not attribute his belief to a "confidential informant" and get a search warrant that would provide the proof? Agent Herman knew in his heart that Dominc Cortina and Donald Angelini were running sports gambling in Chicago. What harm then to make up some facts that would enable him to obtain a wiretap that would trap such devils?

If the investigators could not see the harm, it was the prosecutor's job to have the objectivity and common sense to see the truth. Bad enough they did not realize that the whole idea of Tony Galano being invited to meet with Angelini and Cortina so they could tell him what big bookmakers they were was incredible—how could they possibly fail to realize something was terribly wrong when they discovered that betting records and surveillance photos were missing, supposedly destroyed by accident, and then found that Agent Herman *had not made a single contemporaneous report of the meetings Galano had supposedly told him about?* And, one must ask, how, after the withheld documents were "discovered," could they put Herman on the witness stand and vouch for an explanation so ludicrous, as Judge Grady said, that no one with the slightest sophistication could believe it.

How could the same thing happen again eight months later, beginning with the story that Bill McGuire sat down with a part-time file clerk and told her all about his criminal enterprise—a story that once again appeared nowhere in the agent's contemporaneous investigative reports. At least this time, the prosecutors recognized the problem before jeopardy attached—but then, even though the search-warrant affidavit was belied not only by Brown's contact reports but also by the testimony of Pamela Bridges herself, they continued to argue that the bulk of the affidavit was true. How could they be so "charitable" when even J. Edgar Hoover was rolling over in his grave?

I believe that it is the nature of target prosecutions for the participants to be blinded by the virtue of their cause in pursuing the evil subject of their efforts.

But what would the prosecutors say? I couldn't locate Mike Groark, but Jeff Johnson and Alex Kwoka, both long departed from the strike force, agreed to talk to me. Understandably, they had forgotten many details, but both recalled how the cases had ended with the judges finding that an FBI agent had lied about an important matter. Both rejected my theory that the problem was attributable to a "strike force mentality." Johnson, who was involved only in the Cortina-Angelini prosecution, said that he had ultimately come to believe Agent Herman had lied about the supposed meetings between the informant Galano and the defendants. He attributed his failure to question the story earlier to the fact that he had worked with Dave Kelley, the supervising agent on other cases, and had confidence in him and any investigation he supervised. Alex Kwoka also cited her confidence in the integrity of the FBI agents, as well as her "uncynical" personality. In fact, Kwoka told me, while there were clearly mistakes made in record keeping, *even now she is not convinced that either Agent Herman or Agent Brown really lied.* In both cases there was lots of other evidence the defendants were guilty, she said, so why would the agents lie?

It is true that the relationship between prosecutors and law-enforcement officers is different from that between a lawyer and some stranger (especially where the prosecutor frequently works with the same officer—which is part of the problem of elite units). But there is also a difference between an FBI agent and your friend and law partner. ("If someone told you Tom Sullivan was lying, would you believe it?" Kwoka challenged me.)

FBI agents, like any client or witness, present the lawyer with "facts" and often testify to them or swear to them in an affidavit. The lawyer must evaluate those facts objectively—even cynically—or he is likely to present a story no one will believe and lose a case he could have won. That objectivity is always difficult to maintain in our adversary system—it is a bad idea to establish procedures and organizations that make it even harder.

Nor is the integrity of the criminal justice system helped by the all-to-common tolerance of perjury by law-enforcement agents. So far as I could determine, Agent Brown, like Agent Herman, suffered no discipline, much less prosecution, for his conduct.

Following dismissal of the bet-messenger case in 1981, Dominic Cortina stayed out of trouble for eight years. Then, in 1989, he was indicted in Florida and Maryland and was under investigation again in the Northern District of Illinois. I was able to bundle the three cases into a series of pleas for concurrent sentences totaling twenty-four months in prison. While incarcerated he was diagnosed with cancer and operated on at the Mayo Clinic. After his release, Dom lived peacefully with his family until his cancer returned and he died in November 1999. A year later, his lifelong friend and partner, Donald Angelini, also died of cancer.

Other than their promises to retire, which, like Muhammad Ali's, were good only for the day they were made, the only thing I thought Dominic and Donald ever lied to me about was the nature of their connection with "the outfit." It was never a real issue in the cases I handled, and if the subject cropped up they usually just ignored it. When the "mob expert" on a Chicago newspaper would write a story claiming Dom and Donald were among the bosses of the outfit, they would scoff and insist they were bookmakers, and nothing else. For the most part, the FBI agents attached to the strike force took a kind of middle position. Dom and Donald were important members of the Chicago Mafia, they asserted, and were in charge of its gambling interests wherever "Chicago" operated, but they weren't involved in any of the "heavy stuff." Unlike members of mob "crews" whose activities included gambling, prostitution, juice lending, cartage theft, collecting "street taxes" from independent bookmakers, and other "Mafia"-type crimes, it was conceded that Donald and Dominic did nothing but gambling and never used force or threats to collect money from their customers. Even Bill Roemer, a former FBI agent who wrote two books about the Chicago outfit, described them as "gentlemen." At the same time, Roemer claimed they were the mob's most important "capos," especially after Joe Ferriola became the overall operating boss in Chicago.

It is certainly true that Dom and Donald had to have permission from the outfit to operate their business, and that the permission came at a price. Neither man denied it, but neither did they talk about what the price was. Finally, in the fall of 1999, with both of them truly retired and ill, I asked them to tell me how it had worked. After much hemming and hawing they said all they were going to say. Yes, there came a time when they had to share profits with someone, but that was all. It was just one guy. No one ever told them what they could do or where or when they could do it. They just had to share the proceeds.

"When did you have to start sharing?"

"I don't remember. Maybe in the sixties."

"Who did you share with?"

"He's dead."

"Well, who was it?"

Exasperated: "Why would you want to know that? He's dead."

"Well, I want to put it in my book. If he's dead, what does it matter?"

"You want to put it in your book! It wouldn't be right. There's family, other people."

"Well, if it was just one person I assume it was Joe Ferriola." (He had died in 1990 and been a close friend of both men since childhood.)

"Joe was a close friend. We knew him since we were kids. We were never in business with Joe Ferriola."

I felt bad. By pressing, I was pretty sure I had made them lie to me. Besides, I could be wrong. Over the years, an awful lot of stuff was written about Dom and Donald that I know for certain was wrong, so who can say what Roemer or anyone else actually knew? And it really doesn't matter. What I know is true is that Dominic Cortina and Donald Angelini were some of the best clients a lawyer could have. They were fun, they were smart, they were interesting, they were honorable in their dealings, and they always did what they promised to do. As Bill Roemer said when they died, "They were gentlemen, and I enjoyed meeting them."

Me too.

CHAPTER 9

LEAVINGS

The success I had representing Dominic Cortina resulted in opportunities to represent several other men allegedly involved in "organized crime." Some I agreed to represent; some I refused. Some were nice people and good clients; some were neither. I took those and other "white collar" criminal cases for lawyers, doctors, and businessmen because I liked trying cases, and unlike the civil cases that made up the bulk of my practice, the criminal cases almost always went to trial. Some I won, some I lost.

While I was engaged in trying various criminal cases, my civil cases were moving along at their usual leisurely pace, with most disposed of without trial. One of my clients in a criminal case had ties to the Teamsters Union and its Central States Pension Fund, which resulted in my representing the trustees of the fund in a complex civil case brought by the U.S. Department of Labor. Cases for firm clients General Dynamics Corporation and Bally Manufacturing were settled on favorable terms. Every year I had new cases involving some kind of educational issue or claim of discrimination from the University of Illinois, its medical school, Northern Illinois University, or the Evanston public-school district. All were disposed of on motion or settled.

A major lender-liability case I had filed against Chicago's Continental Illinois National Bank for Fred Sahadi, a California entrepreneur, had been pending for several years and looked like it would actually go to trial when, contrary to my expectations, it was dismissed on the bank's motion for summary judgment. On appeal to the Seventh Circuit Court of Appeals the decision was reversed. The Court of Appeals opinion made my chances of winning the case considerably better than they had been before it was dismissed. Lawyers should be careful what they wish for, especially before asking for summary judgment where it may not be justified. If, like Continental Bank, you win and then get reversed you're often worse off than if you'd bit the bullet and tried the case.

Then one day my wife called my bluff. From the time I graduated from college, I had told myself and everyone who would listen that I was going to spend part of my life as a full-time writer—books, stories, articles, whatever (except legal briefs). And I intended to do it before I was so old I couldn't remember what I wanted to say. Jayne had been a young partner at my law firm when we were married. When Harold Washington was elected mayor, she left to help lead an effort to reform Chicago's corporation counsel's office—the hundred or so lawyers who represented the city. Her two-year commitment to the task was coming to an end. By eliminating patronage hiring, insisting that the lawyers work full time without a private office on the side, firing the most incompetent regardless of their political sponsorship, and hiring good young lawyers based on merit, in two years the office had improved beyond anyone's expectation. Now, she suggested, would be a good time for her to find a job teaching law where living was less expensive, and I could begin writing.

I backed and filled and hemmed and hawed and raised a hundred objections. We couldn't afford it—she had already cut her income in half by leaving the firm; if I left, our joint income would be cut by 90 percent. I had some cases that had to be tried. The firm needed me. I wouldn't know anyone, and worse, no one would know me. But gradually I came to realize she was right. We could do it now—three of my four children were through college and living on their own. The youngest had only a year to go, and I had enough savings to take care of that. Neither of us cared about being rich and, in truth, there was no reason we couldn't live on her income and my savings. If we couldn't, I could continue to do some legal work—I had already promised my client in the *Continental Bank* case I would come back and try it if necessary. I would also continue to supervise the *Central States Pension Fund* case. Between them, those cases would produce a decent income for the next several years. Most important, I realized that if I didn't do it now, I probably never would. It was as good a time as any would ever be if I meant what I had always said. I decided I meant it. Jayne accepted a teaching job in Virginia, and in April I told my partners I planned to leave on September 1.

When the word of what I was planning began getting around, it became obvious that a lot of people thought there must be more to it than met the eye. Well-paid fifty-one-year-old partners in major law firms don't just quit. I could tell from the sober looks and inquiries of some of my friends that one common theory was I must have some incurable illness I wasn't telling anyone about. Other rumors were that I had done something awful and was being kicked out of the firm, or that something having to do with my representation of some mobster made it necessary for me to leave town.

But the most surprising reaction came from a number of lawyers I didn't even know. Jim Warren, who was then the *Chicago Tribune*'s legal correspondent, had covered several of the cases I tried. When he learned of my plan, he devoted one of his weekly columns to describing my career and commenting on how unusual it was for someone in my position to just up and leave. (It was much like reading my own obituary.) Within a few days I began to receive the expected smattering of letters of good wishes from people who had not previously heard of my plans, but mixed in were a significant number of letters saying how much the writer wished he had the "nerve" to do what I was doing. Some were quite agonized in their expression of feeling that they were caught in a rat race they despised but felt unable to abandon, primarily for reasons of money and lifestyle.

I knew there were lawyers who felt that way, but since I loved what I had been doing and was leaving it with reluctance and only because of a long-held promise to myself (and a wife who had called my bluff), I hadn't thought about it that way. I felt a little scared, but hardly heroic. Of course, I had advantages some of my correspondents lacked: a wife who was both sympathetic to the idea and herself a professional capable of earning a decent income, a lack of desire for fast cars and huge houses, kids who were mostly grown and self-sufficient, and some invested savings.

It turned out to be less traumatic than I expected. Several of my partners had predicted I would be bored and come back in six months. I did miss the courtroom, especially when I read about an interesting new case I thought I might have been involved in, but my biggest problem in the first several years after I left was ego. A trial lawyer can be quiet or loud, gregarious or shy, pretty or ugly, and just about anything else you can think of except lacking in self-confidence. Every good courtroom lawyer I know has a healthy— some might say unhealthily healthy—ego. Suddenly unknown and unappreciated, I found myself spending an embarrassing amount of time making sure my new friends and acquaintances understood what a big-shot lawyer I had been back in Chicago. Fortunately, most people were tolerant, if unimpressed.

The other, unexpected problem was an utter lack of the self-discipline essential to writing anything longer than a few pages. My discipline had always been supplied by the demands and schedules set by clients and judges. With no schedule or deadline—indeed, with no one caring whether I wrote anything or not—I found my many other hobbies and interests irresistible. I still have trouble keeping to a writing schedule until a deadline approaches, as the editor of this book will surely testify. Even so, I am doing what I set out to do, and I love it.

The point—for those who wrote and anyone else who wants to do something new but feels trapped where they are—is that it's not as hard as you think. There is life after the law and, I am confident, whatever else you are doing. There is nothing so invigorating as a second career.

But this is a book about what it's like to become a courtroom lawyer, so it is only fair to close with a few comments about how the experiences I have described may differ from those of other lawyers, especially at a time when law practice has changed—in some ways, dramatically—from when I was practicing.

For one thing, maximizing profit has become far more important in most big-city law firms than it was forty or even fifteen years ago, and there is no sign it will change. The "rainmakers" are demanding and often receiving larger and larger shares of the firm's profits, taking down incomes unheard of in the past, even adjusting for inflation. The days when lawyers almost always began and ended their careers with the same law firm are over. Firms that once would not consider "lateral entries" now freely raid each other by offering a bigger share of the profits to lawyers with large, profitable billings. It will be difficult, but idealistic young law graduates should try hard to avoid working for lawyers who refer to their loyal clients as "a book of business." The term perfectly symbolizes the conversion of the practice of law from a profession to a common commercial enterprise in many big law firms in big cities, and plenty of smaller ones in smaller cities as well.

The consequences of these changes are bad in every way, unless your only objective is to make the most money possible, and in that case, you would be better off becoming an investment banker. If you're smart enough to get the kind of grades in a good law school that will get you hired by a prominent big-city law firm, you're plenty smart enough to be an investment banker, so please do.

The current emphasis on the bottom line has a special impact on trial lawyers. Profit expectations require hourly rates to be set so high that only major corporations can afford them, and their cases almost never go to trial. You may get moderately rich as a "litigator" for big companies, but if you try a case only once every five years, you won't become much of a trial lawyer. You also won't meet as many interesting people or have as much fun as I did. I suspect it is at least in part for this reason that in recent years many of the best trial lawyers in the country, like David Boies, have left their large firms to form litigation boutiques, where they can decide for themselves what cases to accept or reject, and how to strike the balance between income and an interesting professional career.

Another problem is the negative impact of the profit motive on the willingness of lawyers in large law firms to satisfy their professional obligation to provide services for persons and entities who need legal representation but cannot afford it. The reader will have observed that many of the cases described in this book were undertaken on a pro bono or reduced-fee basis. I concede that is in part because during some years of my practice I did a volume of pro bono work that most law firms would not have tolerated. But it is also because the cases a lawyer accepts to fill an unmet need or lend support to a cause the lawyer believes in will be the most interesting and personally gratifying experiences of that person's career.

Gratifying or not, providing a reasonable amount of pro bono legal work is an obligation every lawyer undertakes when he or she accepts the monopoly conferred by the license to practice law. Every student emerging from law school who considers joining a law firm should have a clear understanding of that firm's policy and practice (not just its rhetoric) regarding pro bono work, and should decline to join any firm that refuses such work or penalizes lawyers who undertake it. Those who proclaim that American lawyers have no obligation to serve the public are not worthy of the title "lawyer." They have misunderstood their study of "law and economics" and falsely concluded that they are—or ought to be—the same thing.

But if you remember that the law is a profession and a lawyer's fundamental goal is not the maximization of personal profit but the ethical, zealous, effective representation of his clients, the life of a courtroom lawyer is wonderfully interesting and rewarding. I hope these pages have provided some understanding of what trial lawyers do, and how—by trial and error—they learn to do it.

APPENDIX

TABLE OF REPORTED DECISIONS
AND COMMENTARY

CHAPTER SIX
Cousins v. Wigoda 419 U.S. 477 (1975)
Young v. Mikva 66 Ill. 2d. 579, 363 N.E.2nd 851 (1977)
Shakman v. Democratic Organization et al., 435 F.2d 267 (7th Circ. 1970)
Illinois State Employees Union v. Lewis 473 F.2d 561 (7th Circ. 1974)
Burns et al. v. Elrod 509 F.2d 1133 (7th Circ. 1975)
Elrod v. Burns 427 U.S. 347 (1976)
   90 *Harvard Law Review* 186 (1976)
   78 *Columbia Law Review* 468 (1978)

CHAPTER SEVEN
Jones v. Mayer 392 U.S. 409 (1968)
Contract Buyers League v. F&F Investment Co. 300 *Fed. Supp.* 210 (N.D. Ill. 1969)
Clark v. Universal Builders et al. 501 F. 2d 324 (7th Circ. 1974)
   88 *Harvard Law Review* 1610 (1975)
   10 *Harvard Civil Rights and Civil Liberties Law Review* 705 (1975)
   "My Fathers House Has Many Mansions" (April 1972 *The Atlantic Monthly*).
   An Alley in Chicago: The Ministry of a City Priest, Margery Frisbie (2002
   Sheed and Ward)

CHAPTER EIGHT
U. S. v. Cortina 630 F.2d 1207 (7th Circ. 1980)

CHAPTER NINE
Sahadi v. Continental Bank 706 F.2d 193 (7th Circ. 1983)
Donovan v. Fitzsimmons et al. 778 F. 2d.298 (7th Circ. 1985), on rehearing 805
   F.2d 682 (7th Circ. 1986)

❧ ACKNOWLEDGMENTS ❧

Hardly any of the events described in this book would have happened to me without the guidance, support and friendship of my fellow courtroom lawyers, especially Jim Sprowl, Bert Jenner, Prentice Marshall, Tom Sullivan, and Jerry Solovy. Words cannot adequately express my gratitude to them.

In addition, Pren Marshall, Tom Sullivan, and Jerry Solovy read all or substantial portions of the manuscript and provided valuable suggestions and corrections of my faulty memory.

In an effort to obtain independent perspectives and recollections I made an effort to contact the people who played a significant role in the events I describe. Without exception everyone I was able to contact agreed to talk to me, even when they had been on the opposite side of a case and knew I would write things they disagreed with. Their cooperation has contributed to the accuracy of the book and enriched many of its stories. I am grateful to all of them.

My wife, Jayne Barnard, read the manuscript as I produced it and provided expert editorial advice and much needed encouragement. My daughter Katie Trippi and my sister Patty Wroclawski also read the manuscript and made valuable editorial suggestions.

Mathew Colman and Lloyd Sullivan researched court files, newspaper morgues and other records with diligence and imagination. Without the records they uncovered this book would contain many more inaccuracies. Unfortunately, no records are available for some of the events described, so I could only rely on unaided recollection. I apologize for any inaccuracies.

Once again Della Harris performed the miraculous task of converting my handwritten revisions into a final manuscript. I doubt anyone else could have done it.

My editor, Philip Turner, not only contributed a useful line edit to the final product, it was his concept for the structure of the book that inspired the creation of this volume. And my agent, Judith Riven expertly negotiated the deal and provided support and encouragement as the writing progressed.

✦ INDEX ✦

ABOUT THE AUTHOR

John C. Tucker graduated from Princeton University and The University of Michigan Law School before joining the Chicago Law firm Jenner & Block, where he specialized in the trial of complex civil and criminal cases. In 1974 he was elected to The American College of Trial Lawyers and in 1984 was named one of the country's best criminal defense lawyers in the first edition of *The Best Lawyers in America*.

In addition to his private practice Tucker has served as special counsel to the U.S. Civil Rights Commission, The Lawyers Committee for Civil Rights Under Law, The American Civil Liberties Union, and Independent Voters of Illinois. He has taught trial practice to practicing lawyers at the National Institute of Trial Advocacy and lectured or taught courses in trial and appellate practice for law students at The University of Chicago, The University of Illinois, Northwestern University and the College of William and Mary.

In addition to writing the critically acclaimed *May God Have Mercy* about the controversial execution of Virginian Roger Coleman, Tucker has published articles in *The Washington Post, The Chicago Tribune, The New Republic,* and various other newspapers and legal journals. He lives in Virginia with his wife Jayne Barnard, a law professor.